Total Quality Management
Mastering Your Small Business

Jill A. Rossiter

Upstart
Publishing Compa
a division of Dearborn Publishing Group
Chicago, Illinois

This publication is designed to provide accurate and authoritative information in regard to the subject matter covered. It is sold with the understanding that the publisher is not engaged in rendering legal, accounting, or other professional service. If legal advice or other expert assistance is required, the services of a competent professional person should be sought.

Publisher and Acquisition Editor: Jere L. Calmes
Editorial Assistant: Becky Rasmussen
Production Manager: Karen Billipp
Cover Design: Joni Doherty
Cover and Interior Illustration: Timothy Gibbons

Published by Upstart Publishing Company,
a division of Dearborn Publishing Group, Inc.

Printed in the United States of America
96 97 98 10 9 8 7 6 5 4 3 2 1

Author: Jill A. Rossiter

Creative Writer: Mary G. Shuter

Based on an original manuscript by: Jim Holly

Produced under the direction of: Richard O. Schafer, Ph.D., Director, Distance Learning, Wisconsin Small Business Development Center, University of Wisconsin-Extension and Jeannette McDonald, DVM, Research Assistant

Content Advisors: Richard O. Schafer, John Mozingo, Sandy Lewandowski, and Fred Waedt

Contribution by: William H. Pinkovitz, Past Director; Erica McIntire, Director, Wisconsin Small Business Development Center, University of Wisconsin-Extension, Donald E. Hanna, Chancellor

Library of Congress Cataloging-in-Publication Data
Rossiter, Jill.
    Total quality management : mastering your small business / Jill A. Rossiter.
       p.   cm.
    Includes bibliographical references and index.
    ISBN 1-57410-039-4
    1. Total quality management. 2. Small business. I. Title.
HD62.15.R68 1996
658.5'62--dc20

96-28742
CIP

Contents

Preface

Welcome to the
Business Mastery Certification Series

Total Quality Management: Mastering Your Small Business is one of five units from the **Business Mastery Certification Series**.

- **Total Quality Management**

- Marketing

- Finance

- Human Resources

- Business and Legal Issues

These materials have been designed to lead the learner through the process of mastering the business concepts necessary to a successful small business owner or manager. The structure of the materials, featuring the Challenges and the Personal Workshops, coach the learner through the decision-making and growth process that is the basis for the mastery of these concepts. It is anticipated that the self-paced learner will take about 120 hours to complete the Challenges included in each unit. The flexibility of these materials also makes them a perfect instructional tool for use in classroom or distance education alternatives to independent study. If you are interested in the possible pursuit of either of these options, please contact the Business and Economics Section of the Independent Learning Program at the University of Wisconsin-Extension, at (608) 262-4876. You may also write to them at 432 North Lake Street, Room 201, Madison, WI 53706-1498 for more information.

The Small Business Mastery Certificate is awarded to the learner by the University of Wisconsin-Extension Department of Continuing Education upon satisfactory, accredited completion of the five courses in the Small Business Mastery series. This award signifies the learners proficiency in the management skills necessary to the successful small business owner or manager in the 21st century.

Your Challenge Begins

The purpose of this course is to help you gain the knowledge and develop the skills needed to implement the total quality concept in your small business. You will learn what total quality means and why it is important for the survival of any business. You will be given tips and tools for implementing quality and continuously improving processes. And, you will learn how to build your business around the needs and wants of your customers, which is critical to your success in a competitive environment.

This course is organized into four learning Challenges:

Challenge 1: Leading Your Company to Quality

Challenge 2: Putting Your Customers First

Challenge 3: Employee Involvement and Team Building

Challenge 4: A Cycle of Continuous Improvement

Mastery Learning

This course has been designed for you to master quality management concepts outside the classroom. The Personal Workshops that you find in this guide encourage a different type of learning. You are no longer just reading a book. *You* will be actively involved in the learning process of what it takes to develop a sound management program. The mastery of the concepts presented in *Total Quality Management: Mastering Your Small Business* will prove beneficial as you apply your newly acquired knowledge and skills to your own business. This is your personal project. Enjoy!

What Are Personal Workshops?

Personal workshops are not tests, simply exercises and information-collecting forms designed to assist you in applying newly acquired techniques to your specific business. There are no right or wrong answers to these Personal Workshops—each one is designed to take you one step closer to making your business a quality organization.

You're Not Alone

To guide you as you learn about quality management, you will be joined by four small business owners whose personal experiences will model and illustrate key points presented in your learning activities. Meet Pete Jones, Denny and Mabel Wellman, Kiki Hermann, and Lindy Hernandez.

 BestBuilt Construction Company/Pete Jones: BestBuilt was founded in 1970 by Pete Jones. BestBuilt, a minority-owned business, started out as a builder of moderately priced homes in a bedroom community of St. Louis. In the past 25 years, BestBuilt has grown significantly and now employs nearly 80 construction workers and 12 managers and support staff. BestBuilt still builds single family dwellings in the moderate to upper price range, but it also does business in the construction and remodeling of multi-family housing, shopping strips, and small commercial buildings. BestBuilt decided to make the move to quality management two years ago. Management and the support staff are comfortable with and actively involved in continuous improvement, but the construction workers have pretty much ignored all quality efforts, probably hoping the concept would go away.

Denny's Hometown Market/Denny and Mabel Wellman: Hometown Market was the only large grocery store in its town of 10,000 people until six months ago. Now a major competitor has come in with a new store, one in a chain of fifty across the state. Hometown's owners, Denny and Mabel Wellman, feel they must make some major changes if they are going to keep their customers. Hometown Market employs ten full-time and 24 part-time employees.

Quali-Temps Inc. /Kiki Hermann: Quali-Temps is a brand new business offering a new twist in the temporary employment market. All of Quali-Temps's associates, as the company calls its pool of workers, have expertise in computer systems and business applications. Quali-Temps gets called when a business needs high-tech computer help on a short-term basis (less than one year). Quali-Temps is located in a major West Coast city, and it is owned by Kiki Hermann. Kiki is determined to get the business started right— he wants every client to be 100 percent satisfied with his or her choice of Quali-Temps.

Recycled Paper Wholesalers/Lindy Hernandez: RPW transforms old newspapers and office waste into cellulose, which is then sold to companies that make recycled paper products or "blow-in" type insulation, depending on the grade of the fibers. RPW's owner, Lindy Hernandez, decided to start the company when she worked for an insulation manufacturer which was having a difficult time finding reliable vendors of cellulose. RPW has been in the recycling business for five years and employs 22 people. Lindy recognizes, though, that unless she can get her costs down, RPW will soon be out of business.

Learning Aids

Additional sources of information and points worth emphasizing are highlighted in the margins of this guide.

For Your Information: Notes, quotes, and noteworthy information is located in an FYI box at the bottom of the page.

Call Out: Information worth pointing out or remembering is called to your attention.

Resource Tip: Others probably already know what you want to know. You will discover valuable resources where you see this library icon.

Key Words/Phrases: Business terms that are important to the understanding of the topic at hand are defined in the margin of the text.

Step Back: Occasionally you will be asked to refer to an earlier step or workshop for purposes of review.

 Profiles: The concepts of total quality management have taken shape over the past half-century. Many management theorists and practitioners have helped define quality through their work and writings. Some of the "gurus" of quality management are profiled in this book. These profiles will give you some history and a sense of the contributions made by some of the more significant people in the quality movement.

 Quality Tools & Techniques: Several tools and techniques, some statistical and some not, are used to gather information and assess change in quality organizations. Whether or not you have ever taken a statistics course, you should find most of the tools used in total quality management fairly simple to understand and useful for measuring process results and making decisions. Many of these tools and techniques are outlined for you in this Challenge. When you see the icon for Quality Tools & Techniques, you will find a guide to what the tool or technique is, when you should use it and how you make it or do it.

 Challenge Summary: At the end of each Challenge, you will find a summary of what you learned in four key areas. These designations are used throughout the four Challenges so you can systematically build on each technique.

 Information: This guide will provide you with pertinent business information as it relates to you on day-to-day matters as well as for strategic plans for your business.

 Tools: Personal Workshops are the tools you will use to help you test and analyze your business ideas and strategies.

 Learning: Running a business successfully involves you in ongoing learning. This learning will be selective and appropriate, fitting your business's needs and your skills, prior knowledge, experiences, and resources.

 Networking: You will not be alone as you make your business decisions. You will be given access to additional outside resources to contact for support and assistance.

Self-Assessments

You are encouraged to complete the self-assessments that are located at the end of each Challenge. Self-assessments are tools designed for you to check your understanding of the materials covered. If during your self-check, you find that you do not fully understand something, you will be directed to take another look at the material you have read. The guide will direct you to specific pages for review or to additional resources for help.

How to Read this Guide

Spend a few minutes previewing all of your materials before you begin. Become familiar with the guide and the accompanying Personal Workshops. Begin formulating questions in your mind that you want answered as you complete this guide.

Acknowledgments

Many thanks and a great deal of appreciation goes to Shelly A. McLaughlin at the University of Wisconsin SBDC. She labored tirelessly to give this book its "look" and freshness.

We would also like to extend our gratitude to Paul G. Hall, Director, Arlington SBDC, George Mason University in Arlington, VA and Tracy Dranginis, Research Associate, University of Missouri in Columbia, MO.

Challenge 1
Leading Your Company to Quality

"Quality is not only right, it is free. And it is not only free,
it is the most profitable product line we have."

– Harold S. Geneen, former ITT Chairman
in Phil Crosby's *Quality is Free*, 1979

What is all the fuss about quality? What is this TQM thing, and why should a small business owner even care? Isn't it just for big-time businesses? And isn't it just for manufacturing companies?

Perhaps these are the questions you've been asking yourself for the past few years, every time you hear something about "quality." Maybe you're one of the people who believes **Total Quality Management**, or TQM, is a passing management fad. And, yet, you keep hearing about it in various ways—Total Quality Control, Continuous Quality Improvement, Statistical Process Control, Quality Leadership, and so on. It seems that all of that "quality talk" will just never go away. And so, you have decided that maybe you'd better find out what the fuss over quality is all about. Good move. . .

Key Word

Quality management is about having a *shared vision* which will give your employees direction and their work meaning. This vision is a picture of what the company is trying to become, and it will come about when you involve employees in planning and problem solving, when you give them the knowledge, tools and authority to do the right thing at the right time, and when they have a clear understanding of their importance in achieving the goals of the company. Quality management is about building systems—using methods, tools and processes to achieve that vision. And it is about solving problems—eliminating errors and obstacles which threaten quality and an organization's existence.

"Production is not to be esteemed so much by quantity as by quality."

—Aesop's Fables

The purpose of Challenge 1 is to answer many of your basic questions about quality and to provide an overview of the principles of quality management. In addition, you will learn some practical ways to apply those principles and the tools of TQM to your small business, to help it become more productive, more vital and, ultimately, more profitable.

> *"'What is our business?' is not determined by the producer but by the customer."*
>
> —Peter Drucker

Successfully completing this Challenge should not be difficult– there are Personal Workshops and case study examples to guide you. Successfully implementing the principles of quality management in your small business, though, won't be so easy. It will require a major attitude adjustment by you and by every employee in your company. Total quality management is a philosophy, not a managerial "quick-fix." Implementing the quality concept in your business, whether you wish to call it TQM or not, needs to happen by evolution, not by revolution. It will take your dedicated leadership, the education and training of every employee, practice and more practice, and a great deal of patience to make it work for your company. Every worker in your business, management and non-management, will need to learn to work together as partners, and they must do it for one reason—to meet or exceed your customers' needs, because the customer is at the heart of the quality concept.

If you become a "quality" convert—if you apply what you learn in this book to your business *and* you stick with it, your business will never be the same. And neither will your employees.

Upon completion of Challenge 1, you will be able to:

- Define quality

- Explain the need for quality in a competitive environment

- Identify the benefits of the quality concept for small business

- Identify the foundation principles of total quality management

- Recognize the key names and terms that have helped define the quality concept

- Assess your company's strengths, weaknesses, and possible obstacles to implementing the quality concept

- Begin the quality transformation process in your small business

What Is Quality and the Quality Concept?

Key Word

Quality, like beauty, is in the eye of the beholder. And in business, the only "beholder" who matters is the customer. Quality is whatever your customers want it to be. Simply put, quality is the goodness of your product or service as perceived by your customers. Therefore, to understand what quality is for your business, you need to know who your customers are, and you need to develop a clear understanding of what those customers want, need and expect from your business. Whether yours is a service business or a manufacturing firm, "high tech" or "low tech," you need to be concerned about quality—about what your customers need and want, when they want it, and how they want it.

To illustrate this point, assume you are the customer at a barber shop or beauty salon. What is important to you when you go in for a haircut? A friendly stylist? A reasonable price? A clean shop? A great cut, or at least not looking scalped when you walk out? Or maybe you want to be offered a cup of coffee while you get your hair cut;

Profile

"Everything is one of a kind."

– W. Edwards Deming , *Out of the Crisis.*

W. Edwards Deming was an American economist and statistician and is probably the best known of the "quality gurus" in America. He led the Japanese in the rebuilding of their economy after World War II using the concepts that have come to be known as Total Quality Management. He later worked with hundreds of U.S. companies to teach them what he had so effectively taught the Japanese. Deming became well known as a leader in quality management in the U.S. soon after he was featured on a 1980 NBC television program entitled, "If Japan Can, Why Can't We?"

Deming suggested that the quality of a product can't be "inspected in." Instead, it needs to be "built in" during the manufacturing process. He is probably best known for his Fourteen Points for Management, which are his version of the "Ten Commandments" for managers who want to implement the quality concept in their organizations. Those points are discussed later in this Challenge. He is also well known for the Deming Cycle, a model for implementing continuous process improvement. Deming remained active in the quality movement, teaching and consulting well into his nineties, until his death in 1993.

or you want the stylist to do a scalp massage before the wash and offer you a glass of wine. Whatever it is that you want or need or expect, it is the responsibility of the shop owner and employees to know it and to provide it; or better yet, exceed your expectations. Otherwise, they may lose you as a customer.

Does this mean that every hairdresser must offer a scalp massage and a glass of wine to his or her customers? Of course not. That's like saying that every car dealer must offer Cadillacs, because everyone wants to drive a Cadillac. Customers have various wants, needs, and expectations for the products and services they consume. It does mean that business owners need to make decisions about which customers they want to serve, and then do everything within reason to meet the needs and expectations of those customers. If the business owner succeeds in doing that, the business will be perceived by those customers as a quality organization.

As every business owner should know, what most customers want is value for their money. In many cases, a customer will give up a certain product feature or level of service in order to save some money—consumers make such choices every day. Don't confuse the concept of quality with the concept of price. For example, you cannot assume that an economy car is of poor quality just because it has a lower price. The fact is that there are higher quality economy cars and lower quality economy cars, just as there are higher quality luxury cars and lower quality luxury cars. If your product or service is of the "economy" type, you want to strive to have the best quality for your type of product, because that will give your customers what they want—value. Providing a quality product, even a perfect product, does not guarantee your business will be successful. You need to be just as concerned about the quality of your work processes—about producing that product or service in an efficient way.

The term **quality concept** refers to an attitude about how to conduct business, no matter what business it is. That attitude centers on two things (1) meeting or exceeding the customers' wants, needs, and expectations and (2) doing it in an efficient way. It does no good to produce an excellent product that nobody wants, just as it does no good to produce a high quality product using inefficient processes. The quality concept, then, refers not just to the product or service provided, but also *how* it is provided.

Key Words

Quality management has been said to have a "hard side" and a "soft side." The hard side refers to the use of measurement and statistics for quality control. Several statistical tools and processes have been developed to help a business understand how it is performing and whether it is improving. The soft side of quality management emphasizes the need for excellent interpersonal and communication skills to make the quality concept a reality. Employee and managerial training and development are critical to the success of any quality effort in any organization, since everyone needs to become familiar and comfortable with team processes, empowerment, and serving the customer.

FYI

Although consumers may need to give up certain product features for a lower price, they still want and deserve a "perfect" product. The old excuse of "nobody's perfect" isn't good enough. For many products and services, even 99.9 percent isn't good enough. If all of America worked on the 99.9 percent perfection principle:

- 22,000 checks would be deducted from the wrong bank accounts in the next hour

- 1,314 phone calls would be misplaced in the next minute

- 12 babies born today would be given to the wrong parents

- 2 million documents would be lost by the IRS this year

- 2.5 million books would have the wrong cover this year

- 2 plane landings at O'Hare airport would be unsafe today

- 18,322 pieces of mail would be mishandled in the next hour

- 20,000 prescription medicines would be written incorrectly this year

- 315 entries in Webster's Third New International Dictionary would be misspelled.

Source: The Hope Health Letter, published by the Hope Heart Institute, Seattle, WA, Nov. 1993.

Personal Workshop Preparation # 1: What Is Quality?

Quality is a relative concept. What you consider good quality may be totally different than what someone else considers good quality. Why we consider some products or businesses to be good varies from person to person, also. Answer questions #1 through #5 based on *your* perceptions of quality; and try to express why you hold that perception. When you get to Question #6, try to answer based on what you believe *your customers* think.

Personal Notes

_____

_____

_____

_____

FYI

There are several different approaches to quality management and each has its own name and/or acronym. Here are a few of the more common ones you will read and hear about:

- **Total Quality Management (TQM):** Probably the most commonly used and understood term. The name TQM originated with the quality movement in the U.S. military. The word "Total" refers to the fact that the quality effort needs to be implemented by every employee at every level of the organization.

- **Total Quality Control (TQC), Continuous Quality Improvement (CQI) or Total Quality Improvement (TQI):** Variations in name which emphasize one of the major elements of the quality concept: the continuous improvement of processes and systems in the company. The term "quality control" has been used in American business for decades, but it normally refers to the practice of inspecting for quality, at some point in the process or after the product is made.

- **Zero Defects Management:** A concept developed by Philip Crosby, one of the quality gurus, and based on the premise that it is possible to have systems which are totally error free.

- **Statistical Process Control (SPC):** SPC involves the use of statistical analyses to control quality in work systems. Specifically, SPC entails setting control limits for a process and reducing variations that exceed those limits. The foundation for SPC was set by research at Bell Laboratories in the 1930s by a man named Walter Shewhart.

Personal Workshop #1
What Is Quality?

1. What is the best automobile manufactured today?

   What makes it the best?

2. What company do you think of when you think of high quality computer software?

   Why?

3. What company would you hire if you wanted to be absolutely, positively sure something would be delivered the next day?

   Why?

4. What is the best restaurant in your town?

   What makes it the best?

Bonus question:

5. What brand of watch do you consider the best?

   What country was famous for making quality watches prior to 1970?

Personal Workshop #1, continued

What country has taken over that role in the past 25 years?

Why?

Toughest question (Be honest!):

6. Who do you consider the major competitor for your business?

How do you think your customers view the quality of your product or service compared to that competitor (better or worse)?

Why?

Workshop Follow-Up

✔ With the possible exception of parts of question five, there are no right or wrong answers to the questions in this workshop. Your perceptions of what is quality and what is not are based on your personal wants and needs, as well as your experiences as a consumer. Take particular note of how you answered the "why?" questions. In some cases, your perception of quality has to do with product features, while in others it probably has to do with how the product or service is delivered (convenient or timely), or how it makes you feel (confident, happy, smart or satisfied). Consider your answers to question six. The reasons why your customers patronize your business over your competitor's business, or vice-versa, are also based on their personal needs and wants and experiences. How does your company or product make them feel?

Why Quality Is Important to Your Small Business

There is really only one reason to implement the quality concept in your small business—survival. If you are able to continuously meet or exceed the needs of your customers better than the competition, those customers will stick with your business, your market share should grow, and you will have a better chance of surviving as a business. That goes for both large and small businesses. Most large businesses and many smaller ones are facing international competition—especially high quality, lower-priced products and labor from Asia, Europe, and Central and South America. Gradually over the past 30 years, America's largest corporations have watched their costs rise, while market share and profits have slipped. American business leaders began to realize in the 1980s that drastic changes would be needed if they were going to survive in the new global market. Many began looking at the principles of total quality management, because it was obvious that the quality concept had helped pull the Japanese out of a state of total devastation following World War II to a position of world leadership in the production and delivery of quality products.

Key Word

As large American businesses began to implement the practices and teachings of W. Edwards Deming and others, they recognized that they could never succeed unless they had the cooperation of their suppliers. After all, a product is only as good as the materials that go into it. Some began to require **supplier certification,** a process buyers use to encourage quality in their suppliers. This helped assure that the small and medium-sized businesses which supplied manufactured components or raw materials or services to large businesses would meet their quality standards. The quality concept, then, has really been forced on many smaller businesses, because their customers demanded it. And, today, many large and medium-sized businesses will simply not do business with any supplier who refuses to be certified as meeting minimum quality standards.

> *"If the rate of change inside an organization is less than the rate of change outside the organization, the end is in sight."*
>
> —Jack Welsh,
> CEO, General Electric

If you do not supply goods or services to other businesses, you may be thinking, "so what?" But, no matter what your business, you need to attract customers, and you probably have competition. Why should you be interested in quality? Because individual consumers, just like big businesses, are demanding it.

Profile

"It is now clear that upper managers have a vital role to play in the quality planning process. This role requires extensive personal participation. It cannot be delegated, since a major change in company culture is needed."

–Joseph Juran, "Juran Quality by Design" (*The Free Press,* 1992).

Joseph M. Juran, another American who worked closely with the Japanese after World War II, is best known for helping to clarify the manager's role in quality and the cost of quality. He defined the **Cost of Poor Quality** as the sum of all costs that would disappear if there were no quality problems. He showed management how profits would rise as quality improved, since the costs of poor quality would be lowered. Juran helped develop the principle of knowing the customer and meeting the customer's needs.

Juran has written extensively on quality and is probably best known for his *Quality Control Handbook* (McGraw-Hill, 1951), which includes directives for management to achieve quality. For example, Juran believed it was management's responsibility to set goals for quality improvement, and then to organize and train employees to achieve those goals. His philosophy also emphasized measuring and communicating results, and giving recognition to those responsible for continuous improvement in the organization.

Key Word

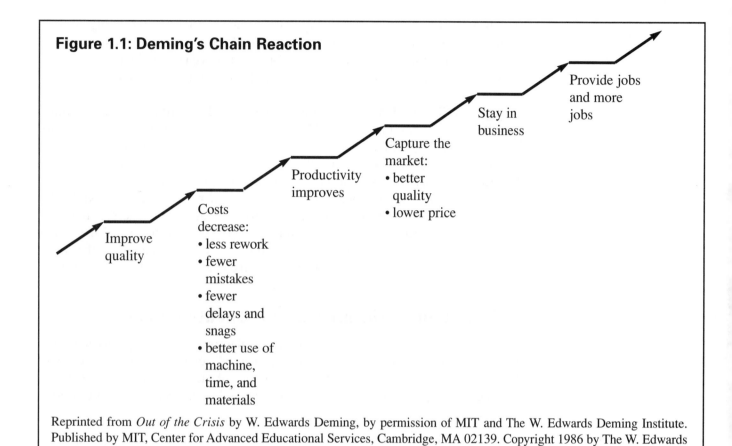

Figure 1.1: Deming's Chain Reaction

Improve quality

Costs decrease:
• less rework
• fewer mistakes
• fewer delays and snags
• better use of machine, time, and materials

Productivity improves

Capture the market:
• better quality
• lower price

Stay in business

Provide jobs and more jobs

Reprinted from *Out of the Crisis* by W. Edwards Deming, by permission of MIT and The W. Edwards Deming Institute. Published by MIT, Center for Advanced Educational Services, Cambridge, MA 02139. Copyright 1986 by The W. Edwards Deming Institute.

Customers are becoming more assertive, and they expect better service from you, no matter what your business. You should be concerned about quality in your business, because you should have the overriding goal of being the best business of your type in your market. And, if you are, you will attract more customers and clients as well as better employees.

Even if your customers don't demand it, does quality make sense for your small business? Yes. W. Edwards Deming described a chain reaction for companies that implement the quality concept, which shows that quality improvements can lead to a better return on investment (see Figure 1.1).

FYI

Regarding the Bonus Question in Personal Workshop #1, the Swiss, of course, have always been recognized worldwide for excellent workmanship in watches. They dominated the world market until the quartz watch was introduced, giving consumers exactly what they wanted: better accuracy at a lower price. It was a U.S. company, Texas Instruments, that introduced the quartz watch, but it was the Japanese who excelled in developing the product to meet the needs of watch consumers worldwide—ever hear of Seiko? The irony is that the Swiss are the ones who invented the quartz movement, but they chose not to manufacture it. Do you think they were paying attention to what their customers wanted and needed?

The benefits of becoming a "quality" small business are overwhelming—better products, lower costs, more customers, better employees, and a workforce dedicated to serving your customers. All of these factors will help you build a better small business, one capable of surviving in an increasingly competitive environment.

 Recycled Paper Wholesalers/Lindy Hernandez: After carefully studying the Deming Chain Reaction, Lindy believes it is the key to RPW's turnaround. She knows that they have many problems with their systems. Specifically, their process for sorting old papers is weak, which makes it difficult to consistently produce the various grades of cellulose (the longer the fibers, the higher the grade). And while old newspapers are plentiful, they are having difficulty finding reliable suppliers for higher grades of paper, which they need to make the better cellulose. Those problems have caused unacceptable delays for their customers. Lindy sees the logic behind the chain reaction and is convinced that the quality concept is the answer.

The Foundation Principles of the Quality Concept

There are three basic principles which serve as the foundation for quality management and will guide your development as a "quality" company. If you, as the small business owner/manager, cannot buy into any one of these principles, you may not be successful in implementing the quality concept in your business. These principles are:

- The customer comes first

FYI

ISO 9000 refers to a set of international quality standards which were established by the International Organization for Standardization (ISO) in 1987 and have been adopted by the European Community (EC), which will soon require companies selling products in Europe to comply with these standards. In essence, ISO 9000 certification ensures that a company meets certain quality production and quality assurance standards. Becoming certified as an ISO 9000 company may offer you a strategic advantage if you compete in the global market or serve a customer who does. ISO also has issued other standards (ISO 9001 - 9004) which offer specific guidelines and models for quality assurance for specific processes.

For information about how to become ISO 9000 certified, contact one of the following:

- American Society for Quality Control, 611 E. Wisconsin Ave., Milwaukee, WI 53202

- National Center for Standards and Certification Information (NCSCI), National Institute of Standards and Technology (NIST), TRF Building, Room A163, Gaithersburg, MD 20899

- Office of EC Affairs, International Trade Administration, Room 3036, 14th and Constitution Ave. S.W., Washington, DC. 20230

- Employee involvement and education to develop unity of purpose
- The continuous improvement of processes and systems

The Customer Comes First

Henry Ford's famous words represent the usual philosophy of America's product-driven economy, where businesses put products on the market with little consideration of what customers really want. The incredible thing is that they got away with it for so long, primarily because affluent American consumers seemed to have an insatiable appetite for new products and new technologies.

> *"The customer can have any color car as long as it's black."*
> —Henry Ford

But times are changing. Putting new products on the market is an expensive and risky business. Consumers have so many options for spending their money on products and services, and they are so overwhelmed with the marketing blitz of today's advertising, telephone and mail solicitations, that most businesses, especially new businesses, find it is very difficult to get the attention of their intended customers. Unlike any time in history, the burden is on the business to find the customer, to understand the customer's needs and wants, and to provide what the customer wants when it is wanted. The smart business person recognizes that we have moved from a product-driven economy to a customer-driven economy, and management practices need to adapt to the new economic order.

The customer is the most important element of your business. All other elements exist to support and sustain your customers. You need to have a clear vision of how your business will serve the customer, and you need to educate every employee in your business regarding how you will all work together to achieve that mission. The service systems you set up must provide everything employees need to deliver the best "customer-friendly" products and service possible. The people who deliver

---

Profile

"The customer is whoever gets your work next."
– Karou Ishikawa

Karou Ishikawa is probably the best known of the Japanese gurus in quality. His work supported W. Edwards Deming's and Joseph M. Juran's in helping to rebuild the Japanese economy with quality. Ishikawa is best known for developing the Fishbone Diagram, one of the seven basic tools of TQM. Ishikawa is also credited with clarifying the concept of customer as "whoever gets your work next," whether inside or outside of the organization. That idea has evolved into the concept of Internal Customers and External Customers. Ishikawa, who died in 1989, was the author of the book Guide to Quality Control, which today is one of the most widely read books on how to use statistics for quality.

these services to customers include everyone in the organization—front-line employees, and all levels of management and support staff.

Employee Involvement and Education

The quest to satisfy the customer is not just the job of management or the front-line employees. A business committed to quality must involve every employee of the company. Gone are the days of rivalries between work units and the "us-versus-them" attitudes of management and non-management. If a company is going to succeed in implementing the quality concept, then *every* employee must rethink his or her position and relationship to every other employee. The game has changed, the stakes are higher, and teamwork is essential to achieving your vision and satisfying the customer.

If everyone in your small business is to become part of the team and a champion for the customer, they will need to be educated. Your goal is to achieve unity of purpose, therefore every employee must learn about that purpose, his or her importance in the organization, and how each job relates to the overall goal of serving the customer. Every employee must be given the skills and knowledge needed to make sound decisions whenever and wherever those decisions need to be made, and every employee must have an unwavering commitment to excellence. As owner/manager, it is your job to train employees in what constitutes excellence and to lead the charge.

Not only is it necessary to "team up" with other members of your organization, you also must establish partnerships with the suppliers of goods and support services that serve your business, along with other businesses in your community, government and regulatory agencies, etc. Cooperation with these organizations can help you better meet the needs of your customers.

The Continuous Improvement of Systems and Processes
Systems

Key Word

According to Peter M. Senge, author of *The Fifth Discipline* (New York: Doubleday, 1990), a **system** is a set of related entities that receives inputs, adds value to them, and produces outputs to achieve a defined system purpose, mission or aim. Every small business is a system with a defined purpose—and that purpose is to serve the customer. Every small business is a sub-system of the larger systems to which it belongs. For example, a restaurant is part of the larger food service industry, its community, and perhaps the entertainment industry. A small manufacturer of steering wheels is part of a larger system of automobile manufacturers. Every system contains sub-systems. The restaurant may have systems within it for food preparation, marketing, catering, and business operations. The steering wheel manufacturer may have systems for production, safety, and shipping its products.

Processes

A **process** refers to a series of activities to obtain results. Systems typically receive inputs, add value to them through certain processes, and produce outputs. Systems typically have a number of processes going on at any one time. In a restaurant, the transformation of raw vegetables into a beautiful salad involves a process, as does the setting of a table. Every small business involves a number of processes, which are performed to meet the needs and wants of the customer.

Key Word

W. Edwards Deming attempted to show the flow of production through a system with the following diagram:

Figure 1.2: The Deming Flow Diagram

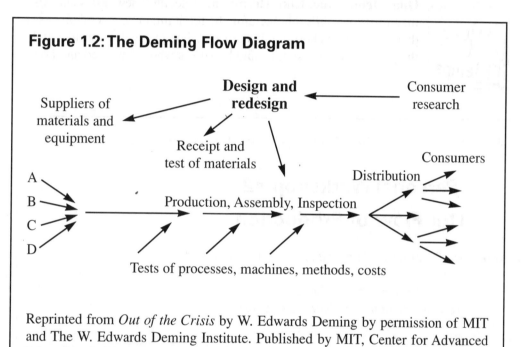

Reprinted from *Out of the Crisis* by W. Edwards Deming by permission of MIT and The W. Edwards Deming Institute. Published by MIT, Center for Advanced Educational Services, Cambridge, MA 02139. Copyright 1986 by The W. Edwards Deming Institute.

Whatever comes into a production line from suppliers will be transformed and improved in some way before it is distributed to the customer. According to Deming, a flow diagram can be made for any job, any production process, anywhere in the world. The purpose of doing so is to understand how everyone connected with the production process is interdependent, from product designers to suppliers to assemblers to distributors; and therefore must work together to continuously improve the process.

> *"The significant problems we face cannot be solved at the same level of thinking we were at when we created them."*
>
> —Albert Einstein

Personal Workshop Preparation #2:
Our Flow of Production

To help you understand the concept of the flow of production through a system, think of a single, simple process in your company, and develop a flow diagram for it. Replace the letters and general descriptions in Deming's diagram with names and words that help describe the process. Don't worry if the diagram you develop isn't perfect—the point of this exercise is just to familiarize yourself with the diagram format and to point out the relationships between people and functions in the process. Start simple!

Quali-Temps Inc./Kiki Hermann: Selecting new associates is a major part of Kiki's job, therefore he felt it might be a good process to diagram. Before choosing this process, though, he also considered that the process is fairly simple, and he knows who is involved and how.

THE PURPOSE OF THIS WORKSHOP IS TO DIAGRAM THE WORK FLOW IN A PROCESS.

Personal Workshop #2
Our Flow of Production

The work flow diagram for: the selection of new associates.

Process Flow Diagram
Process: Selection of New Associates

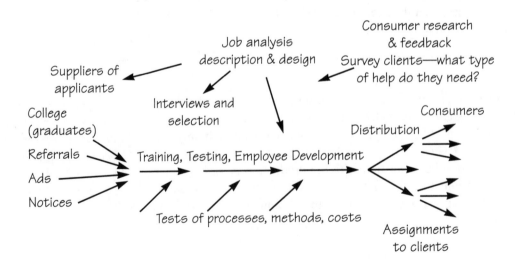

THE PURPOSE OF THIS WORKSHOP IS TO DIAGRAM THE WORK FLOW IN A PROCESS.

Personal Workshop #2
Our Flow of Production

The work flow diagram for: _____

Process Flow Diagram

Process: _____

Workshop Follow-Up

✔ By drawing this diagram, you should have a better idea of how work and people flow through the process you selected. As noted earlier, a similar diagram could be drawn for every job and every process in your company. Once you get into the business of educating your employees about systems, a good learning exercise might be to ask each person to draw a diagram for his or her own job. This will help the employees understand their relationships to the entire system.

Systems Thinking

Key Word

Systems thinking requires an appreciation for the fact that all parts of a system, small or large, are interrelated and interdependent. Once again, using a restaurant as an example, a decision to change the menu and prices could affect the systems for preparing food, ordering produce, advertising the products, etc. It could also affect the larger systems. For example, a change in prices or cuisine could attract or discourage the competition, could compliment or hurt the businesses around the restaurant, and could positively or negatively impact the labor market. Systems thinking requires that every person in the system understand how *what* they do and *how* they do it might impact every other person in the system.

The quality concept requires a thorough understanding of the systems and processes in your business by everyone in the business. It also requires systems thinking—understanding how your job is influenced by those who come before you in the process, and how your work and decisions affect those who come after you in the process. The goal of every business with a quality concept is to constantly improve processes and systems by eliminating glitches, or variation, in the system—in other words, to achieve continuous process improvement. The philosophy of "if it ain't broke, don't fix it" has no place in a company with the quality concept. There is always room for improvement, and every employee should be held responsible for finding and making those improvements.

Profile

"Do it right the first time."

—Philip Crosby

Philip Crosby was influential in bringing the quality movement to American corporations. As an executive, he helped both Martin Marietta and ITT move into quality management, and he has worked with countless other companies around the world since forming his own organization for quality. Crosby is best known for his belief that people are the key to quality, not statistics, and that quality should be achieved through prevention rather than inspection. He believes that it is possible to achieve **Zero Defects** in production, and he believes that adopting the quality concept should be fairly easy for organizations, unlike most of the other gurus in quality management.

Crosby's philosophy on quality is described in his book Quality is Free, which was published in 1979. Crosby offers a Fourteen Point Process for Quality Improvement, which includes ideas such as forming a quality improvement team, conducting zero defects planning, goal setting, and using quality councils within an organization.

Applying the Principles of Quality Management

In the Challenges that follow, you will have an opportunity to apply the principles and tools of quality management to your small business. To prepare you for those Challenges and the even greater challenge of implementing the quality concept in your business, you need to develop a clear understanding of what an organization committed to quality looks like. You also need to assess your readiness to make the move to quality management. The remainder of Challenge 1 is dedicated to helping you understand the characteristics of a quality company, as well as the characteristics of your own company.

Quality Management and Attitude Adjustment

With the exception of Phil Crosby, most of the leaders in quality believe the transition process is a difficult one. That is because quality management requires a change in philosophy—a thought revolution—by the owner, the managers/supervisors, and each and every employee. If you choose to implement quality management in your company, understand that many old habits will need to be broken, and many of your current beliefs regarding how a business should be run will need to change.

The traditional American business was built for the purpose of growing return on investment and maximizing the owner's wealth. The purpose of a company with a quality concept is to develop people so they can better meet the needs and wants of the customers. This is not to say that profit is no longer important—without it, you are out of business. But in a quality company, profit should never be the overriding reason for a company's existence. The differences in philosophy, purpose and the roles of employees are highlighted in Table 1.1 on pages 18.

B ecause many of the practices of quality management are so different from the traditional American way of doing business, you should make the change very gradually, perhaps over a 2-3 year period. Introduce the concepts of quality management to your employees through education and, at the same time, begin to involve them in some teamwork to solve process problems. Start with problems that are relatively simple. As everyone in the company begins to understand and apply the concepts, and after they have experienced some success in improving processes and making decisions, it will become easier to move them to the next level.

W. Edwards Deming believed that a company needed to adopt the quality concept in total in order to succeed at quality. But, if you are not ready to make a total commitment at this time, consider applying just a few pieces to start—the concepts or tools that you think will be most helpful. After all, **the reality for the small business owner is that the business has to keep running, no matter what you decide to implement.** So, take your time, gain some confidence, and then take another step. Remember, quality needs to be an evolution, not a revolution.

Table 1.1: A Changing Paradigm for Small Business

	The Traditional American Company	The New Quality Company (A new paradigm)
Purpose of the Business	To grow return on investment and maximize owner wealth. To put a product or service on the market.	To create a learning organization, where employees work cooperatively and share a vision for meeting customer needs at a profit.
Role of the Customer	The customer is the market and exists to buy the product or service.	The customer is the reason for the company's existence and the basis for all decisions.
Role of the Manager	Decides what should be produced and how, sets strategy and goals, makes decisions, controls costs through economies of scale, resource consumption, and price manipulation; directs and controls activities of employees to carry out duties to meet goals.	Communicates vision and values, models commitment to customer and quality improvement, develops employees through education, team-building and coaching; relinquishes most decision-making to teams and individuals; develops human resources; empowers others to do what's right to serve the customer.
Role of Other Employees	Follow directions, do their jobs, meet the production goals set by management; leave decision-making to management; leave quality control to the inspectors.	Understand the vision and system and their role in it. Learn all about the customer and do whatever is right to satisfy the customer; take pride in workmanship and build in quality; look continuously for ways to improve processes and products.
Organizational Chart		
Results	Short-term profit perspective; "us-versus-them" attitude between management and non-management; the product drives the company.	The needs of the customers drive the company, long-term vision guides decision-making, always improving.

Other Key Concepts of Quality Management

Other key concepts for understanding quality management include the theory of variation, the theory of knowledge, and the psychology behind quality management.

• **Theory of Variation**: Quality is threatened when there are variations in a process or system. Errors and inconsistencies will always exist, and in the traditional organization, people try to fix those problems by working on the product rather than the process. To eliminate errors and raise quality, you must concentrate on minimizing variations in processes. For the small business, this theory suggests that systems and processes must be studied, and quality must be built into those processes, rather than depending on inspection and rework for quality control. Variation in the processes threatens quality, but variation in any process can be spotted and eliminated through statistical analysis, allowing the small business to deliver the best products or services possible.

• **Theory of Knowledge**: Knowledge comes from theory and from putting that theory to use. Knowledge helps businesses to predict, to act accordingly, and to interpret the results of that action. For the small business, this theory suggests that you cannot learn about quality by copying another company—it is a process that your company must develop for itself. You will learn by doing—by making predictions about how various improvements might affect the business, by making those changes and measuring their results, by changing again or reinforcing any positive changes. Change now will produce improvement in the future.

• **Psychology**: Psychology helps managers understand people—employees, customers, or anyone else—and their needs. Deming believed that people inherently want to improve their own performance. Rather than pitting employees against each other, he suggested that management teach employees how to measure things, because then they will continually try to improve on their own standards and accomplishments. For optimal products and services from the small business, it is important to understand the behavior and motivations of the individuals and groups associated with the company. It also suggests eliminating ratings and ranking systems and rewards which promote internal competition and destroy the natural instincts of employees to do a better job within the system.

The Importance of Leadership

Deming believed that the responsibility for quality ultimately rests with top management. In fact, he said that 85 percent of all quality problems were due to management, while only 15 percent could be attributed to the other workers. Only management can establish a commitment to quality and provide the incentives and support needed to make it happen. As an owner/manager of a small business, you are key to your company's quality efforts. Simply put, it will not happen, unless you want it to happen.

Deming is probably best known for his **Fourteen Points for Management**, which are directed to managers who want to implement the quality concept in their organizations. Table 1.2 on pp. 20-21 gives a brief description of each of Deming's Fourteen Points with some possible implications for small business.

Table 1.2: Deming's Fourteen Points for Management

Reprinted from *Out of the Crisis* by W. Edwards Deming by permission of MIT and The W. Edwards Deming Institute. Published by MIT, Center for Advanced Educational Services, Cambridge, MA 02139. Copyright 1986 by The W. Edwards Deming Institute.

1. Create Constancy of Purpose Toward Improvement of Product and Service.
It is top management's job to establish constancy of purpose through "unshakable commitment to quality and productivity" (Deming, 1986) and to satisfying the customer. *Constancy of purpose requires the small business owner to clearly define the company's mission, vision and operating philosophy, and to build commitment to long-term goals to meet the needs of the customers. Supervisors should encourage ideas and innovation, and every employee should be involved in developing strategies for continuous improvement.*

2. Adopt the New Philosophy.
Learn the new philosophy and adopt a plan for continuous improvement. Recognize that we are in a new age of global competition, and customers do not have to tolerate poor quality. *Small business owners must recognize that they cannot insulate themselves from the quality movement. They should change their management philosophy and lead their employees into a never-ending cycle of continuous improvement of products and services, as well as personal pride in workmanship. To ignore quality is a high risk proposition.*

3. Cease Dependence on Mass Inspection to Achieve Quality.
Mass inspection at the end of a process does not guarantee quality or improve the product. Instead of depending upon inspection, teach every employee involved in the process how to build quality into the product as it is made. *As a small business owner/manager, you know that production errors are costly. Instead of spotting the problems and trying to fix them after they are made, examine the process being used to make the product, and train your employees to constantly work to improve that process.*

4. End the Practice of Awarding Business to Suppliers Based on Price Tag Alone.
Vendors should be viewed as partners for long-term relationships. Select vendors carefully—consider the quality of their products or services, as well as the price, their dependability and capabilities. *As a small business owner, recognize that the quality of your product can be no better than the quality of the products that go into it. Pick suppliers based on value, not price. Be clear about your needs and expectations with your suppliers (you are the customer!), and demand quality. Develop and nurture long-term and reliable relationships with those suppliers who meet your quality standards.*

5. Improve Constantly and Forever the System of Production and Service.
An ongoing commitment to the continuous improvement of every process in the system is paramount to achieving quality and will help lower costs. Deming suggested using the **Shewhart/Deming Cycle (Plan-Do-Study-Act)** to make improvements. *The small business owner must recognize that the quest for quality is a never-ending process. There are always more ways to improve the processes in your business, and it needs to be the goal of everyone in the business, every job in every department, to look for those ways and make quality a reality throughout the system. Challenge 4 will guide you through the continuous improvement process.*

6. Institute Training on the Job.
Employees at all levels need skills and knowledge to do their jobs correctly and efficiently. Orientation and training, including training in quality and process improvement, are a necessary part of the quality management equation. *Examine your orientation and training programs. Are they giving your employees the tools they need to deliver quality products and services to meet the needs of your customers? If you want employees to be committed to quality, they must be trained in the concepts of customer service and quality management. Employees need the skills to do their jobs today and in the future.*

7. Institute Leadership.
The role of any leader is to help others do a better job. Managers and production workers need to be trained to be leaders in the quality improvement effort. The approach of management needs to include support, coaching, feedback, mentoring, cheerleading, sharing responsibility, and not blaming. *In the small business, as in any business, management may need to take a serious look at how it views and communicates with non-management personnel. The quality concept requires effective teamwork. Management must support team building in all of its decision making and actions. Managers need to develop the skills to inspire and influence all employees.*

8. Drive Out Fear.

Fear of making a mistake, fear of asking questions, fear of taking risks—all of these fears are common in the traditional organizational structure, and all of them are destructive to the individuals and the company which wants to be able to respond to customer needs. Fear must be eliminated, and a climate of trust and innovation must be nurtured. *If your small business has historically placed blame on individual employees and relied on punishment when things went wrong, then driving out fear will be one of your most difficult challenges. It takes a long time for people to trust once they have been burned. You will need to demonstrate again and again that innovation, risk-taking, and decision-making are not to be feared but celebrated.*

9. Break Down Barriers Between Staff Areas.

Competition or non-cooperation between work areas (divisions, departments, functional or geographical areas, etc.) is not in the best interest of the customer or the business as a whole. Employees at all levels, in all areas, should be working together to solve problems and provide the best possible customer service. *If your small business has different departments or functional areas, it is important that the people communicate openly and solve problems using cross-functional teams. Train people in the common purpose of the organization and teach them how to use teamwork to achieve that purpose. Eliminate the "us versus them" attitude—beginning with management.*

10. Eliminate Slogans, Exhortations, and Targets for the Work Force.

Deming believed that such fluff tends to promote competition between teams, is usually meaningless or arbitrary, and often tends to have the opposite affect on motivation. *If your small business uses slogans, T-shirts, or other motivational gimmicks, examine them closely: Do they really mean anything or make a difference? Are your targets realistic or just wishful thinking? Instead, instill teamwork and a sense of pride in your employees.*

11. Eliminate Numerical Quotas and M.B.O. (Management by Objectives)—Substitute Leadership.

Quotas, production standards, incentive pay, and M.B.O. don't help people do a better job. Instead of guiding performance with meaningless numbers or objectives, guide your employees to continuous quality by helping them learn about processes and how to improve them. This is more difficult than simply measuring outcomes, but it is the key to quality improvement. *In your small business, consider how you are measuring productivity—do you count beans? If so, does it tell you anything about the true quality of your products or services? Instead, learn about processes (the means, not the ends) and establish baseline measures for quality and productivity. Then work to improve them.*

12. Remove Barriers that Rob Workers of Their Right to Pride of Workmanship.

Many of the merit-based and incentive systems that exist reward quantity, not quality. Management must create an environment which allows workers at all levels to excel, to provide quality products and services and to develop their natural sense of pride in their work. *The small business manager must provide training in quality improvement, give workers the tools, skills and coaching needed to develop quality products, and they must remove the barriers that prevent quality, such as vague directions, rewards for quantity, and/or mixed messages.*

13. Institute a Vigorous Program of Education and Self-Improvement.

The quality organization must become a learning organization and maintain a state of constant self-evaluation and change—with the goal of continuously meeting customers' needs. Employees need to improve their skills and increase their knowledge so they can actively contribute in the quest for system and product advances that lead to continuous improvement. *No business is too small to educate and develop its employees. The small business owner/manager must offer employees the opportunity to learn, so that they can better apply their skills and knowledge to the continuous improvement of the company.*

14. Take Action to Accomplish the Transformation.

Taking action begins with understanding and applying the Fourteen Points. Deming recommends that top management develop a plan of action for implementing the quality concept, but it will be the job of every employee to make the transformation happen. *Transformation at the small business level must begin with the unwavering commitment of the owner to the quality concept. Management and non-management alike must be trained and must work together to transform the company, since a change in culture and process is required. Teams must be formed and systems and processes must be examined for understanding and opportunities to improve. Don't wait for your customers to "force" quality on you— take the initiative.*

Personal Workshop Preparation #3: How Do We Measure Up?

This workshop will give you the opportunity to assess the status of your company in relation to Deming's Fourteen Points. Use the descriptions on the previous pages to identify examples of the things you are doing right in your company and the things on which you need to improve. Whether you are already involved to some extent in quality management or just beginning, this exercise will help you to better understand the strengths and weaknesses of your company, as well as to identify certain obstacles you will face in the transformation process. This information can help you prepare to face those obstacles and set priorities.

 Recycled Paper Wholesalers/Lindy Hernandez: Since Lindy has been in business for 5 years, she recognizes that a strong organizational culture already exists. Most of her managers have been with her since the beginning, and they tend to be pretty traditional in their thinking. By completing Workshop #3, Lindy got a better sense of RPW, its people and the challenges facing it.

Personal Notes

_____

_____

_____

_____

 **Profile**

Armand Feigenbaum, a former manager of manufacturing and quality control for General Electric, became significant in the quality movement when he proposed that the responsibility for quality extends beyond the manufacturing function. He suggested in his article entitled "Total Quality Control" (*Harvard Business Review,* Nov.-Dec. 1956) that the quality of any product is affected at many stages of the industrial cycle, by marketers, engineers, purchasing, manufacturing and shipping personnel.

In other words, quality and quality costs are influenced by the entire industrial cycle. Inspection from above doesn't work, since all elements are critical in controlling quality.

THE PURPOSE OF THIS WORKSHOP IS TO DETERMINE HOW YOUR COMPANY IS DOING ON DEMING'S FOURTEEN POINTS.

Personal Workshop #3
How Do We Measure Up?

	Things We're Doing Right	Things We Need To Improve	Obstacles We Face
1. Constancy of purpose	• Revised mission and vision last year. • Owner is committed to quality.	• Goals need to be long term. • Change in philosophy to quality	• Supervisors need to change attitude about workers.
2. Adopt the new philosophy	• Owner is committed. • Everyone understands that we need to change if we want to survive.	• Knowledge of supervisors and all employees	• RPW is very traditional – both supervisors and other workers will need an attitude adjustment.
3. Cease dependence on mass inspection	• Nothing.	• Mass inspection at end of process • Inspection at start and throughout process	• Our system doesn't currently support "building quality in." We'll have to do some serious changes.
4. End practice of awarding business on lowest price	• We do offer different prices for different quality paper.	• Check our prices to see if they contribute to fact that we can't attract suppliers.	• Finding suppliers of higher quality paper.
5. Continuously improve the system	• We need to learn how to do this.	• Processes –.we need to learn how to evaluate and improve them.	• Attitude about whose job it is to assure quality.
6. Institute training	• We revamped our orientation program last year.	• Regular training –.in past it's been haphazard.	• Getting everyone together for training. • Lost production time.
7. Institute leadership	• We have some good people who are willing to learn.	• Leadership training in quality concepts. • More team building.	• We have one very negative manager who needs a change in attitude.

Personal Workshop #3, continued

	Things We're Doing Right	Things We Need To Improve	Obstacles We Face
8. Drive out fear	• I don't think we have much fear at RPW.	• We need to talk about this to see how our employees feel.	• Employees might be afraid of the negative manager.
9. Break down barriers between departments	• We have an annual holiday party.	• Getting departments together for planning, strategizing and learning.	• Staff might be suspicious at first; tread lightly.
10. Eliminate slogans and fluff	• Not much fluff here.	• Examine production targets – do they promote quality?	• Finding meaningful goals.
11. Eliminate quotas	• Nothing.	• Need to learn about processes.	• Get rid of "quantity over quality" attitude.
12. Remove barriers to pride of workmanship	• We've started to talk about what "pride" means.	• People don't totally understand how they can make a difference.	• Leadership needs to learn how to support workers.
13. Provide quality education programs	• This Challenge!	• Education for ALL levels, not just management	• We need to find a good TQM facilitator.
14. Take action in the transformation	• I'm determined to make this happen.	• Need to get all management committed to new philosophy	• We have so much to learn! Some people don't buy the concept yet.

THE PURPOSE OF THIS WORKSHOP IS TO DETERMINE HOW YOUR COMPANY IS DOING ON DEMING'S FOURTEEN POINTS.

Personal Workshop #3
How Do We Measure Up?

	Things We're Doing Right	Things We Need To Improve	Obstacles We Face
1. Constancy of purpose			
2. Adopt the new philosophy			
3. Cease dependence on mass inspection			
4. End practice of awarding business on lowest price			
5. Continuously improve the system			
6. Institute training			
7. Institute leadership			

Personal Workshop #3, continued

	Things We're Doing Right	Things We Need To Improve	Obstacles We Face
8. Drive out fear			
9. Break down barriers between departments			
10. Eliminate slogans and fluff			
11. Eliminate quotas			
12. Remove barriers to pride of workmanship			
13. Provide quality education programs			
14. Take action in the transformation			

Workshop Follow-Up

✔ How well did your company do? Or more accurately, how well does management do on each of the Fourteen Points? Remember that it is the responsibility of management to lead your company through the transformation to quality. If you have listed any member of management as an obstacle to your progress, you need to address that problem early.

How Leaders Behave in Quality Companies

To lead a company into quality takes a special type of person. The quality leader must believe, first of all, that employees are a tremendous asset, worth developing, trusting and nurturing. And, a quality leader must be honest and trustworthy as well; otherwise, the company environment will not support the quality concept. Beyond trust, there are a few other critical characteristics of a quality leader.

The quality leader:

- Stays constantly focused on the goal of satisfying the customer through continuous process improvement

- Is committed to and effectively communicates the mission, vision and values of the company and can inspire others to accomplish the company's goals

- Is constantly involved in quality activities through team building, supporting others in their decision-making, removing barriers for creativity and continuous improvement, developing a supportive environment and modeling the quality concept

- Keeps employees apprised of the plans and activities of the company, and provides clear and accurate feedback to employees and teams to keep them informed and help them learn

- Recognizes that education and training are key to the success of employees and the company, and provides the resources needed (time and money) to develop employees

- Is willing to give up some control by involving employees in decision-making and problem-solving

- Promotes teamwork by eliminating competition between individuals and departments, and by developing a work environment which supports and rewards cooperation, information sharing, and team accomplishments

- Understands that a leader's job is to support, coach, mentor, guide, build relationships and teach

- Understands that a manager's job in a quality organization is to promote continuous improvement of the system, not to control the employees

Personal Workshop Preparation #4: Quality Leadership Assessment

As owner/manager, you need to be aware of your leadership style. So does every other manager in the small business. The next workshop is designed to help you assess your own readiness for leading your company to quality. Try to be as honest as possible in your answers to the following questions. And, if you have a trusted employee—one who isn't afraid to tell you the truth—let that person assess your leadership style as well. Compare your opinions, and then discuss how you can build on your strengths and develop your weaknesses to become more like the quality leader described above. Soliciting feedback from an employee may seem rather threatening to you, but do it in the spirit of learning and improving yourself. If your assessments are distinctly different, you may need to do some serious thinking about how you relate to your employees.

 Quali-Temps Inc./Kiki Hermann: Kiki already knows that he wants to implement quality management into his new business—otherwise, his chances for successfully competing with the "big guys" for the big business will be poor. Kiki took the Quality Leadership Assessment to determine if he had what it takes to be a quality leader.

THE PURPOSE OF THIS WORKSHOP IS TO ASSESS YOUR LEADERSHIP STYLE.

Personal Workshop #4
Quality Leadership Assessment

1. Do you believe that every employee is an asset to your company?
   Definitely!

   If not, why not?

   If so, what have you done lately to help develop these assets?
   Regular training programs to learn new skills on computers; involve them in decision making.

2. Do you have a clear vision and clear values for your company?
   Yes.

   If so, how do you communicate that vision and those values to your employees?
   We have regular planning sessions and we check on progress at weekly staff meetings.

3. Do you involve your employees in decision-making?
   Yes and no.

   If so, how?
   Associate supervisors serve as my executive committee—we make all decisions together. Other employees—not involved.

Personal Workshop #4, continued

4. Are you comfortable letting other people solve problems without your supervision?
    Yes and no.

    If yes, give an example.
    Associate supervisors. I'm not comfortable with others making decisions.

5. Do you promote teamwork in your company?
    Yes—but we need more work.

    If so, how?
    We have a plan to get everyone involved in a quality improvement team this year.

6. Do you effectively communicate with your employees about the plans and activities of the company?
    Yes.

    If so, how?
    E-mail, weekly meetings, electronic newsletter to associates in field.

7. Do you provide your employees with opportunities for education and training?
    Yes.

    If so, what has been done in the last six months?
    Monthly training sessions for all associates.

8. Do the managers/supervisors in your company consistently treat employees with respect and nurture their growth?
    As far as I can tell, yes.

    If so, how do you assure this?
    We need to do more leadership training.

9. Do you promote an unwavering commitment to meeting customer needs in your company?
    Yes!

    If so, how do you know what those needs are?
    We interview clients, extensive questionnaire about needs. Also performance evaluations of associates.

10. Do you promote an unwavering commitment to quality in your company?
    I think so—we keep talking about it.

    If so, how?
    Will start TQM training.

Personal Workshop #4
Quality Leadership Assessment

1. Do you believe that every employee is an asset to your company?

    If not, why not?

    If so, what have you done lately to help develop these assets?

2. Do you have a clear vision and clear values for your company?

    If so, how do you communicate that vision and those values to your employees?

3. Do you involve your employees in decision making?

    If so, how?

4. Are you comfortable letting other people solve problems without your supervision?
    If yes, give an example.

5. Do you promote teamwork in your company?

    If so, how?

6. Do you effectively communicate with your employees about the plans and activities of the company?

    If so, how?

7. Do you provide your employees with opportunities for education and training?

    If so, what has been done in the last six months?

Personal Workshop #4, continued

8. Do the managers/supervisors in your company consistently treat employees with respect and nurture their growth?

   If so, how do you assure this?

9. Do you promote an unwavering commitment to meeting customer needs in your company?

   If so, how do you know what those needs are?

10. Do you promote an unwavering commitment to quality in your company?

    If so, how?

Workshop Follow-Up

✔ The intent of this workshop wasn't to intimidate you. Hopefully, it provided some insight into your own leadership style, and it made you aware of the rigid demands on leaders in a company with the quality concept. The fact remains that, as good as some of these leadership characteristics might sound, they are somewhat contrary to how managers have traditionally run the American workplace. Look at your results again and give yourself a star by those questions that you believe reveal your strengths as a quality leader. Then put a circle around those areas where you need more work. Don't expect to be able to change your total philosophy and management style overnight. Educate yourself, try out the quality concepts, gain skills and confidence, and gradually keep moving ahead. And through it all, focus on "continuous improvement to please the customer."

How to Get Started with the Quality Transformation

Change is never easy, no matter what size your business is. You may be able to clearly and logically explain the benefits of the quality concept to your employees, even in terms of "what's in it for them." That still doesn't guarantee they will embrace the quality philosophy or practice continuous process improvement—and your management personnel may be more difficult to convince than everyone else! Peter Scholtes and Heero Hacquebord offer the following guidelines (Table 1.3 on p. 32) for transforming an organization into a quality management company.

> *"There is nothing more difficult or perilous than to take the lead in the introduction to change."*
>
> —Machiavelli

Table 1.3: Guidelines for Change

©1987 Joiner Associates Incorporated. Used with permission.

1. Recognize the informal organization.

Every company is made up of groups of people with strong relationships and loyalties. Transformation will be much easier if these groups and the informal leaders of these groups accept the quality concept. To implement change, recognize the strength of these groups and their leaders, and work to win their support.

2. Seek the active support of a critical mass.

Chances are you will never win unanimous support for the quality concept. Use your most enthusiastic supporters to win over the neutrals, and gradually build momentum. Ask the skeptics to withhold judgment for a reasonable period of time, so that the company has a chance to try on the quality concept.

3. People don't resist change, they resist *being* changed. Allow people to deal with the need for change and the planning of change. Help people to let go of the old way as gracefully as possible.

Recognize that the transformation to quality will be an emotional change, not just a logical one. Allow your employees the time needed to deal with the dynamics of such a dramatic change; and give them the resources and support needed to learn about quality, practice their new skills and feel comfortable with the change.

4. When possible, organization change should be planned and treated like a courtship—with a mixture of gradualism and surprise.

Give people time to adjust and permission to make mistakes and feel a little awkward. Change gradually or in increments; consider starting on an experimental basis. Replace symbols of the "old way" with new symbols which reflect the change in philosophy and vision. "Woo" the undecided, and listen carefully to people's concerns, especially those of the formal and informal "movers and shakers."

5. Efforts to implement change should be "anchored."

Provide a network of support services and resources, team projects, and quality activities involving many people. This will help those involved feel competent, confident and able to learn from others.

6. The more profound, comprehensive, and widespread the proposed change, the more absolute is the need for the deep understanding and active leadership by the top managers. The transformation to a quality organization is such a change.

If top management is not totally committed, the rest of the company employees will either not fully accept the quality concept, believing it is a temporary fad, or will become very frustrated in their efforts. Top management must provide the inspiration, the direction, and the model for quality transformation.

Personal Workshop Preparation #5: Action Steps for Quality Transformation

Use the Guidelines for Change in Table 1.3 to help you decide how to start the transformation process in your small business. This workshop will give you an opportunity to identify specific action steps that can be taken to get things started. Ideally, you should involve other people in this workshop. Pull together the proponents of quality management and brainstorm steps you can take to get the organization moving toward quality. If you are the only quality champion so far, your first step might be to have some of your trusted and open-minded company leaders go through the entire first Challenge. Then tackle this workshop together. Good luck!

> *"Change would be easy if it were not for all the damned people."*
>
> —Peter Scholtes

Quali-Temps Inc./Kiki Hermann: Kiki sat down with his Business Manager and the three Associate Supervisors at Quali-Temps to complete the next workshop. For each question, they tried brainstorming to come up with a multitude of ideas. Then they discussed the ideas and settled on two or three action steps for each question. Here is what they came up with.

Personal Notes

_____

_____

_____

_____

_____

Personal education is important to your success as a quality leader. At the end of each Challenge in this book, you will find a suggested reading list to help you further develop your quality leadership skills. You might also consider taking more classes on quality management, hiring a consultant to help you develop your quality program and leadership skills, or talking with other small business managers who are involved in quality management.

Personal Workshop #5
Action Steps for Quality Transformation

1. Recognize the informal organization.
   a. List below any informal groups that exist in your company, as well as their leader(s).

Group(s)	Leader(s)
1. South College recent graduates	Jan and Joe
2. The engineers	Mavis

   b. What action steps can you take to win the support of these groups?

   #1 Meet with Jan and Joe to determine their attitudes about quality management and what they might have learned at South College about TQM.

   #2 Meet with the entire engineering group to find out how *their* backgrounds fits in with TQM and whether any of them have previous experience with it. Ask them to help with systems studies and statistical analyses.

2. Seek the active support of a critical mass.
   a. To the best of your knowledge, who do you expect to be the most enthusiastic supporters of quality? Who will be neutral? Who will be the dissenters? List those people below.

Supporters	Neutral	Dissenters
Joe	Susan	David
Adam	John	Karen
Leslie	Jack	Howie
Erica	Jean	Lela

   b. What action steps can you take to win over the "Neutrals?"
   #1 Hire consultant to do a one-day training session on TQM, with special emphasis on the benefits to the employees and the company.
   #2 Follow-up with an information session to address questions and concerns.
   #3 Ask supporters who know them best to meet with them one-on-one to ask about their reservations.

   c. What action steps can you take to negotiate with the dissenters?
   Involve dissenters in training with neutrals, however, ask them to withhold judgment until a few things have been tried out.

Personal Workshop #5, continued

3. People don't resist change, they resist *being* changed.
   a. What action steps can you take to understand people's fear of this change?
   #1 Same as item 2b above.
   #2 Supervisors should meet with all associates to discuss the meaning and possible implications of the change, and to allow individuals to express their concerns.

4. When possible, change should be planned.
   a. What action steps can you take to ease people into this change?
   #1 Begin weekly training meetings to learn about quality.
   #2 Start people on quality improvement teams for simple problems of their choosing.
   #3 Associate Supervisors will work closely with teams to guide them through the process.

   b. What is your timetable for implementing this change?
   #1 Begin training immediately and continue over next two years.
   #2 Begin team building activities immediately.
   #3 Have all associates involved in a quality improvement team within six months.
   #4 Aim for total implementation within three years.

5. Efforts to implement change should be "anchored."
   a. What action steps can you take to assure that people have the support and resources needed to make the change?
   #1 Provide ongoing training to supervisors, quality leaders and team members as needed.
   #2 Expand library resources in total quality management.
   #3 Management will continuously encourage teams to think in terms of what they can do to improve, not what they can't do because of limited resources.

6. The more profound the change, the more absolute is the need for the deep understanding and active leadership of top managers.
   a. What action steps can you take to assure that managers have a "deep understanding" of the principles and practices of quality management?
   #1 Managers will meet weekly for leadership training and attend all quality training sessions.
   #2 Managers will read at least one additional quality management resource or engage in some other self-study activity each week.
   #3 Managers will have a "problems and solutions" session with other managers each week.

   b. What can you do to assure that managers develop the leadership skills needed to assure the success of your quality transformation?
   #1 Managers will remind each other of the characteristics of a quality leader as needed.
   #2 Owner will totally support quality leadership efforts of managers.

Personal Workshop #5
Action Steps for Quality Transformation

1. Recognize the informal organization.
   a. List below any informal groups that exist in your company, as well as their leader(s).

   Group(s)   *Leader(s)*

   b. What action steps can you take to win the support of these groups?

2. Seek the active support of a critical mass.
   a. To the best of your knowledge, who do you expect to be the most enthusiastic supporters of quality? Who will be neutral? Who will be the dissenters? List those people below.

   Supporters   Neutral   Dissenters

   b. What action steps can you take to win over the "Neutrals?"

   c. What action steps can you take to negotiate with the dissenters?

3. People don't resist change, they resist *being* changed.
   a. What action steps can you take to understand people's fear of this change?

Personal Workshop #5, continued

4. When possible, change should be planned.
   a. What action steps can you take to ease people into this change?

   b. What is your timetable for implementing this change?

5. Efforts to implement change should be "anchored."
   a. What action steps can you take to assure that people have the support and resources needed to make the change?

6. The more profound the change, the more absolute is the need for the deep understanding and active leadership of top managers.
   a. What action steps can you take to assure that managers have a "deep understanding" of the principles and practices of quality management?

   b. What can you do to assure that managers develop the leadership skills needed to assure the success of your quality transformation?

Workshop Follow-Up

✔ You now have some concrete ideas for moving ahead with your company's transformation to quality—congratulations! You can use the action steps you have identified as a basis for more detailed planning. For example, if your action step is "provide weekly training on quality management," you or your "quality action team" can now decide exactly how you want to accomplish that task. For example, if you plan to hire a consultant, you should start interviewing possible candidates. If you plan to conduct the training yourself, start reviewing materials to support the learning process. Decide what topics you want to cover and when.

So What's Next?

First, you need to learn as much about quality management as you can. By tackling the Challenges that follow, you will learn a great deal more about the fundamental principles of quality management. You will also have an opportunity to try out the tools on your real business problems. Chances are, you may even find that it is fun! But, in any case, you will find that the quality concept can help your business become or remain vital in a highly competitive world.

You Have Completed Challenge 1

By completing Challenge 1, you have built a foundation for constructing a vital company committed to quality. You now have a new perspective on quality and the customer, and you have the background information necessary to move to the next level of learning.

Quality management is about having a **shared vision** which will give your employees direction and their work meaning. It is about **building systems**—using methods, tools and processes to achieve that vision. And it is about **solving problems**—eliminating errors and obstacles which threaten quality and your organization's existence. The Challenges which follow will help you develop those concepts and implement quality management in your business.

You Leave Challenge 1 with the Following

 Information: By working your way through this Challenge, you have gained knowledge in the concepts and terms associated with the quality concept. Many of the Personal Workshops in this Challenge were designed to make the theory of quality more palatable and relevant to your business. The quality gurus featured in this Challenge each had their own spin on quality management. The profiles were designed to give you some background information on these individuals and to help you distinguish between their philosophies of quality management. There was, frankly, a lot of information in this Challenge—but it was necessary to give you a solid foundation for applying the quality concept to your small business. Don't be alarmed if you don't have everything straight in your head. It will take a while to feel comfortable with the terms and the concepts. The Challenges that follow will help you in your development.

Tools: The **Seven Basic Tools of TQM** were introduced in this Challenge. You had the opportunity to use one of those tools, a **Process Flow Diagram,** to identify the elements and flow of a process in your own business. In the Challenges that follow, you will learn how to apply these and other tools to your business. These tools will help you analyze your current situation, measure process improvements, and solve problems.

Learning: By completing the workshops in this Challenge, you have learned a great deal about the characteristics and philosophy of your small business. You have also learned about your own leadership style. This information should help you determine how close you are to the successful implementation of the quality concept and what areas need special attention. You have also learned about a new way of looking at quality. This new perspective should help you as you learn more about satisfying the needs of your customers in Challenge 2. Finally, you have learned the foundation principles of quality management: **The Customer Comes First**; **Employee Involvement and Education**; and the **Continuous Improvement of Processes and System**. These principles will guide the rest of your learning on the quality concept for small business.

Networking: The case studies in this Challenge serve as examples of small businesses that are in transition and involved in quality management. These cases are designed to be a resource to you—you should be able to learn something from each situation described which might apply to your business. Other resource tips are noted throughout the Challenge, as well as a suggested reading list located at the end of this book. Most of the resources listed should be available or can be ordered through any bookstore. If your library doesn't have the book you are interested in, ask about interlibrary loan. Quality Management puts a high value on education and networking. In Challenge 3, you will learn more about educating your employees in quality and developing excellent feedback and communication skills throughout the organization.

Challenge 1 Self-Assessment

After completing this Challenge 1, you should have a good feel for your company's current status and its readiness for the quality transformation. Check your understanding of the quality concept by asking yourself the following questions. If needed, go back and review the concepts of quality where you feel you need more practice.

Define Quality

( ) I can explain what is meant by the phrase, "quality is in the eye of the beholder."

( ) I can identify what my customers think is "quality" for my product or service.

Pages 1 - 4

Explain the Need for Quality in a Competitive Environment

( ) I can identify my major competitors, their strengths and weaknesses.

Pages 5 - 9

( ) I can explain why quality is important for the survival of my business.

Explain the Benefits of the Quality Concept for Small Business

( ) I can describe how improved quality creates a "chain reaction" resulting, in the end, in a more vital business which provides more jobs.

( ) I can identify at least five benefits of implementing the quality concept.

Pages 9 - 10

Identify the Foundation Principles of Total Quality Management

( ) My company is customer-driven—that is, all decisions are made based on what the customer wants, needs and expects.

( ) I am willing to provide my employees with the opportunities and resources needed to develop their skills and knowledge.

( ) My company considers its employees a valuable asset.

( ) I understand the concepts of systems, processes, and systems thinking.

( ) I can create a flow diagram for any job or process in my company.

( ) I understand the concept of continuous process improvement.

Pages 10 - 16

Recognize the Key Names and Terms that Have Helped Define the Quality Concept

( ) I can recognize the names of the quality gurus, and I understand a bit about their approaches to quality management.

( ) I recognize the different names and acronyms for quality management, and have a general understanding of what they mean.

Pages 3 - 22

Assess Your Company's Strengths, Weaknesses, and Possible Obstacles to Implementing the Quality Concept

( ) I have examined my company's philosophy and characteristics and compared it to the "new paradigm" for a quality company.

( ) I have assessed my company's standing on Deming's Fourteen Points.

( ) I have assessed my own leadership skills for quality management.

( ) I have identified possible obstacles to implementing quality.

Pages 20 - 31

Begin the Quality Transformation Process in Your Small Business

( ) I have made a personal commitment to the quality concept.

( ) I have identified action steps for implementing change in my small business.

( ) I am ready to learn more!

Pages 31 - 38

Take Another Look

Review the results of your checklist above. If you feel you need more work in some area, go back into the text and challenge yourself again. Otherwise, move on to Challenge 2 and learn how to know your customers and give them what they want.

Challenge 2
Putting Your Customers First

*"A satisfied customer is not enough. Business is built
on the loyal customer, one who comes back and
brings a friend."*

—W. Edwards Deming (Indianapolis seminar, 1989)

The premise of Challenge 2 is simple: Your first duty as a small business owner—no matter the type of business or where it is located—is to meet the basic needs of your customers. If you fail to do this, you simply won't make it. It doesn't matter how great or new or flashy your product or store or office is. If you don't meet the basic needs of your customers, you will eventually go out of business. Period.

Not only must *you* recognize the importance of your customers, but so must *everyone* in your business. Why? Because every employee is either serving your customers directly or serving someone who is. Unless you and each of your employees, and your suppliers, understand the importance of knowing your customers and meeting their needs, those needs may not be met. And, as a result, your customers are likely to go somewhere else.

Many business owners assume they are doing okay if they don't have many customer complaints. They buy into the myth that few complaints means that customers are satisfied. Wise business owners understand that most dissatisfied customers don't complain—at least not to the business where they received poor service. They are likely, however, to let nine or ten of their acquaintances know of the bad experience they had, and that sort of negative publicity can kill a business.

The purpose of Challenge 2 is to give you the tools and knowledge needed to develop a close relationship with your customers. Why? Because knowing your customers intimately is the only way to truly understand what they need, want, and expect when they patronize a business such as yours. And, because customer needs and wants change frequently, you are more likely to know and respond to those changes if you maintain close touch with your customers.

Upon completion of Challenge 2, you will be able to:

- Calculate the value of a customer to your business

- Differentiate between internal and external customers

- Identify the needs and expectations of each of your customer segments

- Use quality improvement tools to assess your company's customer service performance

- Build a blueprint for exceptional customer service in your business

- Empower employees to deliver exceptional customer service

Why the Customer Must Come First

Have you ever stopped to figure out what each customer is worth to your business? Perhaps you know the average size of a sale for your business (such as $10), but have you ever calculated how much business a loyal customer could bring to you in his or her lifetime?

Personal Workshop Preparation #6: Lifetime Value of a Customer

To complete this workshop, you will need to know (or estimate) the following:

- The average size of a sale in your business (for the purchase of a product or service). This can be done by simply dividing total sales by the number of sales transactions for some period of time. If you experience seasonal sales, compute your average sale for a full year. If you do not experience seasonal fluctuation, you should be able to compute the average using data for a shorter period of time.

- How often your average customer buys from you. If you have been in business for a while, you should be able to get this information by reviewing sales records. If you are in a business where customer names are not on record (such as a retail store or restaurant), you may want to do an informal survey to get this information. For example, you might ask your clerks or cashiers to ask each customer how often he or she visits the store. The cashier could inconspicuously tally the results on a **check sheet,** and within a week or two, you should have a fairly good idea how often customers visit. See the Quality Tools and Techniques box to find out how to develop a check sheet.

Key Word

Before you begin Personal Workshop #6, you may find it helpful to take a look at the check sheet that Denny and Mabel Wellman developed. Then observe how they used their data to compute the lifetime value of their customers.

Denny's Hometown Market/Denny and Mabel Wellman: Denny and Mabel suspected that their average customer visited the store once each week, but they weren't sure. They decided to have their checkers conduct an informal survey for a normal two-week period (excluding holidays). They also thought it might be interesting to study which days shoppers come in, so they decided to gather the information by day-of-the-week. The following is the check sheet they developed to help their checkers keep track of customer responses.

Quality Tools and Techniques
Check Sheet

What is it? A check sheet is simply a form designed to tally data in an organized way.

When should you use it? Use it whenever one or more people will be counting occurrences or compiling data from observation, experience, or historical sources. Use it when you need an organized format for data collection and analysis.

How do you make it?
Step 1: Decide what data needs to be collected and how it will be collected.
Step 2: Design a check sheet format that allows for the organized tallying of information over some period of time. A grid format is most common. If applicable, include a column and row for totals, an area for special remarks, and so on. Include information about what data is being collected, and when and where the data was collected.
Step 3: Collect data for a test period. Revise the check sheet as needed to accommodate the accurate and consistent collection of data by all involved.

Figure 2.1: Sample Check Sheet

Question: How often do you shop with us?

Register # _____ Week of _____

Day	Every day	2x/week	1x/week	2x/month	1x/month	1st time	Total
Sun.							
Mon.							
Tues.							
Wed.							
Thurs.							
Fri.							
Sat.							
Total							

- How many years an average customer patronizes your business. Again, you may have a good sense of this from experience or circumstances. For example, if your business serves local college students, your average customer probably stays with you for about four years. Otherwise, your local library may be a good source of information about the lifestyles of your customers. Check census data or ask your reference librarian for help in locating demographic data about your market area.

- If you are just starting a business and do not yet know the average size of a sale or number of transactions, use the sales projections from your business plan to estimate these figures.

Figure 2.2: Denny's Sample Check Sheet

Question: How often do you shop with us?

Register # ___9___   Week of ___June 3, 1996___

Day	Every day	2x/week	1x/week	2x/month	1x/month	1st time	Total
Sun.	III	₩₩ ₩₩ II	₩₩ ₩₩ IIII	₩₩ I	I	II	38
Mon.	I	₩₩ II	₩₩ I	I	III	I	19
Tues.	I	₩₩ IIII	₩₩ IIII	IIII	II	III	28
Wed.	III	IIII	₩₩ III	III	I		19
Thurs.	II	₩₩ IIII	₩₩ ₩₩	I		I	23
Fri.	I	₩₩ II	₩₩ ₩₩ I	III	I	IIII	27
Sat.	I	IIII	₩₩ II	II		II	16
Total	12	52	65	20	8	13	170

We pulled together the data to compute the lifetime value of our customers. First, we gathered the check sheets for the two weeks studied and discovered that the great majority of our customers shop one or two times each week. For the purpose of computing the lifetime value of a customer, we decided that the average customer probably comes in about 1.2 times per week. With 52 weeks in a year, we figure our average customer shops at Hometown approximately 62 times a year. Next, we studied the store's receipts for the same two-week period as the survey. We found that the average size of a sale for that period was $35. We realize that the average sale probably

THE PURPOSE OF THIS WORKSHOP IS TO CALCULATE THE LIFETIME VALUE OF A CUSTOMER.

Personal Workshop #6
Lifetime Value of a Customer

How much does an average customer spend each time he or she makes a purchase?		$ 35.00
How often does an average customer make a purchase from your business (times per year)?	X	62
Subtotal	=	$ 2,170.00
How many years will that customer return?	X	8
Total: The Lifetime Value of a Customer	=	$ 17,360.00

jumps at holiday times, but for the purpose of doing this workshop, we feel comfortable with this figure. Finally, we know from experience that probably half of our customers have been coming in for ten years or more; but there are always many young families that become regular customers and then disappear after four or five years, probably due to job transfers. For the purpose of doing this workshop, we decided that eight years might be close to the average number of years that our customers patronize the market. Based on our research and intuition, we were able to compute the lifetime value of our customers.

THE PURPOSE OF THIS WORKSHOP IS TO CALCULATE THE LIFETIME VALUE OF A CUSTOMER.

Personal Workshop #6
Lifetime Value of a Customer

How much does an average customer spend each time he or she makes a purchase? _____

How often does an average customer make a purchase from your business (times per year)?   X _____

Subtotal   = _____

How many years will that customer return?   X _____

Total: The Lifetime Value of a Customer   = _____

Workshop Follow-Up

✔ Once you understand the lifetime value of a customer, it should be obvious how important it is to retain each and every customer. After all, if you fail to meet the needs of a customer who has a potential Lifetime Value of $50,000, you most probably will lose that customer and the $50,000 will go to your competitor. And if that customer leaves your business feeling dissatisfied or angry, he or she may tell five or ten friends about the bad experience. Do the math—if each of that person's ten friends thinks he or she is credible, and each has a lifetime value of $50,000, you have probably just lost the potential for an additional $500,000 of business.

On the other hand, if you treat that customer like gold—if you meet that individual's needs and exceed his or her expectations—you may gain a loyal customer for years and years. And, even better, that customer may tell ten friends how great you are, and so they may become loyal customers as well. Suddenly the *real* value of that first loyal customer increases by $500,000. Now that's a customer!

Satisfaction versus Loyalty

Key Words

W. Edwards Deming made the point that a satisfied customer is not the same as a loyal customer, and what businesses need are loyal customers. In fact, research has shown that many people who claim to be "satisfied" will not hesitate to do their business elsewhere the next time. **Customer satisfaction**, it seems, is a short-lived emotion that is tied to the customer's feelings that his or her immediate needs have been met, but is no guarantee of customer loyalty.

"Listening to customers must become everyone's business. With most competitors moving ever faster, the race will go to those who listen (and respond) most intently."

—Tom Peters, *Thriving on Chaos*

Customer loyalty is based on a stronger and longer-term relationship between the customer and the supplier. Customer loyalty grows over time, after the customer has been delighted by the products and services of the supplier again and again. The loyal customer not only patronizes the business regularly, but wants it to survive. The loyal customer often helps the business by referring other people and by offering feedback on how the business can get even better than it is. If something should go wrong in the dealings with

FYI

L ands' End, a direct mail merchant based in Dodgeville, Wisconsin, has developed a reputation for exceptional customer service. Although Lands' End has outgrown its small business status, it still makes every effort to make each customer feel special and completely satisfied. Here are examples of some of the special efforts Lands' End employees have made:

• A customer who had ordered 21 shirts for an auto-racing team—20 for men and 1 for a woman– called late one Friday before the team's first race the next day to inquire where the shirts were. They hadn't been shipped because a problem had arisen in color-matching the woman's shirt to those of the men. Hearing this, the customer said, "Ship what you have." So instructed, a young assistant in customer service chose a woman's shirt most likely to match the others, commandeered a service rep to drive her to Federal Express in Madison (some 30 miles away), and beat the 6 P.M. deadline. Result: The shirts got to the customer at 10 A.M. Saturday, in time for the race.

• A service rep called a customer on Christmas Eve, as promised, to sing, "We wish you a Merry Christmas" in lieu of a back-ordered gift she couldn't deliver. While singing, she could hear the customer scream out in the background, "She did it! She really did it!"

• The mother of a four-year-old with cancer wrote that he had to enter a hospital regularly for treatment. Each time the parents brought Lands' End sheets to brighten his room. Hearing this, the group made a big, bright get well card, has it signed by as many employees whose names would fit the card, and sent it. Result: A note of thanks from the mother saying the card had been mounted in the boy's room, right over his bed so he could see it easily.

Printed with permission of Lands' End, Inc.

the business, the loyal customer will probably give the business another chance. Most other customers will not.

Identify Your Customers and Their Needs

Customers are the most important element in your business. Serving the customer and meeting the customer's needs should be the fundamental reason for your existence and for every decision you make in your business. Perhaps you know who your customers are—but perhaps not. To check your understanding of your customers, consider these points:

Key Words

- A **customer** is any individual or group you serve.

- A **market segment** or customer group is a mass of customers with similar needs or expectations. For example, the needs and expectations senior adults have might be similar, making them a market segment (or customer group). But their needs and expectations are typically quite different than those of young children. Each of these groups could be considered a different market segment. Everyone in your business serves one or more customers. Your company, as a whole, provides goods or services to your **ultimate customers**—the individuals or groups to whom you hope to sell your product. Your ultimate customer might be the end user (the consumer of the good or product) or it might be an individual or company who plans to take your product, add value to it in some way, and pass it on to another customer.

- Every employee in your company serves the ultimate customer either directly or indirectly.

- In addition, al the employees or departments or units in your company serve other customers: the other employees or departments or units which receive their work and/or benefit from what they do.

Your Internal and External Customers

Every organization is made up of a series of relationships between suppliers and customers. You undoubtedly have a clear idea of who your external suppliers are, and you understand that you are their customer. You also probably know who your ultimate customer is. Those relationships were clearly shown in the Process Flow Diagram you prepared in Challenge 1 on p. 15.

If you expand that notion to your entire business, you will see that every individual in your company is both a supplier and a customer to someone else. In fact, it would be a useful exercise to require every employee in your company to prepare a Process Flow Diagram for his or her position. That exercise would help employees understand the customer-supplier relationships they have with other individuals and groups, both inside and outside the company. For example, a buyer in a department store would understand that she is the supplier for the various departments she serves. The managers and employees of those departments are her customers, although the shopper is the ultimate customer. Furthermore, she is the customer of the manufacturers' sales representatives, and they are her suppliers. Customers and suppliers, then, can be either inside or outside of your organization.

Internal customers are the individuals or groups inside the company who use your services or receive the product after your work is done. On an assembly line, your customer is the next person in line, or anyone else whose work builds on your own. If you are a safety manager, your customers are all the employees who rely on your knowledge and services to maintain a safe work environment.

External customers are outside your company. They include the ultimate customer, the end user, or anyone else who directly or indirectly receives products or services from your company.

Serving your internal customers is just as important as serving your external customers. Research shows that there is a strong correlation between customer and employee views of service quality and the internal climate for service. In other words, if you expect your employees to be responsive to the needs of your external customers, then it is important that those employees, all internal customers, be satisfied at all levels. After all, how can any employee strive to satisfy the external customer if he or she does not have the tools, materials, training, information or guidance to properly do the job?

Many businesses also have **indirect customers**, individuals or groups who have some stake in the company. For example, if you received a small business loan to start your business, the lending institution could be viewed as an indirect customer—not your reason for existence, but certainly influential in how you do business. If your business is regulated by an outside concern, that regulatory agency would be an indirect customer. You need to be concerned about meeting the needs of indirect customers, as well as your ultimate customers.

Personal Workshop Preparation #7:
Who's the Customer?

In this workshop, you will develop a Customer Diagram for your business which shows the relationship between your suppliers, internal and external customers. See the Quality Tools and Techniques box for detailed information on how to create a Customer Diagram.

FYI

Quality organizations promote the idea that employees should treat each other as they treat the external customers—with respect, a smile, and a helpful attitude. Recognition of employees for good work and exceptional service to both internal and external customers is important if your company wants such behavior to become the norm. To develop commitment to quality and customer service in your company, try to catch your employees doing something special to better serve others, and then recognize and celebrate their efforts.

Quality Tools and Techniques

Customer Diagram

What is it? A customer diagram is used to identify your customers and to show the relationships between your suppliers and your internal and external customers. You will note that it is similar to the Process Flow Diagram introduced in Challenge 1, but the Customer Diagram shows how specific customers fit into the process.

When should you use it? Create a customer diagram when you need to identify your customers and understand how they fit into the system.

How do you make it?

Step 1: Organize a team of employees, preferably representing different departments and positions in your company, for the purpose of developing your Customer Diagram.

Step 2: As a team, use the Customer Diagram template (figure 2.3) to list your suppliers, internal customers, ultimate customers, and indirect customers, and to show the relationships between them.

Figure 2.3: Customer Diagram Template

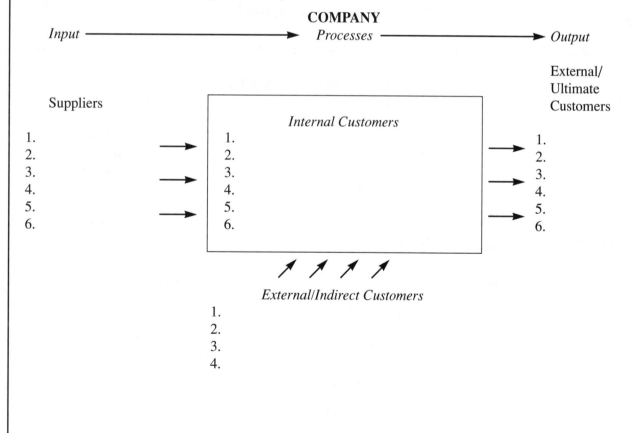

Customers can be identified for your company as a whole, or for the various individuals or departments in your business. Complete this workshop for your company as a whole. Although this exercise can be done by one person, it is better to involve several people. You may find it helpful to see how Pete Jones from BestBuilt Construction Company completed this next workshop.

 **BestBuilt Construction Company/Pete Jones:** We have two major groups of customers we deal with—home buyers and commercial property developers. When we started to think about it, though, we realized that the customer diagram wouldn't change much if we did it separately—we basically work with the same suppliers and internal groups, whether we're building a residence or a commercial building. We put together a team of employees made up of individuals from each of our work areas to

---

THE PURPOSE OF THIS WORKSHOP IS TO IDENTIFY YOUR INTERNAL AND EXTERNAL CUSTOMERS.

Personal Workshop #7
Who's the Customer?

On the customer diagram below, list the suppliers and the internal and external customers for your company as a whole.

BESTBUILT CONSTRUCTION CO.

Input ⟶ *Processes* ⟶ *Output*

External/
Ultimate
Customers

Suppliers

1. Materials suppliers
2. Equipment suppliers
3. Subcontractors
4. Concrete Co.
5. Utilities Co.
6. Missouri realtors

Internal Customers

1. Engineer
2. Architect and Drafters
3. Framing crew
4. Concrete crew
5. Supervisors and management
6. Purchasing and A/P
7. Accounts receivable
8. Sales
9. Finishing crew

1. Home buyers
2. Commercial property developers

External/Indirect Customers

1. Hometown bank
2. SBA (Small Business Administration)
3. Zoning council
4. Inspectors

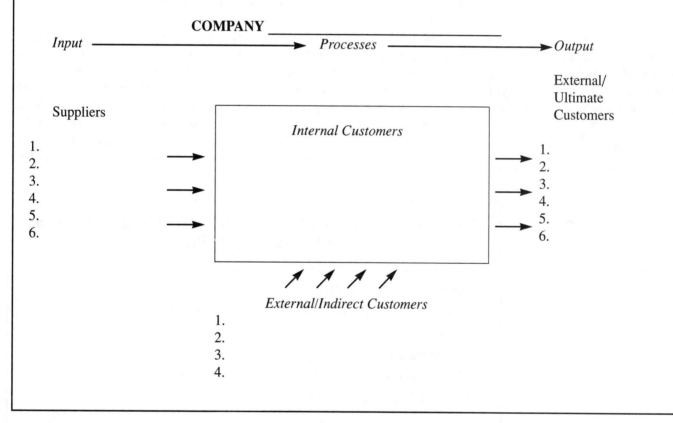

THE PURPOSE OF THIS WORKSHOP IS TO IDENTIFY YOUR INTERNAL AND EXTERNAL CUSTOMERS.

Personal Workshop #7
Who's the Customer?

On the customer diagram below, list the suppliers and the internal and external customers for your company as a whole.

COMPANY _____

Input ⟶ *Processes* ⟶ *Output*

External/
Ultimate
Customers

Suppliers

Internal Customers

1.　　　　　　　　　　　　　　　　　　　1.
2.　　　　　　　　　　　　　　　　　　　2.
3.　　　　　　　　　　　　　　　　　　　3.
4.　　　　　　　　　　　　　　　　　　　4.
5.　　　　　　　　　　　　　　　　　　　5.
6.　　　　　　　　　　　　　　　　　　　6.

External/Indirect Customers

1.
2.
3.
4.

do this workshop. We thought it was important to have every work area represented so we could really get a clear picture of our customer layout.

Workshop Follow-Up

✔ You have developed a customer diagram for your business as a whole. If you think it would be a useful exercise, you could ask each unit or department in your business to develop its own customer diagram. Every group within your company, such as the purchasing department, accounting, the sales staff, or shipping, has its own internal and external customers.

Knowing who your external and internal customers are is an important first step. The next step is much more difficult: identifying the needs and expectations of those customers. You need to develop a relationship with every customer you have identified, internal or external, in order to gain an understanding of all customers' needs and expectations.

Understanding Your Customers' Needs and Expectations

Key Word

It isn't always easy to understand what your customers need. Customers seek **utility** from the goods and services they buy. Utility refers to the condition or quality of being useful. From the customer's perspective, how good or useful a tangible product is usually depends on how it compares to other products on the market. The average customer is likely to ask a number of questions to determine whether a particular product on the market will give him or her the desired utility.

> "What the customer buys and considers of value is never a product. It is always utility, that is, what a product or service does for him."
>
> —Peter Drucker, *Managing for Results*

How good a service is, likewise, depends on how that service compares to the competition. For example, if competing quick copy shops offer the same array of services, are equally accessible, have courteous service, but one is more responsive to rush orders than the other, then the customer will likely patronize the more responsive shop when he or she has a rush order. On the other hand, if time is not important to the customer, that person will probably go to the shop where he or she *feels* more comfortable, all other things being equal. In either case, customers also consider a number of issues in choosing service businesses.

FYI

Questions a Customer Might Ask in Evaluating the Utility and Quality of a Tangible Product

- How functional is the product? Does it do what I need it to do?
- What features does it offer? Is it aesthetically pleasing?
- How durable and reliable is it? How serviceable is it?
- Is it safe?
- Is it affordable? Am I getting value for my money?
- How accessible is it? Can I get it when I need it? Will it be delivered?
- How will it make me feel to use this product?

Questions a Customer Might Ask in Evaluating the Utility and Quality of a Service

- Are the people at this business competent? Would I feel comfortable having them provide this service to me?
- Will they be responsive to my needs? Will they take time to listen to me and answer my questions? Will they give me the individual attention I need?
- Are they reliable? credible? honest? courteous?
- Is this service accessible?
- Will I receive value for my money?
- How will it make me feel to use this service?

When customers ask themselves questions, they are indirectly identifying their needs (convenience, feedback, reliability, and so on). The problem is, most customers aren't able to articulate those needs, nor are they likely to share their thought processes with you as they ask themselves questions.

Observation, Communication, and Speculation

So how can *you*, the small business owner/manager, find out what your customers need? Through **observation**, through **communication** with your customer, and through pure **speculation**.

Observation

Pay attention to the world of your market. How do your customers spend their time and why? Who or what influences their purchasing decisions? Be aware that your customers are directly and indirectly affected by world and local events, economic conditions, and social trends. What are people buying and why? Analyze how environmental factors might influence the demand for your products or services, and then keep yourself informed regarding those factors most likely to impact your business. For example, if you discover that the demand for your product, "Furry Fellows" real fur teddy bears, goes up and down depending upon the activities of PETA (People for the Ethical Treatment of Animals), then you should attempt to stay informed of PETA's activities. If you provide training services to the local health care industry, then you need to keep up with happenings in the insurance industry that might impact your customers, since what influences your customers will eventually influence you.

Watch your customers in action. Try to get a feel for how they make purchasing decisions by observing them throughout their decision-making processes. Who do they talk to? What do they look for in your product? How long does it take them to make the decision? By observing your customers, you will better understand what is important to them, what catches their eye, and how they intend to use the product. Keep you eyes and ears open, as customers will often talk among themselves about what they are looking for, what's important to them as a consumer, and what they like and dislike.

Look at what others in your industry are doing. Pay attention to their production strategies, their advertising or other marketing strategies, their store layouts, and so on. Any information that might help you understand how they are meeting the needs of the customers. If possible, visit the *best* among your competitors and try to understand why they are so successful.

U se your local library as a resource for information about your market area and the characteristics and behavior of your customers. Census data and newspaper and journal articles can help keep you aware of events and economic trends, as well as consumer behavior. If you are not sure where to start looking, tell your librarian the type of information you are seeking, and ask for help getting started. Once you become familiar with the best information sources for your type of business, future research should be much easier.

FYI

> *"The best way to understand your customer is to become your customer and walk a mile in his shoes."*
>
> —Ian D. Littman

Communicating With Your Customers

Allocate time to develop relationships with your customers. Whether your business is service or retail, wholesale or manufacturing, your success in developing loyal customers depends upon the rapport you establish with the people you come in contact with. Rapport is a communication connection, and it can only be established if your customers feel comfortable. It takes time to build relationships— people need to have all of their questions answered and concerns addressed. If a customer feels rushed, ignored or patronized, or if a customer is made to feel unimportant for any reason, that customer will leave your business feeling dissatisfied. Whenever possible, learn the names of your customers and let them know you are interested in them. Keep track of their preferences, purchases and what they are looking for— and then find a way to give it to them.

Listen to your customers (both internal and external). Ask them what they need in a product or service, what their ideal product or service would look like, and what is most important to them in making a buying decision. And then pay attention to what they tell you. Besides having conversations when you come in contact with your customers, there are several other ways to get the information you need. Here are a few suggestions.

- Meet face-to-face with one or more small groups of customers (focus groups) and ask them your questions outright. Keep the meeting relatively short—no more than one hour—and keep it focused. Don't ask them every question you

FYI

Tips for Building Rapport with Your Customers

- Greet every customer in a friendly, non-threatening manner. Whenever possible, learn the names of your customers.

- Establish eye contact and stay focused on the customer. Don't allow outside distractions to send the message that, "something else is more important than you are."

- Learn how you can help the customer by asking open-ended questions about his or her needs, how the customer will use the product or service and what characteristics or product features are most important. Remember that customers buy utility, not products.

- Listen to your customers with your ears, your eyes, and your mind. Try to understand what the customer is really trying to say.

- Solve problems for your customer. Without being defensive or distrustful, accept every customer problem as your own. Help identify possible solutions and fix the problem to the customer's satisfaction.

- Let your customers know that you appreciate their business and you enjoy serving them. Invite them to return.

- Treat every customer as though the survival of your business depends upon his or her patronage. . . . and remember that it does.

can think of; rather, pick a particular product line or service need or problem they might have, and allow them to really discuss the issue with you. Send personal invitations to 6 to 12 of your most valued customers. Consider offering some incentive to these individuals to attend, such as refreshments, a gift certificate, a discount on their next purchase, or a special gift.

• Ask customers to evaluate your product or service using a quick-response survey card. If you own a restaurant, for example, you might have a small card on each table or attached to the bill that asks customers to give you feedback on the meal and the service. Again, keep it very simple, or your patrons will not bother to fill it out—unless they are either very happy or very angry. An example of a restaurant survey follows below.

• If yours is a retail business, you could attach a postage-paid survey card to the receipt or drop one in every purchaser's sack, while saying something like this to the customer:

> *We really appreciate your business today. Will you please let us know how we can serve you better in the future by answering the questions on this card and dropping it in the mail in the next few days? We would greatly appreciate it. This kind of information helps us serve you better.*

• If you are a retailer of more expensive products or products that must be delivered, you can accomplish the same thing by sending a survey card along with a thank you note a few days after delivery. And if you have a service business, you could include your survey card with the invoice or, better yet, a thank you note.

Buster's Bistro

Thank you for choosing Buster's Bistro for your meal today. Our goal is to give you outstanding value—a delicious and hearty meal at a reasonable price. Please let us know how you feel about your meal and the service we provided today:

1. How would you rate the quality of your meal?

☐　　　☐　　　☐　　　☐　　　☐

Very poor　　　　Average　　　　Excellent

2. How would you rate the quality of the service you received?

☐　　　☐　　　☐　　　☐　　　☐

Very poor　　　　Average　　　　Excellent

3. What can we do in the future to make your visit to Buster's Bistro even better?

_____

_____

- Another option is to ask your customers to complete longer surveys or questionnaires. While such questionnaires might give you much valuable information about your customers, keep in mind that it is difficult to construct a good questionnaire, and even more difficult to get people to take the time to complete it. If you decide to conduct a formal survey, you should definitely consider hiring a professional in marketing research to help you.

- Pay close attention to all customer complaints, whether written or verbal. In fact, a customer complaint is truly an opportunity. Don't miss it! First, a complaint is an opportunity to fix whatever is wrong for the customer. For example, if a customer returns a product saying it wasn't suitable for some reason, never argue. Simply try to solve the problem by finding a more acceptable product, returning the money, or implementing whatever solution works best for the customer. In the process, try to learn from the customer why the returned item wasn't suitable. What product features or specifications did the customer need that this particular product didn't provide? If you can get this information from the customer, then you are one step closer to understanding that person's needs and expectations, plus you have developed a relationship with him or her in the process. If handled correctly, nearly every complaining customer can be turned into a satisfied or even loyal customer by your efforts to remedy the problem.

- If a customer takes the time to offer a written complaint, you need to take the time to respond directly to that complaint. An immediate telephone call will be most effective, as it gives you the opportunity to thank the customer for the letter and get more information about the specific problem. Make every attempt to remedy the problem and to impress upon the customer your sincere concern for his or her needs.

- Follow up all major sales of products or services with a telephone call. A few days after delivery of the product or service, take a few minutes to call your customer to be sure everything is satisfactory and to see if the customer/client has any questions. Thank the customer, again, for the business, and ask him or her to let you know if there is any way you can help in the future.

FYI

Letters of praise from customers are also wonderful opportunities to strengthen relationships. Call the customer to thank him or her for the letter and to reinforce the fact that you value the individual's business and comments. Ask the customer to keep you informed of ways you might better serve him or her in the future. If appropriate for your business, ask if you can use the letter in your portfolio, quote the customer in your marketing materials, or list him or her as a reference for future clients.

- Use the telephone to keep regular contact with your customers. Develop a system for following up periodically—how often depends on your business or service—to see how things are going for the customer, how the products you sold previously are performing, and whether the customer has any special needs or problems you might help solve. In addition, any time you have a new product or service to offer, call those customers who might have such a need, and let them know about the new offering. Whether it be routine follow-up calling or telephoning for a special purpose, these are wonderful opportunities to learn more about what your customers are looking for and will be looking for in the future.

Test market your new products or services whenever possible. Ask customers how they like the new product and why. Whether people who try the new product love it or hate it, you will always get helpful information about what your customers want, need, and expect through test marketing

Before responding to a Request for Proposal (RFP) from a prospective customer, consult with suppliers and subcontractors to assess the specifications. Those "partners" may help you better understand the RFP and the customer's needs, and they may offer insight on how to best respond to those needs.

Pure Speculation

Think like your customers think. Try to put yourself in their shoes and answer the questions they might ask to evaluate your product or service. Remember to answer the questions from the *customer's perspective,* not your own.

Talk to other people—your employees, your business associates, your family and friends—about what you believe your customers want, need and expect. Pay attention to their responses, their questions, and their own ideas. Their reactions should tell you a lot about how realistic they think your beliefs are.

Pay attention to your gut feelings—but don't depend exclusively on them. If you know your business and have extensive experience, your intuition can be a valuable tool, but don't discount the facts, the trends and what your customers and employees are telling you. Many a business has closed its doors because the owner/manager refused to acknowledge that what the customers wanted wasn't the same as what the owner/manager thought they should want.

> *"They didn't want it good... they wanted it Wednesday."*
> —Robert Heinlein

Personal Workshop Preparation #8: Customer Needs

To be a successful business person, you need to identify the needs, wants and expectations of your customers. Then, you need to develop a strategy to meet those needs, wants and expectations in your company. Using a modified **flow chart** format, the

Personal Workshop that follows gives you the opportunity to identify what you believe to be the needs of your customers, whether internal or external, and then to identify some actions you might take to meet those needs. This workshop should be completed for each of your significant customer groups or market segments. Do it first for one of the ultimate customers you identified on the customer diagram. If possible, involve a team of employees in this exercise, since such a group can offer a broader perspective and a variety of creative strategies. If, while doing this workshop, you discover that you do not have a clear understanding of what your customers need, want, or expect, then you will first need to gather that information using one or more of the techniques described in the previous sections of this book. For information on what a flow chart is and how to create one, see the Quality Tools and Technique box.

Quality Tools and Techniques

Flow Chart

What is it? A flow chart is a picture of a process. Standard symbols, such as rectangles and diamonds, are connected by arrows to show the flow of events or steps in the process. A flow chart is one of the seven basic tools for quality management.

When should you use it? Use a flow chart anytime it would be helpful to visualize the flow of any process, step-by-step. For example, a flow chart might be developed to help employees understand the process of billing a customer. Such a flow chart could include the steps in the billing process, what people or departments are involved in the process, and the decision points for those people. Flow charts may be very general, or very detailed.

How do you make it?
Step 1: Identify the process to be studied, when and where it starts.
Step 2: List each step in the process in sequence. Beside each step, note what decisions need to be made before moving to the next step.
Step 3: Draw the flow chart using the following symbols, connected by arrows showing the direction of the flow:

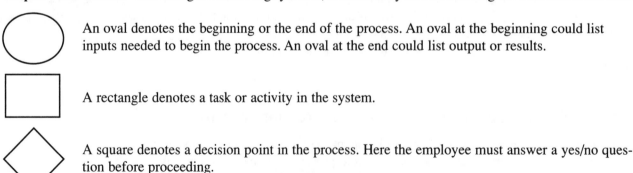

An oval denotes the beginning or the end of the process. An oval at the beginning could list inputs needed to begin the process. An oval at the end could list output or results.

A rectangle denotes a task or activity in the system.

A square denotes a decision point in the process. Here the employee must answer a yes/no question before proceeding.

Some flow charts are drawn from top to bottom, while others are drawn from left to right.

Quality Tools and Techniques, continued

Figure 2.4: Sample Flow Chart

Process: Customer Order Processing

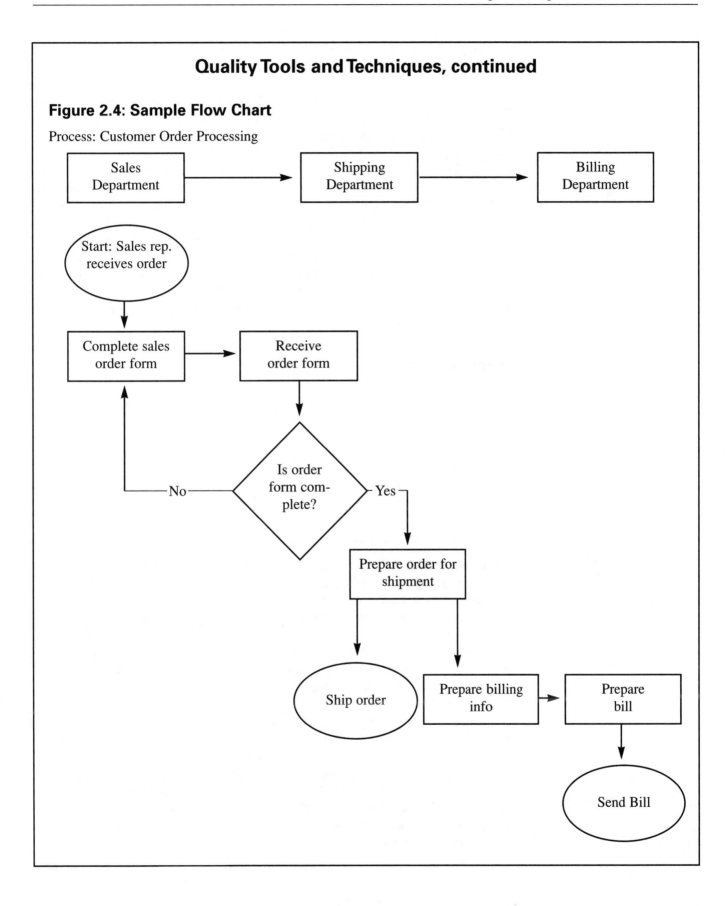

Before you begin this next workshop, you will find it helpful to observe how Pete Jones and his employees completed the exercise.

 BestBuilt Construction Co./Pete Jones: We thought we had a handle on the needs and expectations of our customers, but we really weren't sure. We completed this workshop in two parts. First, we determined that we did not know the needs, wants and expectations of our customers; we needed to spend some time identifying ways we would try to get that information. After we felt we had done enough research and had gathered information about our customers, we completed the rest of the workshop. Completing this workshop was a group effort for us—we really needed the input and ideas of every employee to do a thorough job. For that reason, we decided to work on this at a couple of our monthly company meetings. In fact, we hired a facilitator to guide us through the process. She broke us into four smaller groups, then brought us and our ideas all back together. We are really pleased with the results, and we feel like everyone in the company now has a good sense of what our customers need and want.

Personal Notes

_____

_____

_____

_____

FYI

There is a small beauty salon in West Des Moines, Iowa, called Hair Kutters II. The shop, which caters to working women, recognizes the value of making its clients feel comfortable and special. When they arrive, clients are offered a chance to remove their shoes and slip their feet into some little flannel booties (don't worry— they are freshly laundered) to help them relax. Then they are offered a cup of coffee or tea, a soft drink, or an elegant glass of wine. The wait, if there is one, is never more than five minutes or so. Each professional-looking stylist spends several minutes asking the client open-ended questions in an attempt to understand what cut or style the client is looking for. Questions might include the following: What sort of work do you do, and what type of image are you trying to project? How much time do you have to care for and style your hair each morning? Are you looking for a style for a special occasion? The kicker, though, is that while this discussion is going on, the stylist is giving the client a scalp massage with an exotic, fragrant oil. By the time the client is ready to leave Hair Kutters II, she feels terrific. She has a quality haircut, a classy style and she feels truly pampered and valued as a customer. She may have paid a few dollars more, but it was worth it! She will be loyal for life.

THE PURPOSE OF THIS WORKSHOP IS TO IDENTIFY CUSTOMER NEEDS AND STRATEGIES FOR MEETING THOSE NEEDS.

Personal Workshop #8
Customer Needs

Customer Group: ___Home Buyers___

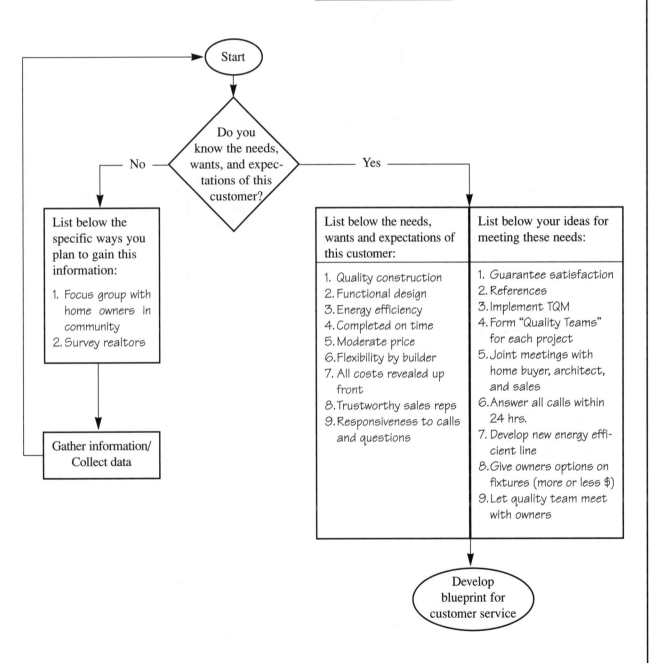

Start

Do you know the needs, wants, and expectations of this customer?

No

Yes

List below the specific ways you plan to gain this information:

1. Focus group with home owners in community
2. Survey realtors

Gather information/ Collect data

List below the needs, wants and expectations of this customer:

1. Quality construction
2. Functional design
3. Energy efficiency
4. Completed on time
5. Moderate price
6. Flexibility by builder
7. All costs revealed up front
8. Trustworthy sales reps
9. Responsiveness to calls and questions

List below your ideas for meeting these needs:

1. Guarantee satisfaction
2. References
3. Implement TQM
4. Form "Quality Teams" for each project
5. Joint meetings with home buyer, architect, and sales
6. Answer all calls within 24 hrs.
7. Develop new energy efficient line
8. Give owners options on fixtures (more or less $)
9. Let quality team meet with owners

Develop blueprint for customer service

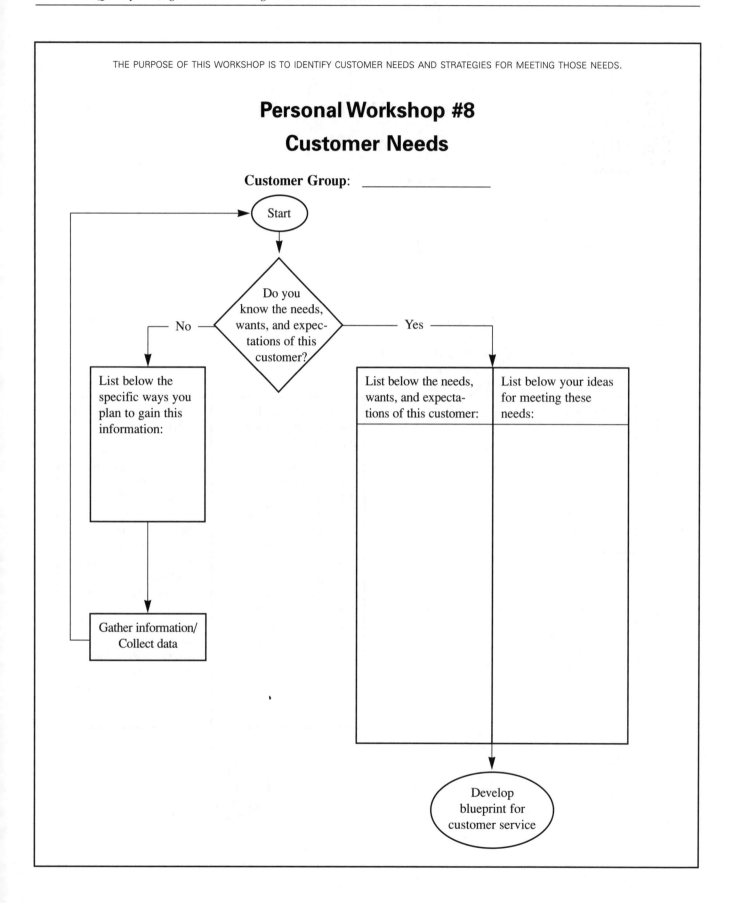

THE PURPOSE OF THIS WORKSHOP IS TO IDENTIFY CUSTOMER NEEDS AND STRATEGIES FOR MEETING THOSE NEEDS.

Personal Workshop #8
Customer Needs

Customer Group: _____

Start

Do you know the needs, wants, and expectations of this customer?

No

Yes

List below the specific ways you plan to gain this information:

Gather information/ Collect data

List below the needs, wants, and expectations of this customer:	List below your ideas for meeting these needs:

Develop blueprint for customer service

Workshop Follow-Up

Don't forget that each of your employees has many customers—those people and groups inside and outside the company that depend on their work. Ideally, in order to really understand the needs and expectations of each of their customers, every employee should do this workshop for every customer group he or she identified on the Customer Diagram. Once you understand the needs and expectations of your ultimate customers, you are ready to build a system for exceptional customer service for those groups.

Build a System for Exceptional Customer Service

No matter what your business is, you have undoubtedly established some sort of a system for serving your customers. That system includes all of the steps a customer must take to purchase your product or service. Within that system, there may be one or several points of contact with a customer. A **point of contact** is any occasion when the customer comes into contact with someone who represents your company. Each point of contact is, in effect, a "moment of truth" for your business, since it gives the customer an opportunity to make a judgment about the level of service you offer. For example, when a customer first contacts your business, whether by telephone, by mail, in person, or some other way, it is a "**moment of truth**." How that customer is greeted and treated could make the difference between developing a loyal customer or losing that customer to the competition. The same is true when the order is taken, when the delivery is made, when the invoice is received, when the product is serviced, and so on. If your system for customer service does not provide exceptional service at each and every point of contact, then you may lose the opportunity to ever serve that customer again.

Key Words

What Does Exceptional Customer Service Look Like?

Every customer has certain minimum requirements and expectations for some level of service, and those requirements change somewhat, depending upon the type of business it is. In a restaurant, customers expect, at a minimum, a clean table and decent food. In a retail establishment, customers want to be able to find the product they desire and help from a sales clerk if they need it. In a hospital, cleanliness and licensed health-care providers are the bare minimum for most customers. And for a manufacturer, products must be delivered to specification.

> *"A little consideration, a little thought for others, makes all the difference."*
>
> —Eeyore to Pooh in *Winnie the Pooh* by A. A. Milne

If you want to provide exceptional service, you must do it at every point of contact. This is important to remember. After all, you may be spending big bucks advertising your business just to get people through your door. If, once they get there, a grouchy receptionist or snippy salesperson chases them away, then you are wasting your advertising dollars.

FYI

"See simplicity in the complicated. Achieve greatness in little things."

—Lao Tsu, *Tao Te Ching*

Providing the bare minimum, though, is probably not enough to stay in business long term. Each customer's standards vary, depending upon his or her personal needs, previous experiences (which create expectations), and the level of service being offered by the competition. As a matter of fact, the bare minimum will probably cause many customers to be dissatisfied.

If a business wants customers to come back, more is certainly better. In the restaurant, good service and reasonable prices are definitely a plus— in fact, they may be considered minimum standards by some customers. In the retail establishment, broad selection, value, and friendly sales personnel are likely to satisfy customers. In a hospital, a short wait and empathetic personnel may bring customers back. And the manufacturer might consider offering just-in-time delivery and good follow-up by sales personnel to keep its customers happy.

Exceptional customer service goes beyond *good* customer service. The business which delivers exceptional customer service recognizes that customers want more than accuracy, friendly people, promptness, value, competence, and quality products. Every customer wants to feel that he or she is important to your business. Every customer wants to feel that he or she can trust you. And every human being loves to feel special. If you and your employees can help your customers feel *important* and *comfortable* and *special*, then you are delivering exceptional customer service. And, if you discover a way to delight your customers by doing something special—something that your competition isn't doing— then you can earn the loyalty of those customers.

Personal Workshop Preparation #9: What Is Exceptional Customer Service?

In this workshop, you will decide what exceptional customer service "looks like" for your type of business. In preparation for this workshop, review your work on Personal Workshop #8 , Customer Needs. The needs and expectations you identified in that workshop will help you define exceptional customer service in this workshop. It would be best to do this workshop with a group of employees. Furthermore, by using the brainstorming technique, the group could develop some excellent and creative ideas for delivering truly exceptional customer service—for making your customers feel very special. For information on brainstorming, see the Quality Tools and Technique box.

Quality Tools and Techniques

Brainstorming

What is it? Brainstorming is a technique for generating a multitude of ideas, opinions and/or solutions surrounding any type of problem in a team or group setting. The outcome of brainstorming is a list of ideas, opinions, or possible solutions to the stated problem.

Quality Tools and Techniques, continued

When should you use it? Use brainstorming when you need to generate a large number of creative ideas or possible solutions in an efficient way. The brainstorming process is intended to be a free-flow of ideas, with ideas building on other ideas, without fear of criticism or judgment about the viability of those ideas.

How do you do it? Typically, someone serves as facilitator for the brainstorming session. The facilitator describes the technique and ground rules to the group, keeps order and enforces the rules during the brainstorming session, and carefully records the ideas as they are given.

Step 1: Define the problem and goals of the brainstorming session.

Step 2: Set the ground rules. Be sure participants understand that everyone is welcome and expected to throw in his or her ideas. No idea is to be criticized or judged as silly, stupid or impossible. In fact, no idea is too ridiculous to mention—the goal is to generate a list of all sorts of creative ideas without discussion. Later, outside the brainstorming session, those ideas will be more carefully considered.

Step 3: Brainstorm. Ideas may be thrown out by any team member at any time, or the facilitator can go around the group, asking each participant for one idea in turn, until the group runs out of new ideas. Throughout the session, all ideas should be recorded, word-for-word.

Step 4: Review the list of ideas. Eliminate duplicates and ask for clarification on any ideas that may be unclear.

Denny's Hometown Market/Denny and Mabel Wellman: We know that the key to competing with the big new store across town is to offer more selection, but keep our prices reasonable and our service "hometown" friendly. We believe that lots of our faithful older customers come here for more than just groceries. They come here for social reasons, too—to have someone ask how they are doing and to carry on casual conversations with their acquaintances in the aisles. That's just fine with us—we want them to feel totally comfortable here. As we thought about what exceptional customer service is in a grocery store, we decided that making our customers feel welcome, relaxed and comfortable is the key.

Observe how Denny and Mabel Wellman completed this next workshop.

Personal Notes

_____

_____

_____

_____

_____

THE PURPOSE OF THIS WORKSHOP IS TO DEFINE EXCEPTIONAL CUSTOMER SERVICE FOR YOUR BUSINESS.

Personal Workshop #9
What Is Exceptional Customer Service?

Type of Business: *grocery store*

List below what constitutes good customer service for your type of business.	**List below the additional things that could be done to provide *exceptional* customer service.**
• Good selection of groceries	• Have a greeter at front door to help shoppers get carts and answer any questions
• Quality meats cut to customer specs	• Build a small "cafe" area for shoppers to meet friends, sip a cup of coffee, rest their feet. Offer free coffee to shoppers. Have pastries, fruit, and a few lunch items for sale.
• Fresh produce	
• Fresh baked goods	
• Special orders	
• Friendly checkers, department heads, and stockers	• Offer free delivery to homes of senior citizens and disabled shoppers
• Honor coupons and food stamps	• Offer a free cookie to children at bakery
• Reasonably short wait in line	• Offer "Most Valued Customer" cards to shoppers, entitling them to a free product gift each week.
• Good sacking	
• Load groceries in car	
• Reasonable prices	• Honor competitor's coupons
• Special promotions	• Accept all returns without question, and offer to replace the item *plus* give something extra for the customer's trouble.
• Cash payroll and personal checks	
• No-hassle returns	
• Community support	• Offer senior citizen discount
	• When a customer asks directions, always take them where they want to go—don't just point.
	• Smile, smile, smile, and focus totally on the customer you are serving at the moment.

THE PURPOSE OF THIS WORKSHOP IS TO DEFINE EXCEPTIONAL CUSTOMER SERVICE FOR YOUR BUSINESS.

Personal Workshop #9
What Is Exceptional Customer Service?

Type of Business: _____

List below what constitutes good customer service for your type of business.	List below the additional things that could be done to provide *exceptional* customer service.

Workshop Follow-Up

✔ Review the needs and expectations of your customers—those that you identified in Personal Workshop #8. Are each of those needs and expectations met through the items you have identified in the left-hand column as the elements of good customer service? If not, think some more about how you might meet every need and expectation your customers have. Unless you satisfy every need and every expectation, your customers may not be satisfied with the service your business provides.

To check how you are doing as a business right now, look again at the items and ideas you listed in the left-hand column, and do the following as Denny and Mabel Wellman have already done for this workshop:

- Put a star (*) by those items or ideas you are currently doing and doing very well.

- Put a plus sign (+) by those items you are doing, but not consistently or very well—in other words, improvement is still needed.

- Put a minus sign (-) by those items you are not currently doing.

Now, study your results. If you have all stars, then congratulations— you are already tuned into your customers' needs and expectations, and now you can concentrate on getting better and better. If you have plus or minus signs, then you know where you need work. Take care of these items before you attempt to implement any of your ideas in the right hand column. After all, a cherry on a sundae isn't going to impress your customers if you have neglected to give them the ice cream or the hot fudge.

In the right-hand column, you should have listed a number of ideas that go beyond your customers' expectations. If you implement any one of these ideas, it should surprise and delight your customers. If you are able to implement several of these ideas, as well as consistently provide each of the items on the left, then you are on your way to developing loyal customers through exceptional customer service!

Empowering Employees to Serve the Customer

The best laid plans and most creative ideas in the world will not lead to exceptional customer service unless you empower your employees to serve the customer. To empower people, you must simply allow them to take responsibility for making decisions and fixing problems without fear of reprisal. You can empower your employees by following this three-step process:

> *"A company is known by the people it keeps."*
>
> —Will Rogers

Step 1: Hire the right people for the job. You need people who have demonstrated a strong work ethic and who care about the quality of work they do. Be sure to select a "people person" for any position requiring contact with the public, and try to discern whether a job applicant has good communication skills, for that is key to understanding the customer. Begin talking about your customer service philosophy during the interview process; you want to be absolutely sure that you hire individuals who are comfortable and effective in "serving" others.

Step 2: Train those people to "eat, sleep, and breathe" customer service. Never assume that people know what good customer service skills are. Make clear to each employee what the company's customer service philosophy is. Be certain that every employee understands his or her critical role in serving the customer and in the company's success. Involve employees in the development of your customer service blueprint, solicit their ideas for delighting the customers, and insist upon everyone's commitment to giving customers what they want. Teach employees how to solve problems for customers, how to ask open-ended questions, how to listen effectively, how to communicate clearly, and how to make every customer feel valued. Finally, owners and managers should model exceptional customer service by treating their own employees as special people.

Step 3: Give employees the authority to do whatever is necessary to satisfy the customer. Let employees own and solve every customer problem they come in contact with, without defensiveness or attempting to place blame. If you have taught them your customer service philosophy and good problem-solving skills, then your employees should have the tools needed to provide exceptional customer service—**so trust them to do so.**

What You Can Accomplish by Empowering Your Employees to Serve the Customer

- **Response time to customer complaints decreases.** Customer problems are solved at the point of conflict, rather than by an anonymous customer complaint representative at some later time or obscure location. By solving problems immediately, customers leave your business feeling satisfied, and they don't have time to tell anyone else about their negative experience before the problem is solved.

- **Red tape is minimized.** There are no hard and fast rules about how to handle every situation. Instead, the employee is trained to solve problems and encouraged to make the best decisions possible given the circumstances, and without fear of reprisal.

- **Employees feel valued and special.** Employees develop new skills that give them confidence and make them more valuable to you, to your customers, and in the employment marketplace. Employees develop self-esteem as a result of the trust and responsibility given to them. Employees understand and appreci-

FYI

To learn more about hiring the right employees and developing those employees through education and training, the book, *Human Resources: Mastering Your Small Business,* is available from Upstart Publishing Company, Chicago, IL. This book is part of the Small Business Mastery Certification Series, and you can order it by calling 1-800-235-8866.

ate their importance to the company, and they tend to live up to your highest expectations.

- **Owners and managers feel relief.** There is no way that owner/managers can do it alone, and there is no reason why they should have to. If an owner/manager trusts enough to empower employees, he or she may actually be able to relax when physically away from the business . . . preferably on a beach in Hawaii.

- **Customers feel valued and special.** Customers want their problems solved with minimum hassle. They want to be listened to, empathized with, and respected. All of these things are possible when employees are empowered to do the right thing for the customer.

Key Word

Designing a Blueprint for Exceptional Customer Service

A **Customer Service Blueprint** is simply a written description or plan for the customer service system you will implement. It combines much of the information you have already gathered—points of contact, customers' needs and expectations, and your ideas for delivering exceptional customer service—into one document. That document might be considered a strategic plan for customer service, which can then be used for training employees and guiding their decision-making, communications and dealings with every customer group.

> *"Excellence stems from a frame of mind. It's caught, not taught."*
>
> —Anonymous

Personal Workshop Preparation #10: A Blueprint for Exceptional Customer Service

You have already laid much of the groundwork for this workshop by participating in the earlier workshops in this Challenge. It is now time to pull all of your information and ideas together into one document, your own Customer Service Blueprint. While the blueprint format may look lengthy, it can easily be compiled, one step at a time.

Key Word

You will start by developing a **philosophy for customer service** for your company— a general statement that will help guide all employees and their decision-making in the future. The philosophy statement should clearly describe the value your company places on its customers, and it should suggest to employees how customers are to be treated. Write your philosophy statement carefully, because once it is written, it needs to become gospel, guiding the everyday worklife at your place of business.

In Part II of this workshop, you will identify specific strategies for delivering exceptional customer service at each possible point of contact with your customers. Every point of contact is critically important— a "moment of truth"— and so your blueprint needs to describe how customers will be greeted and treated and made to feel special by everyone with whom they come in contact.

In this next workshop, you will have an opportunity to examine the Customer Service Blueprint that Kiki Hermann developed for his business.

Quali-Temps Inc./Kiki Hermann: Writing a statement of philosophy for customer service at Quali-Temps was simple. We wanted our employees to understand that customers are the reason we exist and that the customer is always, always right—even when he or she is wrong. Since our associates serve as our ambassadors while on assignment, it was very important that our philosophy statement give them the guidance they need to represent us. Many of our key personnel were involved in building this blueprint. We realize, though, that it is just a start; we plan to talk about it at least once a month, or more often if a particular problem comes up. In fact, we have formed a Customer Service Team for the express purpose of developing and implementing the blueprint throughout the company.

THE PURPOSE OF THIS WORKSHOP IS TO DESIGN A CUSTOMER SERVICE BLUEPRINT TO GUIDE YOUR COMPANY.

Personal Workshop #10
A Blueprint for Exceptional Customer Service

Part I: Develop a statement which describes your company's guiding philosophy on customer service.

Quali-Temps Inc. is dedicated to providing every business client with the best temporary technical assistance money can buy. Every associate at Quali-Temps will focus on solving the client's immediate problem, uncovering the client's special needs and then fulfilling those needs in a professional, friendly and timely manner. We want every client to view Quali-Temps as a caring partner in its technological advancement.

Part II: For each ultimate customer group or market segment you serve, describe what you can do to deliver exceptional customer service at each point of contact. Finally, list who is responsible for carrying out each strategy or activity (individuals, departments, or work groups).

Point of Contact	Activities and Strategies	Who's Responsible?
Yellow pages and direct mail promotions	• Emphasize quality and caring	Joe and Kiki
Sales calls	• No cold calls, appointment only • Ask questions about their needs, frustrations, etc. • Help them trouble-shoot • Empathy and understanding • Provide reference letters	Sally and sales team (training needed)

Personal Workshop #10, continued

Point of Contact	Activities and Strategies	Who's Responsible?
Telephone	• Answer all calls before the 3rd ring—everyone backs up everyone else • Avoid putting clients on hold or transferring, unless you know the next person can answer the question and is available • Take thorough messages and ask appropriate questions to minimize clients having to repeat their stories • Return all messages in the same day • Answer all phones in a friendly, professional manner • Thank every client for calling	Jim, Jane, Kiki, and all office staff as backup (training needed)
Drop-ins	• Greet and welcome all drop-ins immediately • Offer coffee or tea and a seat • Never keep appointment waiting for more than a few minutes • Work in all unscheduled appointments within 15 minutes	Jim, Jane, Kiki and all office staff as backup
Receipt of paperwork	• Get contracts, invoices and evaluation in mail within 24 hours of request or close of work period • All form paperwork is to be accompanied by a formal letter or a personal note • All paperwork must be perfect— no errors • Include stamped, self-addresses envelopes	Sally, Joe, Jim and Jane Sally, Joe, Jim and Jane Jim and Jane Jim and Jane
Placement of associates	• All associates will represent Quali-Temps in a professional manner • Associates check in with home office for technical assistance as needed	Sally (training needed) Sally
Follow-up calls	• Follow-up calls focus on how associates are meeting needs of the client or if they need additional help in some way • After work period, follow-up to thank client for business and to see if we can help in any other way	Sally and sales staff

THE PURPOSE OF THIS WORKSHOP IS TO DESIGN A CUSTOMER SERVICE BLUEPRINT TO GUIDE YOUR COMPANY.

Personal Workshop #10
A Blueprint for Exceptional Customer Service

Part I: Develop a statement which describes your company's guiding philosophy on customer service.

Part II: For each ultimate customer group or market segment you serve, describe what you can do to deliver exceptional customer service at each point of contact. Finally, list who is responsible for carrying out each strategy or activity (individuals, departments, or work groups).

Point of Contact	Activities and Strategies	Who's Responsible?

Personal Workshop #10, continued

Point of Contact	Activities and Strategies	Who's Responsible?

Workshop Follow-Up

 If you involved your employees in this workshop, then you should have accomplished two things:

1. You have a Customer Service Blueprint for your business which will guide all employees and which makes specific employees, departments, and work teams accountable for customer service during their "moments of truth."

2. Employees who helped develop the blueprint understand why customer service is so critical, why each employee is important to the success of the company, and everyone's role in delivering exceptional customer service.

Your Customer Service Blueprint is actually nothing more than a strategic plan for delivering customer service in your business. Like most strategic plans, it is worthless if it gets filed away or reviewed only periodically. The key to exceptional customer service is to use your blueprint on a daily basis as a guide to continuous improvement at every point of contact.

Implementation: Putting Your Blueprint to Use

It isn't enough to have a Customer Service Blueprint—you must provide the coaching and training needed to carry it out. Use your Customer Service Blueprint when you orient new employees and when you train all employees in customer service. It will help each employee understand the customer service system in your business, and it will guide you in setting up training to teach specific customer service skills to your employees.

Continuously Improving Customer Service

Your goal as a quality business should be to continuously improve the service you give to your customers. There are many quality management tools and techniques available to help you analyze your current processes and identify current weaknesses in your customer service system. Histograms and Pareto charts are very effective tools for identifying in-house problems which, in turn, cause customer service problems.

Histograms

For example, a simple histogram (bar graph) could be used to track the reasons why job shipments are delayed in a print shop. Or a histogram could help a retailer or service business better understand the reasons behind customer complaints. See the Quality Tools and Technique Box on pages 76-77 for information on how to create a histogram.

Personal Workshop Preparation #11: Building a Histogram

Think of a problem or question you might be having in your business that is somehow related to customer service. For the purpose of learning how to build a histogram, choose something simple—a situation for which you know you can collect or tabulate the data easily. The following are some ideas you might consider:

- What are the primary reasons for customer complaints in this business?

- Who sells the most service contracts (or something else) to our customers?

- Why do orders get shipped late?

- Which day of the week (or time of the day) do we serve the most customers?

Pull the data you need together before you begin the workshop. As you do the workshop, refer back to the information on histograms in the box on Quality Tools and Techniques.

Quality Tools and Techniques

The Histogram

What is it? A histogram is a bar graph which shows how often something occurs for different reasons over a certain period of time. For example, to understand why customers return products they have purchased, a company might develop a histogram to show how many products are returned for each reason identified: defective item; wrong size; wrong color; customer didn't like it; and so on.

When should you use it? Histograms can be used to collect and analyze data over time in a system, or to evaluate the impact certain changes in the system may have caused. It may be appropriate to use a histogram if you have different categories or classes of information which are mutually exclusive—in other words, when each incidence fits into one and only one category. For example, you could build a histogram to show how many students earned an "A" for a certain course, how many earned a "B" and so on. Since students cannot earn both an "A" and a "B" as their final grade for one course, each grade category is mutually exclusive.

How do you make it?
Step 1: Identify your problem.

Step 2: Determine what categories or classes of data you will collect, then collect the data. As an example, categories might be "A," "B," "C," "D," and "F" for the histogram concerning grades in a course. If applicable, set category ranges (i.e., "A+ to A-," "B+ to B-," and so on).

Step 3: Format the axes. Categories of data are scaled and labeled on the horizontal axis; frequency of occurrence is scaled and labeled on the vertical axis.

Step 4: Build the histogram. Draw a bar that corresponds with the frequency of occurrences in each category for some period of time or set of data. Data may be transferred from a check sheet to the histogram, or data may be collected directly on the histogram template.

Quality Tools and Techniques, continued

Step 5: **Analyze the histogram**. Does its shape suggest a normal distribution (symmetrical and bell-shaped) within the categories? Does the distribution appear to be uniform (all about the same) or totally random? Is the distribution skewed to one side or the other? Any of these situations could suggest good or bad news, or could suggest possible solutions to your initial problem

Figure 2.5: Sample Histograms

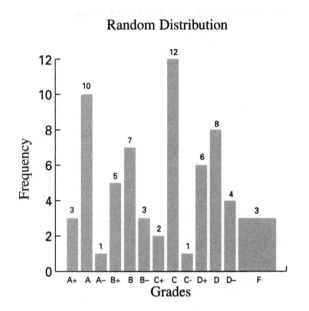

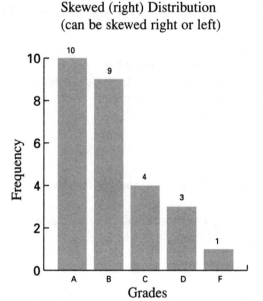

Before you begin this exercise, observe the histogram that Lindy Hernandez created for her business.

 Recycled Paper Wholesalers/Lindy Hernandez: When orders get shipped late, then invoices get sent late, and it costs us money. Usually orders are shipped late because of some delay in the production process. We needed to get a handle on the causes behind late orders and production delays, and so that is the problem we chose to study and plot on a histogram. We collected our data by filling out a late shipment report form—just something we made up to keep track of the reasons for late shipments for a period of three months. In order to get a real handle on late shipments, we plan to continue to collect data over the next year and build more histograms. As we try to eliminate some of the most common causes of late shipments, the new histograms should help us measure our progress.

Personal Workshop #11
Building a Histogram

Step 1: State your problem.

Identify the reasons for late order shipments.

Step 2: Determine what categories or classes of data you will collect, then collect the data.

Categories:
• Mechanical problems on line
• Slowed production due to absenteeism
• Delay in receipt of newspaper
• Delay in receipt of chemicals
• Too many orders to fill
• Other

Step 3: Format and label the axes below.

Step 4: Using your data, build the histogram.
Time Period: March, April, May

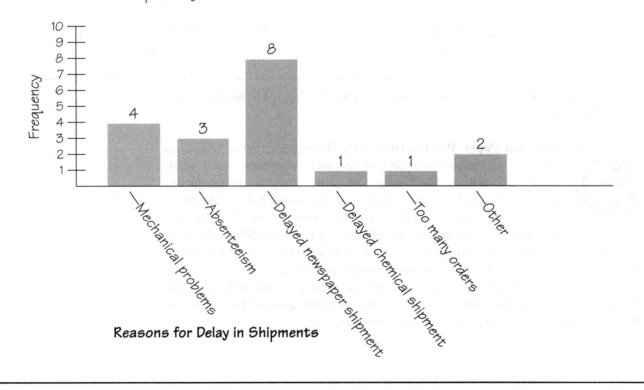

Personal Workshop #11, continued

Step 5: Analyze the histogram.

1. What does the histogram tell you about your data?

The histogram shows a random distribution and suggests that our biggest causes of delay are delayed newspaper shipments, mechanical problems and absenteeism.

2. What conclusions can you draw (if any) from this information that might help you solve your problem or answer your question?

1. All of these problems are within our control and therefore we should be able to drastically reduce the number of delayed shipments over the next year.
2. Delayed newspaper shipments are clearly our biggest problem and should be tackled first. Specifically, we must find more reliable sources for our newspaper or somehow offer better incentives to our current suppliers. We will study this situation.
3. We also need to look carefully at the reasons for mechanical problems and absenteeism.

THE PURPOSE OF THIS WORKSHOP IS TO BUILD A HISTOGRAM FOR ANALYZING DATA.

Personal Workshop #11
Building a Histogram

Step 1: State your problem.

Step 2: Determine what categories or classes of data you will collect, then collect the data.

Step 3: Format and label the axes below.

Personal Workshop #11, continued

Step 4: Using your data, build the histogram.

Time Period: _____

Frequency

Categories or Classes

Step 5: Analyze the histogram.

1. What does the histogram tell you about your data?

2. What conclusions can you draw (if any) from this information that might help you solve your problem or answer your question?

Workshop Follow-Up

✔ Histograms are simple to build and very useful for visualizing the frequency of distinct events or data from a process. Don't limit your use of histograms to customer service issues. Histograms can be very useful in helping you to interpret all sorts of data. For example, you could build a histogram to depict variations in thickness of a manufactured part. With that information, you may be able to adjust your equipment or change some step in your process to eliminate manufacturing parts outside of the acceptable range. A histogram could be a useful tool for analyzing data about equipment breakdowns. By studying the histogram, you might identify the major causes for those breakdowns, and then work to eliminate those causes.

Finally, histograms can be a great way to measure improvement that results from a change in any process. For example, assume you built a histogram that showed the frequency of various causes for customer complaints, and then you make some change in your process to eliminate one or more of those causes. New data—taken after the change was made—and a new histogram could show you just how effective your changes were. Just compare the new histogram with the old one for a clear "before and after" picture.

Pareto Chart

A **Pareto chart** looks very similar to a histogram in some ways. It, too, is a simple bar chart, but it is specifically intended to help you distinguish between significant causes of problems and insignificant ones. See the Quality Tools and Techniques box for detailed information on Pareto charts.

Quality Tools and Techniques

Pareto Chart

What is it? A Pareto chart is a simple bar chart which ranks causes in decreasing order of occurrence so that significant causes can be distinguished from insignificant ones and priorities can be set. Pareto charts are based on the **Pareto Principle,** which states that 80 percent of the problems come from 20 percent of the causes. This chart illustrates that concept and shows which of the causes are creating the majority of the problems.

When should you use it? Use a Pareto chart when data can be arranged into categories and when you need a better understanding of the significant causes of any problem.

How do you make it?
Step 1: Identify your problem.
Step 2: Determine the categories or classes of data you will collect and for what time period, then collect the data. Use a check sheet to tally data in each category.

Quality Tools and Techniques, continued

Step 3: Build a frequency table. List categories in descending order, from most frequent to least frequent in column one. List the occurrences for each category in column two and total them at the bottom. Compute the cumulative occurrences in column three. Compute percentages for each category by dividing the number of category occurrences by the total number of occurrences for all categories. List these in column four.

Figure 2.6: Frequency Table

Categories	Number of Occurrences	Cumulative Occurrences	Percent of Total (Column 2 ÷ Total)
A	10	10	37%
B	9	19	33%
C	4	23	15%
D	3	26	11%
F	1	27	4%
Total	27		100%

Step 3: Format the axes. Categories of data are labeled on the horizontal axis; frequency of occurrence is labeled on the left vertical axis. Percentages are scaled on the right vertical axis.

Step 4: Build the Pareto chart. Transfer the data from the frequency table as follows. **1)** Draw a bar that corresponds with the frequency of occurrences for each category for the established period of time. **2)** Note the percentages for each category on top of the bar. **3)** Draw in the cumulative percentage line.

Step 5: Analyze the chart. Identify which categories are significant and which are trivial for this problem. Develop strategies for addressing those issues which are most significant, for these will result in the greatest improvement.

Quality Tools and Techniques, continued

Figure 2.7: Sample Pareto Chart

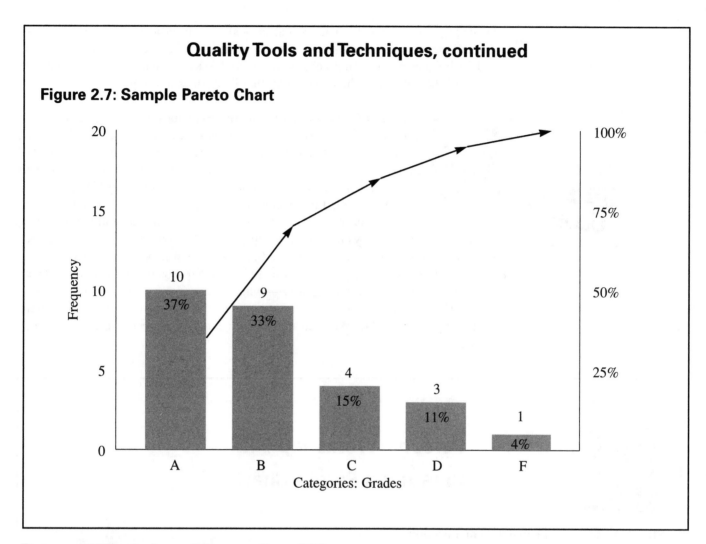

Personal Workshop Preparation #12: Creating a Pareto Chart

You may be able to use the same data from the histogram you developed in the last workshop, or you might choose a totally different topic and set of data to develop a Pareto chart. If you choose a new problem, try again to select one for which the data may be easily gathered. If you are unsure of a problem or question, you might try one of these:

- What are the most significant reasons for customer complaints in this business?

- What are the most significant reasons why order shipping is delayed in this business?

- What are the most significant reasons why sales personnel do not regularly contact their clients in this business?

It is always better to involve a team of employees in the development of a Pareto chart. A group representing several different departments or work levels will be able to suggest several possible causes (categories) for any problem you choose. Work through the steps of the workshop, one at a time; and refer back to the Quality Tools and Techniques box on Pareto charts (pages 81-83) as needed. Before you complete this workshop, examine the Pareto chart that Pete Jones developed.

BestBuilt Construction Company/Pete Jones: We do get a few complaints from our customers. Sometimes they are for very small reasons, such as "I don't like the way the paint looks in the living room." Sometimes they are for major reasons, such as "You are a month behind in construction, and it hasn't even been raining!! What's going on?" We decided to concentrate on that latter type of complaint—not finishing construction on time—and use a Pareto chart to understand the most significant reasons for delays in completion time. To gather our data, we asked the project supervisors to go back through their files and track the various reasons why projects have been late in the past year. If more than one reason contributed to the delay, we told them to mark both categories— what we are trying to do is figure out how to avoid delays in the future, so we want to know about anything that might have contributed to the delay. We used the Pareto chart workshop to work through our problem.

THE PURPOSE OF THIS WORKSHOP IS TO MAKE A PARETO CHART WHICH WILL SHOW SIGNIFICANT CAUSES FOR A SPECIFIC PROBLEM.

Personal Workshop #12
Creating a Pareto Chart

Step 1: Describe your problem or question.
What are the most significant reasons for delayed completion of projects?

Step 2: Determine the categories or classes of data you will collect and for what time period. Then, collect the data.
(a) List below the categories or classes of data you will collect:
Possible reasons for delays: bad weather, waiting for permits or inspection, mistakes in construction, short of help, waiting for materials, equipment breakdowns, client made last-minute changes, poor project planning.

(b) What time period was or will be studied for this chart?
1995

(c) Collect the data. Use historical data already in your records or collect new data. Record data on a check sheet or in some other organized fashion.

Personal Workshop #12, continued

Check Sheet for BestBuilt

Reasons for Delays in Project Completion
Project Coordinator: All-cumulative
Time Span: 1995

Reasons	Frequency
1. Bad weather	7
2. Wait for permits or inspections	6
3. Mistakes in construction	12
4. Short of help	3
5. Waiting for materials	20
6. Equipment breakdowns	2
7. Last-minute changes	6
8. Poor project planning	18
Total Contributing Reasons	**74**

Step 3: Build a Frequency Table. This table will help you organize the data you will need to build a Pareto chart. Use the template below and follow these steps:

(a) In column 1, list categories in descending order, from the category with the most frequent occurrences to the category with the least frequent occurrences.

(b) In column 2, list the number of occurrences for each category. Record the total number of occurrences at the bottom of column 2.

(c) Compute the cumulative frequency of occurrences in column 3. In other words, the first category the cumulative frequency of occurrences will be equal to the number of occurrences in column 2. For the next category, the cumulative frequency will be the total number of occurrences for both the first and second categories, and so on.

(d) Compute percentages for each category by dividing the number of occurrences for that category by the total number of occurrences for all categories. Round off your answers so they total 100 percent. List these percentages in column 4.

Frequency Table for BestBuilt

Reasons for Delays in Project Completion
Time Span: 1995

Categories	Number of Occurrences	Cumulative Occurrences	Percent of Total
Waiting for materials	20	20	27%
Poor project planning	18	38	25%
Mistakes in construction	12	50	16%
Bad weather	7	57	9%
Wait for permits or inspections	6	63	8%
Last-minute changes	6	69	8%
Short of help	3	72	4%
Equipment breakdowns	2	74	3%
Total	**74**	—	**100%**

Personal Workshop #12, continued

Step 4: Format the axes of the Pareto chart on the template below. Categories of data should be scaled and labeled on the horizontal axis. Frequency of occurrence should be scaled and labeled on the left vertical axis. Percentages should be scaled and labeled on the right vertical axis.

Step 5: Build the Pareto chart. Transfer the data from the frequency table as follows:

(a) Draw a bar that corresponds with the frequency of occurrences for each category for the established period of time.

(b) Note the percentages for each category inside its bar.

(c) Draw in the cumulative percentage line.

Pareto Chart for BestBuilt

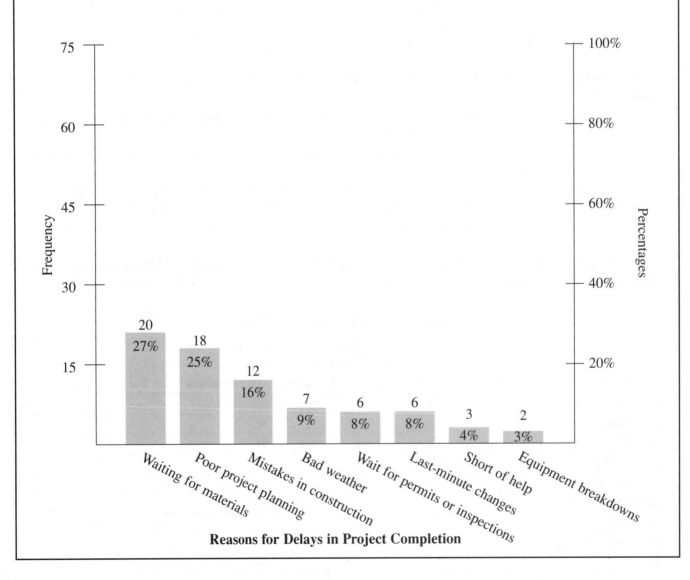

Personal Workshop #12, continued

Step 6: Analyze the Pareto chart you have created and answer the following questions:

(a) Which categories appear to be significant and which appear to be trivial for the problem or question you are studying?

The significant categories are waiting for materials, poor project planning, and mistakes in construction. Bad weather is beyond our control, and the remaining categories are relatively insignificant.

(b) What action or strategies can you adopt to eliminate or minimize the impact in those categories which are most significant?

Waiting for Materials: Except for the occasional item out of stock from the factory, there is no good reason why all materials should not be available when needed. We need to revamp our system for ordering materials and develop better relationships with our suppliers. This could also be considered a poor project planning problem.

Poor Project Planning: A thorough study of our project planning process is called for. With our movement to TQM, project planning/quality teams might make more sense than the project manager approach. We will study this option. In either case, additional training is needed in project management.

Mistakes in Construction: These could be prevented if we get the field personnel to buy into the TQM effort and every employee takes personal responsibility for building the thing right the first time. We need additional TQM training and team building, and we need to look at our incentive system.

THE PURPOSE OF THIS WORKSHOP IS TO MAKE A PARETO CHART THAT WILL SHOW SIGNIFICANT CAUSES FOR A SPECIFIC PROBLEM.

Personal Workshop #12
Creating a Pareto Chart

Step 1: Describe your problem or question.

Step 2: Determine the categories or classes of data you will collect and for what time period. Then, collect the data.

(a) List below the categories or classes of data you will collect.

(b) What time period will be studied for this chart?

(c) Collect the data. Use historical data already in your records or collect new data. Record data on a check sheet or in some other organized fashion.

Personal Workshop #12, continued

Step 3: Build a Frequency Table. This table will help you organize the data you will need to build a Pareto chart. Use the template below and follow these steps:

(a) In column 1, list categories in descending order, from the category with the most frequent occurrences to the category with the least frequent occurrences.

(b) In column 2, list the number of occurrences for each category. Record the total number of occurrences at the bottom of column 2.

(c) Compute the cumulative frequency of occurrences in column 3. In other words, behind row 1 (the first category) the cumulative frequency of occurrences will be equal to the number of occurrences in column 2. For the next category, the cumulative frequency will be the total number of occurrences for both the first and second categories, and so on.

(d) Compute percentages for each category by dividing the number of occurrences for that category by the total number of occurrences for all categories. List these percentages in column 4.

Frequency Table for _____

Problem: _____

Time Span: _____

Categories	Number of Occurrences	Cumulative Occurrences	Percent of Total
Total			

Step 4: Format the axes of the Pareto chart on the template below. Categories of data should be scaled and labeled on the horizontal axis. Frequency of occurrence should be scaled and labeled on the left vertical axis. Percentages should be scaled and labeled on the right vertical axis.

Step 5: Build the Pareto chart. Transfer the data from the frequency table as follows:

(a) Draw a bar that corresponds with the frequency of occurrences for each category for the established period of time.

(b) Note the percentages for each category inside its bar.

(c) Draw in the cumulative percentage line.

Personal Workshop #12, continued

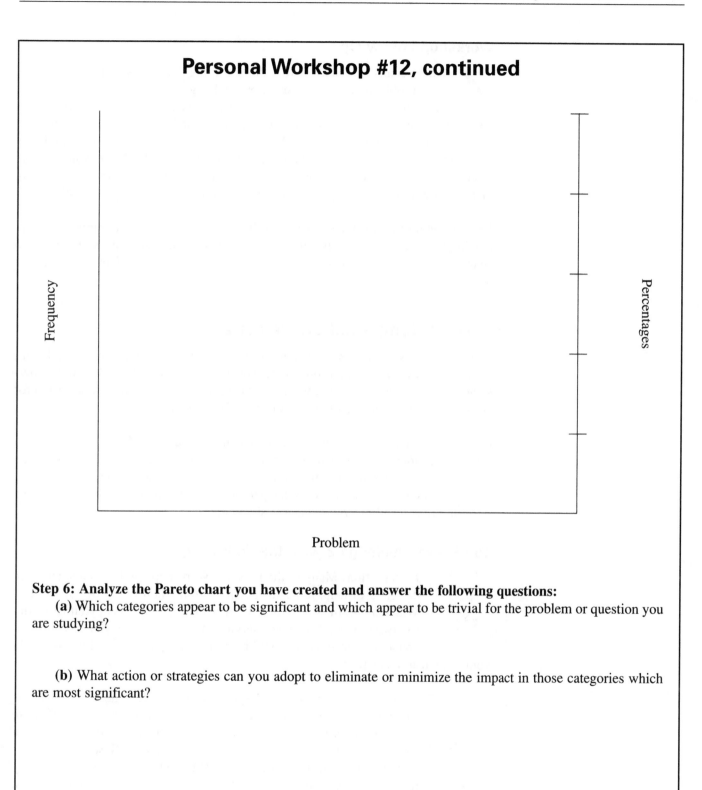

Step 6: Analyze the Pareto chart you have created and answer the following questions:

　　(a) Which categories appear to be significant and which appear to be trivial for the problem or question you are studying?

　　(b) What action or strategies can you adopt to eliminate or minimize the impact in those categories which are most significant?

Workshop Follow-Up

✔ Pareto charts can be a key tool in identifying the most significant causes of your problems. If you discover, by studying your Pareto chart, which circumstances are causing you the biggest problems, and those circumstances are within your control, then you can begin to take action immediately to improve your customer service system. On the other hand, if the categories you originally thought were causing the problem are really trivial, you should change your focus to fixing the more significant categories first. In other words, concentrate on changing things that will have the biggest impact on your total system and your results.

Understanding the real facts is key to solving problems and encouraging continuous improvement in your customer service system. The histogram and the Pareto chart are two effective tools for getting to the root of any problem you might be having.

You Have Completed Challenge 2

Putting your customers first is the key to success in any quality organization. It isn't enough to know *who* your customers are. You also need to develop a thorough understanding of how they think and what they need; then you need to build a system for customer service which assures that their needs are met.

Customer service involves much more than being friendly or offering free gift wrapping. Exceptional customer service requires that you anticipate every customer's questions and problems, and that you deliver solutions and answers on the spot. Exceptional customer service only happens when you and your employees put the customer first each time you make a business decision.

You Leave Challenge 2 with the Following

Information: Many of the Personal Workshops in this Challenge were designed to help you pull together information from several sources. With that information, you are in a position to implement your Blueprint for Exceptional Customer Service. The knowledge you have gained about your customers should help you with planning and marketing in your organization, as well.

Tools: Several quality management tools were introduced in this Challenge, and you were given the opportunity to practice using these tools to assess your business. You calculated the lifetime value of a customer, and developed a customer diagram, a flow chart, a histogram, and a Pareto chart. These last three tools can be used in many ways in your organization and aren't limited to customer service applications. They can help you analyze your current situation or measure improvement over time. Combined with the other basic quality management tools to be introduced in the next two Challenges, they can help you begin your quest for continuous improvement.

Learning: The workshops in this Challenge have helped you learn techniques for gathering valuable information about your customers and evaluating your current customer service system. You learned about points of contact and why each point can be considered a "moment of truth" for your business. You have also learned how to develop a Blueprint for Exceptional Customer Service in the future, and you have been given tips for effectively implementing that blueprint.

Networking: Communication with your customers and your employees is key to your success in putting the customers first. This Challenge has helped you discover ways to learn more about your customers' needs and expectations, a critical first step if you hope to deliver exceptional customer service. Also in this Challenge, you were asked to involve your employees as you completed the Personal Workshops. Your employees are a wonderful resource, with a wealth of knowledge and different perspectives. By involving them, you should know more about your customers, and your employees should be more committed to your company's goals for customer service.

Challenge 2 Self-Assessment

After completing this Challenge you should have a good understanding of who your customers are, what their needs and expectations are, and how you might satisfy those needs and expectations. Check your understanding of the concepts learned by asking yourself the following questions. If needed, go back and review the concepts of quality where you feel you need more practice.

Calculate the value of a customer to your business.

( ) I can calculate or estimate what the average customer spends each time he or she makes a purchase.
( ) I can estimate how often the average customer patronizes my business in a year.
( ) I can estimate the Lifetime Value of a Customer to my business.

Pages 42 - 45

Differentiate between internal and external customers.

( ) I know who my external customers are.
( ) Employees in my company understand that they are both suppliers and internal customers to other employees.
( ) I can diagram the relationship between suppliers, internal customers and external customers.

Pages 47 - 52

Identify the needs and expectations of each of your customer segments.

( ) I have seriously thought about and am prepared to answer the questions a customer might ask in evaluating the utility and quality of my product or service.
( ) I have used observation, communication and/or speculation to find out what my customers need and expect from my business.

Pages 52 - 63

( )   I have developed a list of customers needs and expectations for each customer group I serve, both internal and external.

**Pages
43 - 90**

Use quality improvement tools to assess your company's customer service performance.

( )   I understand how to develop a simple check sheet to tally data in an organized way.

( )   I understand how a Quick-Response Survey can help me gather information about customer service.

( )   I have developed a histogram and understand how this tool can help assess customer service performance.

( )   I have developed a Pareto chart and understand that it shows me the most significant causes of any problem.

**Pages
63 - 75**

Build a blueprint for exceptional customer service in your business.

( )   I understand how to facilitate the brainstorming technique for generating a large number of creative ideas.

( )   I have identified exceptional customer service for my business.

( )   My company has a statement that describes our guiding philosophy on customer service.

( )   I have developed and am prepared to implement a blueprint that includes customer service activities and strategies for each point of contact in my business.

**Pages
68 - 75**

Empower employees to deliver exceptional customer service.

( )   My employees were involved in the development of the Customer Service Blueprint.

( )   My employees understand their importance to customer service and their responsibilities at each point of contact.

( )   I have given my employees the authority to solve problems for customers on the spot.

Take Another Look

Review the results of your checklist above. If you feel you need more work in some area, go back into the text and challenge yourself again. Delivering exceptional customer service means trusting your employees enough to let them solve problems for every customer. If you are comfortable with this concept, you are ready to move on to Challenge 3 and learn about other ways to involve your employees in quality.

Challenge 3

Employee Involvement
and Team Building

*"The achievements of an organization are the results of
the combined efforts of each individual."*

—Vince Lombardi

In Challenge 1, you were told that to be successful, a business committed to quality must involve every employee of the company. Each and every person must be given the skills and knowledge needed to make sound decisions whenever and wherever those decisions need to be made; every employee must be taught how to become an effective team member, and every employee must have an unwavering commitment to excellence.

So, how can you, a small business owner/manager, get your employees involved in teams that are committed to quality?

It starts with you. As owner/manager, you must communicate a clear vision, and you must learn to trust your employees to help move the company toward that vision. Then, you can implement three specific strategies to fully involve every employee in your quality transformation:

- **Strategy: Turn managers into team leaders.** Help every manager develop the skills and assume the roles of quality leadership: teacher, role model, coach, and cheerleader.

- **Strategy: Build a culture that supports team success.** This means that "mushroom management"—keeping employees in the dark and feeding them a lot of manure —must be replaced with feedback, empowerment, and trust.

- **Strategy: Build high-performance teams.** Learn everything you can about how to build effective teams, and then use those teams to solve problems, complete projects, and continuously improve processes in your business.

Nearly every person alive is intrinsically motivated to learn, to become better, and to make a meaningful contribution through work. And yet, many people have never been given the opportunity to make decisions or improvements on the job. In fact, because management has traditionally used fear and coercion to "motivate" employees, people have come to believe that thinking can be dangerous, and that change is almost always for the worse. Such tactics and attitudes are not effective in the long run for any type of organization, and they are totally contrary to the quality concept. It is up to you to lead your people through the transformation to quality.

> "We must be the change we wish to see in the world."
>
> —Mohandas Gandhi

Challenge 3 has been designed to give you the skills and tools needed to develop the people in your company into outstanding, quality-conscious team members.

Upon completion of Challenge 3, you will be able to:

- Identify the roles of management in the quality organization

- Recognize your own team leadership strengths and weaknesses

- Begin building a culture that supports team success

- Identify the types of teams and how to use them in your company

- Apply the following tools and techniques for increasing team effectiveness: nominal group technique, brainstorming, force field analysis, and the cause-and-effect diagram

- Evaluate team effectiveness

It Starts with You

> "The chairman's job is to manage the purse strings, not control the artisans' hands."
>
> —Alfred Sloan

In Challenge 2, you spent a good deal of time thinking about the relationships between your employees and your customers, and you learned that each employee is critical to your company's success. In Challenge 1, you had the opportunity to identify the current characteristics of your business and to assess how your business is doing on each of Deming's 14 points. You also completed a Quality Leadership Assessment, which started you thinking about your own readiness to lead your company into quality management. Before you go on, you might want to take a few minutes to go back to Personal Workshop #4 (pp. 30-31) and review what you wrote.

Now, consider this. How much do you actually know about team leadership? And how effective are you as a team leader? In spite of what you know you *should* be doing, are you really ready to trust your employees enough to empower them to make decisions? Are you truly committed to investing the time, energy and money needed to make your business a learning organization? Are you a positive role model for your employees, and do you see yourself as their coach rather than "the boss?" Finally, are you encouraging collaboration among employees, or does your company tend to pit employee against employee, rewarding individual achievements rather than team accomplishments? If your answer to any of these questions was "no," then "physician, heal thyself." Before you can expect a transformation to the quality concept in your company, you will need to change the way you currently think and act.

Read about how to change managers into team leaders in the next section. Work through the exercises for yourself, first. Identify your strengths and weaknesses as a team leader. Then guide your managers through the same process. Together, you can grow as a management team, helping each other develop as team leaders for your organization.

Strategy: Turn Your Managers into Team Leaders

As owner/manager of a quality organization, you must continuously work to develop your employees and build teams. It is important that you enlist the help of each of your managers in the transformation to quality—an owner/manager cannot do it alone. The managers in your company will need to change their thinking about what they do and how they do it. They will need to think of themselves as team leaders, not as traditional managers. Quality leadership requires a change of roles for managers, from decision makers and work directors to teachers, role models, coaches, and cheerleaders, as shown in Figure 3.1.

> *"The ideal is in thyself; the impediment, too, is in thyself."*
>
> —Thomas Carlyle

Figure 3.1: The Roles of Management in the Quality Organization

Teacher

Role Model

Coach

Cheerleader

Quality Leadership

The Manager as Teacher in the Quality Organization

Every manager in every organization occasionally has to deal with employees who don't do what they are asked to do. While you might assume that the work didn't get done because the employee wasn't motivated, more often than not, motivation has nothing to do with it. It may be simply that the employee doesn't understand what to do or how to do it. There is a learning curve for every job, and seldom will you have an individual step into a position and be fully competent immediately.

One of the most important roles of a manager in a quality company is that of teacher and trainer. At the most basic level, each and every employee must be taught his or her job as well as the correct way to do a specific task. But more importantly, the manager must be sure the employee understands how his or her position fits into the process and system as a whole. Each worker should understand the following:

- What happens before the work gets to my station?

- What happens when the work leaves my station?

- What are the decisions I need to make and the problems I may need to solve in my job?

- What are the performance expectations for my job?

- How does my job affect the overall quality of the product or service delivered?

- How is my job important to the overall mission and vision of this company?

Techniques for Developing Your Teaching and Training Skills

- Read about learning theory and learning styles. Find out how to reach all types of learners by adapting your teaching methods. Use a variety of teaching techniques and learning tools to help you reach all types of learners.
- Take a "train-the-trainer" course through your local college or community education program.
- Contact your area association for training professionals (such as ASTD: the American Society for Training and Development) to learn about opportunities for developing your training skills.
- Explore the library for books and journals on teaching and training.
- Think of the best teachers and trainers you have had throughout your life. Write down what characteristics these people had or the techniques they used that made them effective. Try to emulate their success by using those techniques in your teaching.
- Look for ways to make the concepts being taught relevant to the employee's own life and work.
- Observe other managers involved in teaching and training, and take note of what works for them and what doesn't.
- Consider using the Socratic approach to teaching: instead of directly answering an employee's question, ask the employee a series of other questions to help him or her discover the answer independently.
- Always involve your employees in the learning process. Employees will learn and retain much more if they are "doing it" instead of "writing it" or just "hearing it."

As part of the Small Business Mastery Certification Series, the University of Wisconsin Small Business Development Center offers a program on "Developing Employees through Education and Training," which is one of the Challenges offered in *Human Resources: Mastering Your Small Business*. You can obtain this book by contacting Upstart Publishing Co., Chicago, IL at 1-800-235-8866.

If the employee does not know the answers to these basic questions, then it will be difficult for him or her to embrace or affect the quality concept in your company.

It is equally important that managers teach employees how to function as effective teams, since teamwork is central to quality management. Team members can be taught how to give effective feedback, how to analyze problems and evaluate solutions, how to overcome personal differences, and so on. Each of these skills is critical to the success of a quality organization.

Finally, managers in the quality organization must teach employees how to learn, so that every individual has the ability to gather information, increase knowledge and build his or her skills and productivity. It is every manager's responsibility to be a teacher and trainer to every other employee.

The Manager as a Role Model

The people in your company drive change, whether that change is for better or worse. If you wish to transform your company into a quality organization, then each manager must eat, sleep, and breathe the quality concept every day. Managers must build a climate of trust and team spirit by opening themselves to decision sharing and possible criticism. Managers must constantly talk about the shared vision and the principles of customer service and quality management, as well as the mission of the company and its goals for achieving success. Managers must always look for ways to improve their own performance, so that others will understand that the quest for continuous improvement is never ending.

> *"Change cannot be viewed as the enemy, for it is instead the source of organizational salvation."*
>
> —Warren Bennis

Change is often difficult for people, and employees in small businesses are no exception. It is up to your managers to lead the business through the quality transformation process by demonstrating their own willingness to change. Those managers who are not open to personal change can delay or thwart your efforts to become a quality organization. Quality leaders, on the other hand, consistently model to others how to behave, how to be 100 percent responsible for their own quality, and how to work effectively with others.

The Manager as Coach

The role of coach is central to the quality concept, since decision-making is shared. In the traditional organization, the manager was the decision-maker, and non-management employees were expected to carry out directives for achieving organizational goals. In the quality organization, employees are trained to make decisions and solve problems that relate to their jobs, and it is management's responsibility to coach them through the process—to guide and support employees in their efforts to become better and more productive.

As a coach, each manager needs to be certain that employees have the tools, skills, and support needed to do their jobs. As a coach, each manager helps employee teams and individuals assess the situation, develop alternatives, and solve problems. As a coach, managers provide feedback which either reinforces effective behavior and performance, or guides employees back on track. The purpose of coaching is to build quality teams made up of interdependent and competent employees.

The Manager as Cheerleader

First and foremost, each manager must be a cheerleader for the vision of the organization and its quest for quality. With conviction and sincerity, every manager should talk to employees about what he or she is trying to accomplish and how the quality concept will be implemented.

Second, each manager needs to be a cheerleader for the teams and individuals who are making quality a reality. Through feedback, recognition and the celebration of team accomplishments, the quality leader reinforces the specific skills and actions that result in successful behavior.

Personal Workshop Preparation #13: Team Leadership Skills

Perhaps you have always thought of yourself as a manager—not as a teacher, a role model, a coach, and a cheerleader. Yet, each of these are critical skills for managers in the quality organization. This workshop is designed to accomplish two things: to help you identify your strengths and weaknesses in each of the management roles, and to develop an action plan for improving your skills in each area. Every manager in your company should participate in this Personal Workshop and then, using your new knowledge and understanding, you can begin to build your leadership skills as a management team.

 **BestBuilt Construction Company/Pete Jones:** Even though we've been involved in quality management over the past couple of years, most of our construction workers—the guys in the field—haven't bought it. In fact, they pretty much ignore it. I was meeting with a group of managers and supervisors last week, and after hearing several negative comments about the field workers—things like, "all they care about is getting their paychecks," it occurred to me that we could be a big part of the problem; we haven't really changed from being managers to being team leaders.

FYI

If a manager believes in the quality concept, then the transition from traditional manager to team leader will be much smoother. Undoubtedly, some of your managers have been using each of these sets of skills all along, even before quality became a buzzword in your business. On the other hand, if a manager has been "motivating" people with threats and coercion, or if he or she does not believe in sharing decision-making with employees, then the transition will be a difficult one. As owner/manager, you may need to make some very difficult decisions about individuals on your management team who will not or cannot buy into the quality concept.

There's obviously still this "us versus them" attitude, in spite of all our talk about teamwork. I decided that every manager and supervisor at BestBuilt should complete the workshops in this section to help them develop a better understanding of their new roles in our company. We plan to use this information to assess our own attitude problems and skill weaknesses. We hope to do some training over the next several months to help us all develop better team leadership skills. I used the next Personal Workshop as a self-assessment of my team leadership skills.

THE PURPOSE OF THIS WORKSHOP IS TO HELP YOU UNDERSTAND YOUR STRENGTHS AND LIMITATIONS AS A TEAM LEADER AND TO DEVELOP A PLAN TO SHARPEN YOUR SKILLS.

Personal Workshop #13
Team Leadership Skills

Teacher Skills

Part 1: Self-Assessment of Your Ability as a Teacher. For each statement below, put a mark in the space that indicates your behavior.

	Rarely	Sometimes	Usually
1. I keep all employees informed about overall company goals and activities.		X	
2. I thoroughly explain and demonstrate tasks and proper procedures to employees.		X	
3. I teach my employees effective team skills.			X
4. I teach my employees how to gather and analyze data, how to solve problems, how to think critically, and how to make good decisions.			X
5. I evaluate each person's learning to assure the employee has mastered the concepts.	X		

Part 2: Understanding and Action Plan
1. What strengths do you bring to the role of teacher?
- Experience in training and leading others
- I'm good at explaining things in a step-by-step process
- I make my managers "talk through" their decisions, and I "talk through" my thoughts with them

Personal Workshop #13, continued

2. What are your weaknesses?
- *I don't always make time to train others as thoroughly as I should.*
- *I don't usually follow-up or evaluate the learning. I just assume they understand unless they ask me something or make a mistake.*
- *I don't do orientations in any systematic way. I just mention things as they come up, and sometimes things get missed.*

3. List below at least three specific things that you can do to improve your team leadership skills in this role:
- *Develop an orientation checklist for new employees*
- *Work more closely with employees during the training period to be sure they understand concepts and procedures—better follow-up*
- *Work with managers to develop their training skills. Get them more involved in teaching on a daily basis*

Role Model

Part 1: Self-Assessment of Your Ability as a Role Model
For each statement below, put a mark in the space that indicates your behavior.

	Rarely	Sometimes	Usually
1. I talk about quality, our commitment to the customer, and the importance of teamwork with other employees			X
2. I actively look for ways to continuously improve myself and my work, and I seek input from others on how I might get even better.			X
3. I encourage employees to express themselves openly, even when their views differ from my own.			X
4. I demonstrate to my employees that I trust their judgment and value their knowledge and opinions.			X
5. I do not tolerate negative talk, excuses, blaming others, or disrespect in this company.		X	

Part 2: Understanding and Action Plan
1. In what ways do you positively influence others as a role model?
- *I constantly talk quality and customer service to everyone in the company.*
- *I always encourage employees to participate and share their views and ideas. I let them know I really value their expertise.*

Personal Workshop #13, continued

2. What behaviors or attitudes do you need to change because they might have a negative impact on others?
- Sometimes I don't say anything when others are being negative or disrespectful. This could be interpreted in the wrong way by people who observe it.

3. List below at least three specific things that you can do to become a better role model for other employees:
- Be consistent and adamant about not condoning negative talk, blaming, or disrespect by anyone
- Openly talk about ways that I'm trying to improve my own skills
- Praise good teamwork, and be more careful about criticizing others

Coach

Part 1: Self-Assessment of Your Ability as a Coach.

	Rarely	Sometimes	Usually
1. I work with individuals and teams to set goals and define parameters, but I allow and expect them to solve problems and make decisions with a minimum of interference.			X
2. I am accessible to employees and easy to talk to.			X
3. I give every employee the opportunity to actively participate on teams and be involved in decision-making.		X	
4. I discuss with employees their performance, their aspirations, and ways they can improve their effectiveness on the job.		X	
5. I provide frequent feedback to employees and teams to guide them and reinforce their accomplishments.			X

Part 2: Understanding and Action Plan

1. What skills have you developed that make you an effective coach?
- I have learned to trust and delegate decisions to others.
- I am very clear about performance expectations and help employees find ways to accomplish their goals, if they need it.

2. What weakness do you have as a coach?
- I tend to be more supportive to the people I really like, and not as supportive to the ones I don't have much in common with, even though they're good employees.

3. List below at least three specific things that you will do to become a better coach:
- I will actively recruit more people from the field to be involved in teams.
- I will make the effort to be an effective coach to every employee, not just my favorites.
- I will schedule regular times to meet with the different employee groups to bring them up-to-date on goals and activities and to give them the opportunity to ask questions, state their concerns, etc.

Personal Workshop #13, continued

Cheerleader

Part 1: Self-Assessment of Your Ability as Cheerleader.

	Rarely	Sometimes	Usually
1. I praise employees and teams whenever they achieve significant results.		X	
2. I continually talk about our vision with enthusiasm and conviction.			X
3. I encourage employees and teams to set goals, and I support their efforts to achieve those goals.		X	

Part 2: Understanding and Action Plan

1. When have you exhibited good cheerleading skills in the past?
- When we first got involved in quality management
- When our first round of teams started seeing results

2. What are some instances when you could have provided more enthusiasm and support?
- I think I have let up over time, especially since things are running smoothly for management, even though the construction workers in the field haven't bought in.

3. List below at least three specific things that you will do to become a better cheerleader:
- I will meet with the construction workers to encourage them to get involved on teams and to explain to them how quality management can help them do their jobs.
- I will work with the supervisors to find out who is working on quality in the field, and then do a write-up on accomplishments in the next company newsletter.
- Over the next six months, I will personally meet with all employees to talk about their involvement and to find out about their goals and aspirations for moving up in the company.

Personal Notes

_____

_____

_____

_____

_____

THE PURPOSE OF THIS WORKSHOP IS TO HELP YOU UNDERSTAND YOUR STRENGTHS
AND LIMITATIONS AS A TEAM LEADER AND TO DEVELOP A PLAN TO SHARPEN YOUR SKILLS.

Personal Workshop #13
Team Leadership Skills

Teacher Skills

Part 1: Self-Assessment of Your Ability as a Teacher. For each statement below, put a mark in the space that indicates your behavior.

	Rarely	**Sometimes**	**Usually**

1. I keep all employees informed about overall company goals and activities.

2. I thoroughly explain and demonstrate tasks and proper procedures to employees.

3. I teach my employees effective team skills.

4. I teach my employees how to gather and analyze data, how to solve problems, how to think critically, and how to make good decisions.

5. I evaluate each person's learning to assure the employee has mastered the concepts.

Part 2: Understanding and Action Plan

1. What strengths do you bring to the role of teacher?

2. What are your weaknesses?

3. List below at least three specific things that you can do to improve your team leadership skills in this role:

Personal Workshop #13, continued

Role Model

Part 1: Self-Assessment of Your Ability as a Role Model. For each statement below, put a mark in the space that indicates your behavior.

	Rarely	Sometimes	Usually
1. I talk about quality, our commitment to the customer, and the importance of teamwork with other employees.			
2. I actively look for ways to continuously improve myself and my work, and I seek input from others on how I might get even better.			
3. I encourage employees to express themselves openly, even when their views differ from my own.			
4. I demonstrate to my employees that I trust their judgment and value their knowledge and opinions.			
5. I do not tolerate negative talk, excuses, blaming others, or disrespect in this company.			

Part 2: Understanding and Action Plan

1. In what ways do you positively influence others as a role model?

2. What behaviors or attitudes do you need to change because they might have a negative impact on others?

3. List below at least three specific things that you can do to become a better role model for other employees:

Coach

Part 1: Self-Assessment of Your Ability as a Coach.

	Rarely	Sometimes	Usually
1. I work with individuals and teams to set goals and define parameters, but I allow and expect them to solve problems and make decisions with a minimum of interference.			
2. I am accessible to employees and easy to talk to.			

Personal Workshop #13, continued

	Rarely	Sometimes	Usually

3. I give every employee the opportunity to actively participate on teams and be involved in decision-making.

4. I discuss with employees their performance, their aspirations, and ways they can improve their effectiveness on the job.

5. I provide frequent feedback to employees and teams to guide them and reinforce their accomplishments.

Part 2: Understanding and Action Plan
1. What skills have you developed that make you an effective coach?

2. What weakness do you have as a coach?

3. List below at least three specific things that you will do to become a better coach:

Cheerleader

Part 1: Self-Assessment of Your Ability as Cheerleader.

	Rarely	Sometimes	Usually

1. I praise employees and teams whenever they achieve significant results.

2. I continually talk about our vision with enthusiasm and conviction.

3. I encourage employees and teams to set goals, and I support their efforts to achieve those goals.

Part 2: Understanding and Action Plan
1. When have you exhibited good cheerleading skills in the past?

2. What are some instances when you could have provided more enthusiasm and support?

3. List below at least three specific things that you will do to become a better cheerleader:

Workshop Follow-Up

You have undoubtedly discovered that you are involved in each of these management roles in some form almost every day. Changing behaviors can be difficult—and changing your attitudes can be even more difficult. But if you expect the employees in your company to believe in quality, in their importance to the company, and in their own responsibility to the process of continuous improvement, then people in leadership positions must act as role models. This workshop may have been difficult for you, and some managers may find it threatening. That was not its purpose. Use the information you gained to become a better teacher, role model, coach and cheerleader to others. Ask a mentor or trusted colleague to help you develop better skills by telling you if you become lax in your behavior or enthusiasm for quality. And let other managers know that you will do the same for them. This is an excellent opportunity to build trust and understanding in your organization.

> *"All human progress, like baseball, involves a certain amount of risk. You can't steal second while keeping one foot on first."*
>
> —Anonymous

Strategy: Build a Culture that Supports Team Success

Key Word

> *"Interdependence is a higher value than independence."*
>
> —Stephen Covey, author of
> *The 7 Habits of Highly Effective People*

Developing managers into team leaders makes it possible to build an organizational culture which truly supports team success and the quality transformation. The **quality culture** is customer-focused with a clear vision and goals to guide employees. In the quality culture, there is a commitment to learning and abundant feedback to help teams of employees continuously improve processes and performance. In the quality culture, employees are empowered and entrusted to make decisions and do their jobs without fear of reprisal. The quality culture gives every employee the opportunity to experience the elation of working with others to achieve something bigger and better than could be achieved by any individual alone—and the interdependence of team members makes it possible. This is illustrated in Figure 3.2.

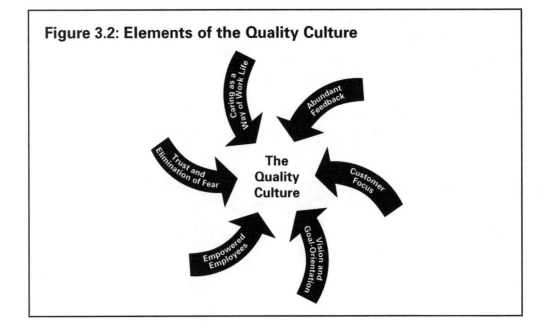

Figure 3.2: Elements of the Quality Culture

Caring as a Way of Work Life · Abundant Feedback · Trust and Elimination of Fear · The Quality Culture · Customer Focus · Empowered Employees · Vision and Goal-Orientation

Customer Focus, Vision and Goal-Orientation

In the quality culture, there is a clear vision to guide employees in their work and decision-making. A quality company's vision and decision-making revolves around meeting the needs of the customers. As you learned in Challenge 2, it is critical that every employee in your company be committed and intent upon serving the customer.

When your company has a clear vision, individuals and work teams can establish long and short-term goals for moving the company toward that vision. The result, then, is a business where everyone understands where they are headed and how they are going to get there—and yet they can adjust those goals and move in a different way, if circumstances in the environment demand it.

Trust and the Elimination of Fear

It has been said that all of our emotions stem from either love or fear. Fear can be paralyzing to individuals and to organizations. And yet, many companies have traditionally used fear to "keep employees in line." The idea, apparently, is to scare employees just enough so that they do what they are supposed to do, but not enough to drive them away. Consequently, employees have lived for years with the fear of being fired, demoted, or otherwise reprimanded or embarrassed for doing something wrong. They have lived with the fear of having their ideas shot down, having access to people or information withheld, or being left out of the decision-making process, even when the decisions directly affect their work. The result of these and other workplace fears is an American workforce with the attitude, "I'll just go to work and do my job . . . I'm not paid to think." What a waste!

If your company is going to succeed as a quality organization, meeting and exceeding the needs of your customers, you must have the help of each and every employee. This means that fear must be eliminated in your company. It means that blaming others and making excuses when things don't go exactly right are unacceptable. It means that competition among employees is discouraged, while collaboration and consensus are known by everyone to be the keys to success. It means that every person is given the education and tools needed to make a full contribution through work.

The term **strategic planning** refers to a company's effort to develop long and short-term goals, and action plans for achieving those goals, with the mission and vision of the company as the basis and guide for that action. A strategic plan should, in theory, be a dynamic document, reviewed and revised frequently, as the organization responds to changes in its internal and external environments. While the term strategic planning is no longer vogue in many management circles, the concept of goal setting and action planning is just as critical to the quality organization as it has always been. But, rather than setting quotas or arbitrary targets for production, the goals of your quality organization should focus on constantly improving the systems of production and service.

Key Word

And it means that every employee understands that his or her skills and knowledge are valued by the company.

Keeping employees informed, providing specific and frequent feedback, and involving employees at every level in decision-making and on teams will help drive fear out of your workplace and build trust between management and non-management, as well as between work units and individuals.

Abundant and Supportive Feedback

In the quality organization, giving and using feedback are important skills for all employees. Getting feedback can be a threatening concept for many people, especially those who have been in an organization where negative feedback is far more prevalent than positive feedback.

Key Words

Feedback can be either corrective or affirming. Both forms have value, if they are provided in an honest and considerate manner, and if they are given in the spirit of continuous improvement rather than to place blame. **Affirming feedback** can reinforce performance and build confidence. **Corrective feedback** can help employees focus or redirect their efforts, search for better solutions and/or improve their skills. Giving corrective and affirming feedback in a positive way is an important skill for every team member. Accepting and using feedback for continuous improvement is, likewise, an important skill for team members in the quality organization.

As an owner/manager of a small business, you must be willing to make yourself vulnerable. Set the example by eliciting feedback from others, and then accept and use that feedback to become a better leader. Feedback is a critical element in the quality culture, and so you must teach employees how to give, receive, and use feedback in a productive way.

There are different levels and types of feedback that may be useful to your employees and your company. Some feedback is impersonal and relates to how systems are working. For example, you may want to know how your billing system is working. To get this information, you could seek feedback from your accounts receivable clerk, your customers, and/or other personnel who work with or are affected by that system.

Some feedback relates specifically to how individuals are performing or relating to others in the company. Because it is more personal, it is much more difficult to give or receive feedback of this type, and it may require careful thought and sensitivity to avoid defensiveness. It is important that employees at all levels know and understand how their behaviors and skills are helping or hindering the quality efforts of the company. Feedback may be sought from supervisors or team leaders, peers, mentors, customers, or anyone who has personal contact with the individual.

Receiving Feedback

There are many ways to ask for feedback. A written or oral survey could be developed and distributed to gather data about systems or employee performance.

Employees or teams could be asked to submit periodic reports on their activities or findings. Managers, supervisors, peers or internal customers could be asked to provide written summaries or reports evaluating processes and other people. Or, verbal feedback can be solicited. For example, as an owner/manager who is interested in becoming a better team leader, you might approach several employees this way:

I am asking several members of our team to give me some feedback on my team leadership skills. I am wondering if we could spend about ten minutes together so that you can share with me, confidentially, what you see as my strengths and weaknesses as a team leader. I hope to use the information I gather to develop a plan to improve my skills. Would you please help?

FYI

Key Word

360-Degree Feedback

It is often useful to seek feedback from a circle of people, rather than one or two. This is called **360-degree feedback**, and it can provide you with a more thorough picture of your performance and effectiveness. For example, the Personal Workshop you just completed on Team Leadership Skills could, with a few word changes, be used as a 360-degree feedback instrument. You could then ask a number of co-workers to complete the workshop with you in mind—assessing your skills, strengths, and limitations, and sharing their ideas on how you could become a more effective team leader. While this might sound threatening, 360-degree feedback is an effective way to gain true understanding of how others perceive your behavior. Everyone has blind spots, and everyone has an ego. The goal of 360-degree feedback should be to help individuals recognize their blind spots without destroying their self-esteem. This type of feedback can be painful, and yet this technique will help you see the truth so that real improvements can be made.

Figure 3.3: 360-Degree Feedback

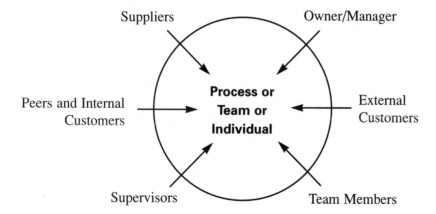

360-degree feedback will give you multiple view-points, which is important to a true understanding of how well a system or an individual or a team is performing.

Whether you have formally requested it or not, you can get the most from feedback by following a few simple rules:

1. **Pay close attention when you are receiving feedback.** If it is verbal feedback, give the individual speaking your full attention, and listen carefully for understanding. If written, try to interpret what is being said and why. Jot down any questions you might have as you read through the material. Make every attempt to remain objective when receiving feedback, and do not allow your emotions to take over. Stay focused, do not interrupt, and avoid body language that might suggest defensiveness.

> *"It's not what you don't know that hurts you, it's what you know that just ain't so."*
>
> —Satchel Paige

2. **Seek true understanding.** Ask questions or request specific examples to help clarify your understanding. Paraphrase what you think you have heard or read, and ask for confirmation from the individual giving the feedback.

3. **Consider the source.** Understand that feedback is a reflection of a person's experiences, knowledge, and understanding of the issues. Never automatically discount feedback; nor should you automatically accept it. Weigh the value of all feedback on the basis of the validity and reliability of the information received.

4. **Take appropriate action.** Don't ignore feedback. Always acknowledge the value of what you have received and, when appropriate, consider how you can use that information to become more effective or efficient. Remember that feedback is a gift. Whether you use it or not, express your appreciation for the new information.

Giving Supportive Feedback

Whether corrective or affirming, all feedback should be given in a supportive way. Remember that all feedback should be given in the spirit of continuous improvement and reinforcement, not to place blame. As with receiving feedback, following a few simple rules will help you develop good supportive feedback skills:

1. **Think about what you want to say and how to say it.** Carefully plan what needs to be said and the best way to deliver the feedback. If necessary and if time allows, write out and rehearse what you are going to say in advance. Again, don't let emotions rule. Select your voice tone and volume and body language as carefully as you have selected the words.

2. **Give feedback at the right time and in the right place.** If you are giving affirming feedback, the right time is whenever and wherever you become aware of good performance. Immediate feedback and praise will help reinforce the good performance and give employees the recognition they deserve. If you are giving corrective feedback, you may need to select the time and place more carefully. Promptness is still important, but a private setting may be important to save the recipient from embarrassment.

3. **Always be respectful and courteous.** If you are anything else, the feedback will be lost on the recipient. Remember that your goal is to provide information that will *help* someone. There is no room for sarcasm, insults or rudeness when giving supportive feedback.

4. **Focus on the behavior of the individual or team, not on personality characteristics.** Instead of saying to an employee, "You don't get along with the members of our team," focus on the behavior that illustrates that point: "When you put down the other members of the team, I feel embarrassed and angry, and not much gets accomplished." While hearing this may still be painful, this approach suggests that the behavior of the person is objectionable, not the person himself or herself. Be specific when giving feedback, rather than making general comments such as, "Good job," or "Could have been better."

A Commitment to Learning

Education is an important element in the quality concept. A quality organization needs to become a **learning organization**, a company which recognizes that continuous learning is the key to continuous improvement and staying ahead of the competition. A learning organization is constantly looking for ways to give its employees new information, new ideas and better skills through learning experiences. A learning organization supports the personal and professional growth of its employees through training and education.

Key Word

Everyone in your company needs to be involved in learning, because *not* learning is like sitting still. It is like waiting for the competition to run you over. A commitment to learning is central to developing trust, empowering employees, and staying customer-focused, and it is critical to the quality concept.

> "Even if you are on the right track, you will get run over if you just sit there."
>
> —Will Rogers

Strategy: Build High Performance Teams

Team building isn't just a buzz word among management theorists—it is a critical skill for any owner/manager in today's competitive environment. Well-managed companies, both large and small, are discovering that effective teams can produce higher quality products more efficiently. In fact, some studies cite productivity

---

FYI

BFR Statements
Behavior - Feeling - Results

A BFR statement is often an effective way to give corrective feedback without making the other person feel defensive or under attack. A BFR statement has three basic parts. First, you state the behavior. Second, state how that behavior makes you feel. Third, state the results of the behavior. The format is as follows:

"When _____(state the behavior)_____, I _____(state the feeling)_____, because _____(state the results of the behavior)_____. For example, instead of saying, "You did a sloppy job on that project," say "When I saw the mistakes in your figures, I felt very concerned, because incorrect figures could really throw our final calculations off."

increases up to 50 percent, and reduced production costs of up to 25 percent, in firms using high performance work teams.

Team building involves more than simply putting a group of people together to work on a project. To be effective, a team must learn how to communicate and work together. A high performance team uses synergy, combining the talents of each team member to solve problems, find creative solutions, and improve processes. Effective teams are clear about what they need to accomplish, they are committed to certain values and team goals, and they share responsibility for their tasks and their accomplishments. Every member of a high performance team is interdependent, making unique contributions, while supporting the other members of the team through feedback and reinforcement.

Advantages and Limits of the Team Approach

Effective teams can help your company make gains in quality and productivity. An experienced, effective team can move through the quality improvement process like a well-oiled machine. An effective team will come up with better decisions and more creative solutions than an employee working alone. The members of an effective team will pool their skills, knowledge, and talents, and because they share a common commitment and values, they support one another and are motivated to achieve their goals. Team members have the opportunity to use their talents and to develop better communication, problem-solving, and decision-making skills through their work on teams. Finally, employees who work on effective teams have a better understanding of the system as a whole, and a better appreciation for the perspectives and needs of other people.

Building effective teams, however, can be time consuming and tumultuous. Teams need to have a clear purpose and goals, and roles and ground rules must be clearly understood. Teams need good leadership, and they need to go through several stages of development before productive results can be expected. Some problems or decisions simply can't wait for the team to work through these dynamics before productive action is taken.

Any time you expect people to work together, there is the potential for conflict. Teams are no exception, and yet the benefits of building effective teams far outweigh the disadvantages. Individuals can be trained, conflict can be managed, and teams can become the driving force in your company for improved quality and production.

Understanding Team Development

Teams go through a life cycle, or five stages of development:

- *Forming*: As a team forms, individuals are typically cautious and uncertain about what lies ahead. The mission and goals of the team may be unclear, and the relationships between individual members have not yet been established.

- *Storming*: As team members begin to understand more about the team's goals, they begin to form independent ideas about how to proceed. In this stage, disagreements and conflict are common, as team members begin to test ideas, size up other team members, and jockey for position on the team.

- *Norming*: At this point, the team begins to come together. Ground rules are set, goals and roles are clarified, and team members begin to communicate with one another effectively.

- *Performing*: The group finally begins to function as an effective team, and members value other members and their involvement with the team as a whole. Individual strengths are recognized and utilized, and limitations are accepted. The team begins to achieve its goals, solve its own problems and demonstrate achievement. This is the most productive stage in team development, and moving the team to this stage is an important function for any team leader.

- *Adjourning*: Depending upon the purpose and goals of the team, it may be dissolved after a period of time.

A team's developmental process may be slow or relatively fast, depending upon how experienced team members are, how effective the leadership is, and the personality dynamics within the team. It is also possible that, once a team is performing, it could slip back into a less functional stage in the process in response to some significant event or change in the system (such as a new person being added to the team, new leadership, a change in goals, and so on).

Types of Teams

Teams are formed for various purposes and for various periods of time: short-term or long-term. There are four primary types of teams common in the quality company:

- **Project teams** are developed for the purpose of planning and implementing specific projects or events. The members of a project team could come from any level in the organization. It isn't uncommon for team members to represent the different work units in the company which need to be involved in the project or event. An example of a project team would be a team formed for the sole purpose of developing an employee handbook.

Key Words

- **Process improvement teams** are developed for the purpose of examining and improving a specific process in the system. For example, in a pizza bakery, a process improvement team could be set up with team members representing different departments and with the goal of continuously improving the production process and the products being produced. A process improvement team typically works together over a long period of time.

- **Problem-solving teams** can be developed for the purpose of solving one particular problem. For example, in that same pizza bakery, if the crusts are coming out of the oven with disfiguring air bubbles in them, a team might be developed to explore and solve that one particular problem. Once the problem is solved, the team would be adjourned.

Key Words

- **Management teams** might be formed for various purposes, such as developing a strategic or production plan, learning about and developing effective team leadership skills, or identifying problems or processes needing improvement in the current system. Some management teams are limited to trouble-shooting, and then process improvement or problem-solving teams are developed to analyze and solve the problems.

Personal Workshop Preparation #14: Using Teams in Our Business

This workshop is designed to help you identify how you could use teams in your small business. In most companies, there is a use for every type of team noted earlier. If you have not used teams in the past, try to keep an open mind during this workshop and think about projects, processes, or other challenges in your company which could benefit from the involvement and creative input of a functional team.

 Recycled Paper Wholesalers/Lindy Hernandez: We haven't really used teams in the past, so I really found this workshop a challenge. Since we're new at this, I plan to start out pretty low key. I'll get the project team on training formed and rolling, and then we'll form the process improvement team. I don't expect to see any immediate results from that team, because I know it will take a while for them to get used to working with each other; but I really believe this team will put us on the right track for the cost savings we so desperately need.

Personal Notes

_____

_____

_____

_____

_____

FYI

Key Word

Self-Directed Work Teams

Self-Directed Work Teams (SDTs) operate, as the name suggests, as autonomous, self-managed groups of employees within a company. SDTs typically do their own planning and coordination of work, and they continuously look for ways to improve and evaluate their work. In some cases, an SDT might even be responsible for hiring, evaluating, compensating, and/or firing team members.

THE PURPOSE OF THIS WORKSHOP IS TO IDENTIFY WAYS TO USE TEAMS IN YOUR SMALL BUSINESS.

Personal Workshop #14
Using Teams in Our Business

Select the type of team you will use. Complete this exercise for each team you selected.

❏ Project Team   ❏ Problem-Solving Team
❏ Process Improvement Team   ❏ Management Team

• Name a specific project or event that could be planned and/or implemented by a project team in your company:

• Describe the purpose for this team:

• Write objectives for this team:

• What people would you put on this team, or which units would you want represented?

Workshop Follow-Up

✔ While you might choose not to implement all of the teams discussed here in your small business, at least you should now have an understanding of how each type of team might be used. If the team concept is new to your company, start out slowly and give team members the training and authority they need to become effective. If you do not, the team might fail, and it will become more difficult to make the transition to teamwork in the future. Always keep other employees informed of the activities and progress of your teams. This will help allay their fears about what might be going on in a select group, and it will give the team members the recognition they deserve for their accomplishments.

Characteristics of High Performance Teams

No matter the type of team, all high performance teams share certain characteristics that help make them effective in whatever they do:

- *Shared vision for the company*: Effective teams understand the vision for the company and how their team is important to making that vision reality.

- *Clear mission and team goals*: Effective teams have a stated mission or purpose and they set goals for team achievement. Effective teams are results-oriented.

- *Effective team leadership and organization*: Effective teams have a leader to guide and manage team activities without dominating other team members. Team leaders handle the logistics of team meetings, facilitate team meetings, keep team members on task and moving forward, keep records of meetings and team action, and help employees become effective team members.

- *Clearly defined roles and responsibilities*: Each member of an effective team makes unique contributions based on his or her knowledge, skills, and special expertise or talents. Special roles, in addition to team leader, might include liaison with an outside group or person, quality expert, marketing expert, or some other role requiring special expertise. Full and balanced participation by every team member is essential and understood in the effective team. Often, team members will also have responsibilities for outside "assignments," such as gathering data or recording feedback from non-team members.

- *Open communication*: Effective teams understand the importance of open communication between team members and with those outside the team. Good listening skills are critical in effective teams, as are good questioning skills. Team members should be trained to state opinions, raise issues, and challenge other team members and the group as a whole in nonthreatening ways.

- *Established ground rules*: Effective teams have a set of ground rules to guide behavior by team members. Some examples of ground rules are: arrive on

> *"The chief objective of leadership is the creation of a human community held together by the work bond for a common purpose."*
>
> —Peter Drucker

FYI

Groupthink

Groupthink occurs when consensus becomes more important to team members than critical analysis. Groupthink is a possible hazard of high team cohesiveness, when team members begin to think alike, and the team becomes more intent on agreeing than on risking conflict by raising important questions. The possible result of groupthink is poor decision-making. One possible way to avoid groupthink is to always encourage dissenting opinions and challenging questions from team members during the problem-solving and decision-making processes. Appointing one or two team members to the role of "devil's advocate" can help a team consider all possible options and consequences of any decision.

time and fully participate in every meeting; do not interrupt other team members; complete all outside assignments on time; and resolve all conflicts immediately.

- *Supportive environment, interdependence, and synergy*: An effective team conducts business in a supportive and non threatening way. The skills and talents of individual team members are respected and utilized, creativity is encouraged and applauded, and team members can count on others to carry through where they are weak. The effective team has synergy, and team members recognize that they can accomplish far more by pooling their knowledge and talents than they could achieve working independently.

- *Trained in group processes*: The effective team understands the stages of team development and guards against the possible pitfalls of **groupthink**.(see the FYI on page 116 for more information on groupthink.) The effective team uses quality tools and techniques to solve problems and make decisions as a group. And, effective teams learn how to resolve conflicts through effective communications and group processes.

Key Word

- *Evaluates its own effectiveness*: Since the effective team is clear about its purpose and sets measurable goals, it is able to evaluate its own effectiveness. The high performance team can document improved quality and productivity, and it can objectively evaluate its own group processes, and then take corrective action to become a more effective team.

Essential Skills for Team Success

There are certain skills that are essential for team success. The team leader should personally develop each of these skills and teach and model them for team members. Each team member should learn these skills through training and practice in the team setting.

> *"A camel is nothing more than a horse that was designed by a committee."*
>
> —Anonymous

Managing Meetings

A **meeting** is a gathering of two or more people for a specific purpose. Meetings can be productive and time-saving, or they can be time consuming and useless. Many people consider all meetings "cruel and unusual punishment"—and yet, the average American worker spends several precious hours in meetings every week. Meetings are called for a variety of reasons, including to solve problems, disseminate information, plan events, get consensus, gather viewpoints, improve processes, or simply to touch base. So why do meetings have such a bad reputation? Because most of them are poorly planned, poorly managed, and nonproductive.

Key Word

Bad meetings are often the result of bad habits formed over time. To break those habits and to develop the skills needed to run an effective meeting every time, follow these **"Ten Commandments of Meeting Management."**

The Ten Commandments of Meeting Management

Used with permission, copyright 1995, Jill A. Rossiter.

I. Thou Shalt Only Hold a Meeting When It Is Absolutely Necessary

Unless you can identify a specific purpose and set concrete objectives for the meeting, forget it. Even then, ask yourself if you can accomplish your meeting objectives in another way, such as making a few telephone calls, having a conference call, sending e-mail or writing a memo. If the answer is no, then begin planning the meeting. Remember that meetings are expensive. They take people away from other productive work, and there are often administrative, materials, or travel costs as well. If the benefits of meeting don't outweigh the costs, don't call the meeting.

II. Thou Shalt Plan for Meeting Results

Carefully plan every aspect of your meeting by setting meeting objectives, developing an agenda and a timetable for agenda items, and by arranging for a meeting time and place, equipment, and so on. Always keep meetings as short as possible; participants are more likely to stay on task if a meeting is tightly scheduled.

Key Word

The Agenda: An **agenda** will guide the meeting participants before and throughout the meeting. In addition to listing the purpose and objectives of the meeting, the agenda needs to tell the meeting time and place, who will be attending, and the time schedule for meeting activities. Actual items on the agenda time schedule might include:

- Review of the purpose and objectives of the meeting

- Introductions of participants

- Establishment or review of ground rules for the meeting

- Review and/or revision of the agenda

- Review and approval of the minutes of the last meeting

FYI

The Top Ten Reasons Why Meetings Are Nonproductive

1. There is no clear purpose or objective for the meeting.
2. There is no agenda, or a poorly planned agenda.
3. The agenda is not followed—people get off the track.
4. The meeting has an ineffective leader/facilitator.
5. The wrong people (or too many or too few people) are invited to the meeting.
6. People are not prepared for the meeting.
7. People do not give full attention to the meeting.
8. The meeting starts late and/or ends late.
9. No decisions are made.
10. There is no meeting follow-up.

- Individual or team status reports
- Problem-solving or decision-making activities
- Discussion
- Development of action plans and making team assignments
- Meeting summary
- Planning of the next meeting
- Meeting evaluation

There are several ways to arrange agendas for meeting effectiveness. For example, you may want to list agenda items in descending order of importance. This will help assure that the most important items are taken care of in the time allotted, and the least important items are deferred until the next meeting, should time run out. An alternate approach is to have team members take care of "quick" business first—items that can be dealt with or decided upon in a short period of time—and then reserve the balance of the meeting time for one or two more significant items. This assures that the minutia is dealt with, freeing the team to concentrate on the more weighty issues for the rest of the meeting. In either case, it is important to consider that meeting participants will eventually run out of steam. Don't try to accomplish too many significant things in a single meeting, or you may get substandard results from your team members.

III. Thou Shalt Be Picky about Whom Thou Invites

For a team meeting, invite only the team members and any outside "guests" who need to attend to provide specific information or feedback. Allow "guests" to join the meeting at a specific time (when their contributions are needed), and to leave when finished. Meetings with more than about eight people may be less productive than a smaller group. On the other hand, if a quorum is needed to make decisions, do not hold the meeting unless you know enough people will attend.

IV. Thou Shalt Send Out a Meeting Announcement and Agenda in Advance

Allow team members enough time to thoroughly prepare for a meeting and make logistical arrangements to attend the meeting. To help participants prepare, note on the agenda who will be responsible for each agenda item, and add handwritten notes to specific people for clarification, if necessary. Supporting documentation might include reports, memos, data output, survey forms, maps or travel information for participants—everything you want the team member to review before arriving at the meeting.

V. Thou Shalt Arrive at Meetings on Time and Fully Prepared

As you review the agenda ahead of time, make note of any materials or other items you need to review, prepare or take with you to the meeting. Then, schedule a time to take care of those matters so they will be fresh in your mind or in your hand when needed. You should always arrive in time to set up and be prepared for the start of the meeting; to arrive late is disruptive and sends a negative message to other team members. If you must be absent or late for some valid reason, send a message to the meeting facilitator in advance, so that the agenda can be adjusted, if necessary.

VI. Thou Shalt Participate Fully in the Meeting

Meetings are most productive when every team member participates fully, mentally and physically. Side conversations, reading unrelated papers or newspapers, interruptions by telephones, beepers, or non-team personnel should be strictly taboo. Guest participants should be free to come and go as needed for the meeting, but team participants should come to the meeting totally committed and prepared so they do not disrupt the team's work by constantly running in and out.

VII. Thou Shalt Begin and End the Meeting on Time, and Stay on Schedule Throughout

The team leader or meeting facilitator is responsible for keeping the meeting and the people on task. Never delay the start of a meeting for latecomers; this is unfair to the punctual people, and it rewards the late person's inconsiderate behavior. Once the agenda has been reviewed and/or revised, make every effort to stick to it. It is sometimes necessary to cut off discussion on a topic, especially when the points being made are redundant or otherwise unproductive. Keep control of the meeting and keep things on target. If the group or an individual gets off track, bring them back to focus on the issue at hand and the meeting objectives.

VIII. Thou Shalt Document the Meeting

It is important that the team have a record of what was discussed and accomplished at each meeting. One team member should take meeting minutes, but every team member should take notes about team activities and actions, as well as note any assignments for the next meeting. Team members should keep a binder or folder of notes and materials from team meetings, and they may want to take those materials to future meetings for easy reference.

IX. Thou Shalt Summarize Meeting Results and Assignments and Evaluate the Meeting

Summarize what was accomplished and decided. Review any assignments made, so that team members leave with a clear understanding of what they need to do to pre-

FYI

One trick for keeping attention focused and a short meeting on task is to remove the chairs in the room where the meeting is to be held. No kidding. By not allowing team members to get too comfortable, you will see them get into the meeting, get to the point, and get out in almost record time. While this technique will not work for longer working or strategy sessions, it is great for short staff meetings and information updates.

pare for the next meeting, if applicable. If another meeting is needed, discuss the schedule and possible agenda items for that meeting. Spend a few minutes talking about the dynamics of the meeting and the team members. What tools or techniques were helpful? Did everyone fully participate and why or why not? Was the meeting well-managed? Finally, discuss what can be done to improve meeting management and group dynamics in the future.

X. Thou Shalt Provide Meeting Follow-Up

At the very least, minutes to the meeting should be sent out a few days prior to the meeting date. Additional follow-up items might include an action list of team assignments (who is doing what and when), data or other materials requested at the last meeting, draft reports or correspondence, etc. In some cases, follow-up with other parties may be necessary. For example, a report on team activities may need to go to management, or data may need to be requested from someone inside or outside the workplace.

Listening Intently

Hearing is no problem for most people. Listening is another matter. It has been estimated that we filter out at least 50 percent of what we hear on a daily basis. We ignore it, consciously or unconsciously, we misinterpret it, or we give it the proverbial "in one ear and out the other" treatment.

> *"You know what you said; you don't know what you heard."*
>
> —W. Edwards Deming

And yet, active, intent listening is a critical skill for leaders and team members, as well as for anyone whose success depends upon the ability to effectively communicate with others. Listening intently increases our understanding of the message being sent, provides us with vital information for decision making, and builds stronger relationships with other people. Active listeners are a rare breed in many companies, and "managers who don't listen" are often cited as one of the primary reasons why employees aren't motivated and companies fail.

The good news is that effective listening skills can be practiced and learned. Listening intently involves concentration and sensitivity to the speaker. It involves using our eyes and mouths as well as our ears to understand what other people are really trying to say.

Here are some tips for learning to listen intently:

- Make a connection with the speaker through eye contact and facial expressions. Let the person know that he or she has your attention and you are ready to listen.

- Concentrate on what the other person is saying. Don't let your mind be distracted by noise, by other people or activities in the area. If necessary, move to a less distracting place to continue the communication.

- Pay attention to intonation and inflection in the speaker's voice. Try to "listen between the lines." Also be aware of the individual's body language. Often, even when the verbal message isn't clear, voice or facial expressions or hand movements can help you interpret what the other person is saying.

• Try to understand the speaker's perspective. Think about who this person is, where he or she comes from, and why he or she might feel a certain way. Open your mind and try to be a "feeling listener," not just a "fact listener."

• Keep your mind in the present and control your emotions. Do not allow highly charged words or statements to break your concentration. Do not begin composing your response in your mind while the person is still talking. Instead, think about what the person is saying and how it is being said, and hang onto any questions that come to mind while the person is talking.

• Don't interrupt. Allow the person to finish his or her thought and stop talking. Then, if you aren't clear on something, ask questions or paraphrase what you think you heard and ask for clarification. In some cases, you may want to invite the speaker to expand on what was said by saying, "Give me more information about…"

Questioning for Clarity

Questioning for clarity is a form of feedback and an important communication skill in any team setting. Effective questioning can build trust, promote understanding and strengthen team relationships. Ineffective questioning, however, can be annoying or even intimidating, sending the message that trust is lacking.

There are two major types of questions that should be used:

• **Closed questions** are those that can be answered with a simple and direct response, such as yes, no, or a simple statement of fact. Asking closed questions is appropriate when you need a straight answer without detail or opinion. Examples of closed questions include the following: How many items did we ship? Has Bob left yet? Do you want me to put the book on your desk?

• **Open-ended questions** cannot be answered with a yes or no, but typically require more thought and detail by the respondent. Open-ended questions

FYI

To test your listening skills, try this exercise. Find a partner and ask that individual to spend about three to four minutes telling you a story about his or her childhood. Do your best to listen intently without interrupting or asking any questions. When finished, tell your partner, in your own words, what you heard him or her say—as much as you can remember. Ask your partner to grade your listening skills from "A" to "F." Then repeat the exercise with your partner as he or she tells a new story. The difference this time is that you are allowed to ask your partner questions or seek clarification about what was said. Again, tell your partner what you heard, and ask to be graded on your listening skills. Did you improve? Most often, the opportunity to ask questions increases one's ability to understand what is being said.

should be used when you need more information, when you are interested in opinions, and when you want to encourage discussion and participation. Examples of open-ended questions include the following: How did the accident happen? What are some things we could do to improve our supplier relationships? Tell me how you feel about working with this team?"

Effective questioning is a skill which can and should be learned by all team members. A short training session on questioning for clarity could be a valuable investment for your company. Understanding the types of questions and techniques for clarifying communication can go a long way to building better team relationships.

Bringing Out the Best in Others

Initially, it is the responsibility of the team leader to help each employee grow in the role of team member. Eventually, as the team matures, every team member should help bring out the best in his or her teammates. While every person is motivated by different factors, most everyone feels good about achieving something significant, either as an individual or as a member of a team. Most everyone wants to be appreciated and recognized in some way for his or her accomplishments, and most everyone wants to be given opportunities to grow personally or professionally, and to advance in his or her position at work and in life.

There are many specific things that can be done by the team leader and team members to help other people grow and achieve their goals. Here are a few that should be commonplace in the quality organization:

- **Recognize individual strengths and celebrate differences**: While most of us are "average" at most things, everyone is "above average" at some things. Make a point to discover what people's strengths and special talents are, and then give individuals a chance to use them to help the team achieve its goals. Diversity of ideas and talents and people is essential if a team is to remain vital and productive. Celebrate those differences and point out the ways that team members complement one another in their work together.

- **Involve members in the team's work**: Keep members active by drawing them into team discussions and planning sessions, by involving them in data collection and interpretation, by asking their opinions, by making them an integral part of the decision-making process, and by asking them to accept certain responsibilities, such as completing a specific task, following up on some detail, giving a presentation, and so on.

- **Promote creativity**: Set ground rules and develop meeting activities that get people thinking in new and creative ways. Whether you use brainstorming, as described in Challenge 2, or some other technique is not important. What is important is that team members feel confident enough to share their thoughts and ideas without fear of being criticized, laughed at or ignored. Every new idea should be acknowledged, recorded and considered for its possible merit. Team members should be encouraged to build on other team members' ideas, because this is how creative ideas evolve.

> *"Imagination is more important than knowledge."*
>
> —Albert Einstein

• **Recognize good performance**: When a team member makes a meaningful contribution to the team, puts forth his or her best effort, or helps the team reach its goals, he or she should be recognized. Likewise, when the team as a whole accomplishes something, whether a significant project or just one step in a complex process, its progress should be recognized. Recognition could be a note of appreciation, a team pizza party, a simple acknowledgment and "thank you" at a team meeting, or possibly a material reward of some sort. A note to the owner/manager about the team's accomplishments, or an article in the company newsletter could also be effective means for recognizing the performance of the team.

Dealing with Conflict

> *"In my experience, people can face almost any problem except the problems of people."*
>
> —W. Edwards Deming

Dealing with the "problems of people" is never easy, but it is necessary in a quality organization. Conflict is a normal part of team development and group dynamics. It is important to acknowledge any conflict that arises and deal with it—otherwise, the team may cease being productive and the self-esteem of individual team members can suffer.

Conflict might arise for a number of reasons. In some cases, the conflict is between people, and in other cases the conflict exists because one or more individuals disagree with the team process in some way.

• **Conflicts between people.** Conflicts between people might arise because of a disagreement that occurs within the team, or it could be totally unrelated to what the team is doing. Some people-to-people conflicts may have developed prior to the team's existence and most likely will continue after the team adjourns. The sources of conflict between people might be personal and stem from power struggles, envy, or simply from incompatible personalities. Or people may disagree for less personal reasons, and have a conflict regarding work-related issues. No matter the reason, conflicts between people can be disruptive to the team, block consensus and result in little productive activity.

• **Conflicts between people and team processes.** Sometimes team conflicts arise because one or more team members disagree with the goals of the team, the roles of the members, or how the team is proceeding. There might be disagreement about methods used, conclusions drawn, data gathered, or the responsibilities of the team members. Conflict might arise because a team member attempts to dominate or refuses to participate or compromise. Such conflicts can sidetrack or stall a team and deflate its members, and they usually force the team to take a step backward before it can move forward again.

People tend to respond to conflict in different ways. Emotions tend to run high, and team members may become confrontational, stubborn or sarcastic, assuming a "fight" response. Other team members may choose the "flight" response, and withdraw their participation or contributions to the team effort. The group as a whole might delay taking any action on an issue, because it wants to avoid the conflict that is sure to come to the surface if it does.

It is the job of every team member to recognize the symptoms of conflict and to nip it in the bud, so to speak, before the group becomes unproductive or dysfunctional. Once conflict has been acknowledged, the team leader can guide the team members through a resolution process. That process typically involves identifying the root of the problem, giving team members an opportunity to express different points of view on the issue, exploring options and agreeing, as a team, on the best way to resolve the issue. The biggest mistake a team leader can make is to ignore the signs of conflict or refuse to deal with the issues, even when they might be personally threatening. Such behavior is likely to escalate the problem—creating a forest fire that eventually will consume far more time and energy than the spark that started it.

 Recycled Paper Wholesalers/Lindy Hernandez: As a business owner, I've learned the hard way that it doesn't pay to ignore conflict. Although I encourage employees to work out their own problems, sometimes you just have to intervene. For example, it became obvious to me that there was a major tiff going on between a few of our process improvement team members. At first, everyone tried to ignore it, and I thought they would eventually work things out, but the whole team began to suffer and couldn't make any decisions, because the team became so divided. I thought about just dissolving the team, but that would have been like cutting off your nose to spite your face—and it wasn't going to make the problem go away. So I sat down with the whole team to try to get to the source of the problem and work out some solution. It turned out that with a neutral party there, everyone was willing to talk about their problems. To avoid placing any blame, I started by asking everyone to write down what was bothering them. Then I asked them to write down some BFR statements (refer to the FYI on writing BFR statements on page 111) that would help them explain their feelings to the rest of the group in a nonthreatening way. Then, everyone shared their BFRs with the group. It all came down to two issues. A few

In recent years, as team building has become an important issue for business and industry, many training companies have developed programs for team development. Several are offered to the public in major cities across the country, and most are reasonably priced. The content of these programs varies and may be largely a repeat of what you have learned in this Challenge. There are also independent consultants and trainers who will come directly into your company and help employees develop team skills. These training services cost a little more, but generally are more effective than public programs, since team members have an opportunity to practice their new skills together. There are even team-building programs that involve such exercises as paint wars (playing "war" with guns that shoot paint pellets), falling off ladders blindfolded into team members' supportive arms, and other physical exercises for building trust and camaraderie. Before selecting any training program in team-building, carefully consider what the long-term impact of the learning experiences will likely be. Choose programs that give participants an opportunity to apply what they are learning to their real work. This will increase the odds that your employees will use their new knowledge and skills when brought back into the daily schedule.

people felt that one of the team members, Krista, was not very sensitive or respectful to the employees from production, and several felt they weren't getting enough information to help them prepare adequately for team meetings. We talked about both issues and outlined some solutions. It was a bit painful for Krista, but she accepted the feedback and is now working very hard to improve her people skills. It has taken a little while for trust to build, but now the team is getting back on track.

Tools and Techniques for Team Effectiveness

There are many tools and techniques available to help you build more effective teams in your company. Some of these tools are designed to help team members become a more cohesive and supportive group. Others can be used to stimulate creativity or improve the decision-making skills of the team.

Improving Team Effectiveness with Team-Building Exercises

There are many excellent team-building exercises available that are designed to build cohesiveness in the team. One good approach to team building is to give team members an opportunity to complete some sort of personality or behavioral profile and then to talk, as a group, about their different personal styles and how those differences are important for team effectiveness. For example, some people may discover that they are "idea" people, but not especially good at turning ideas into reality. Other people might discover that they are good with detail—that they can take any good idea and provide the follow-through needed to make it happen. By discovering this information about themselves, employees learn to feel good about their own strengths, recognize their limitations, and appreciate how other team members complement their own work and personality styles.

Diagnosing with a Cause-and-Effect Diagram

The **cause-and-effect diagram** is one of the Seven Basic Tools for Quality Management, and it is an excellent way for team members to diagnose any problem. For example, if a company team is having difficulty understanding why orders are being processed late, developing a cause-and-effect diagram will help them identify and categorize the possible causes for the problem. See the Quality Tools and Techniques box for information on how to create a cause-and-effect diagram.

FYI

There are many excellent personality or behavioral type profile instruments on the market, including the *Personal Profile System®* published by Carlson Learning Company of Plymouth, MN, and the *Myers-Briggs Type Indicator®*, published by Consulting Psychologists Press, Inc. of Palo Alto, CA, to name a few. Most of these instruments need to be administered and interpreted by trained professionals. To locate a trainer, check with your area chamber of commerce; look in the yellow pages under management training and consultants; or call the publishing company and request the name of a qualified trainer in your area.

Quality Tools and Techniques

The Cause-and-Effect (or Fishbone) Diagram

What is it? A cause-and-effect diagram is a tool used to aid a team in identifying and classifying the root causes of any problem or existing condition.

When should you use it? The cause-and-effect diagram is an excellent tool for helping a team focus on causes rather than symptoms—on what might be causing a problem, rather than *who* is to blame. It is also useful in helping team members understand the complexity of a problem, the relationship between multiple causes of a problem, and identifying the causes of a problem that are within or out of the team's control.

How do you make it?
Step 1: Using a cause-and-effect diagram template, identify your problem in the space at center right.

Figure 3.4: Cause-and Effect Diagram

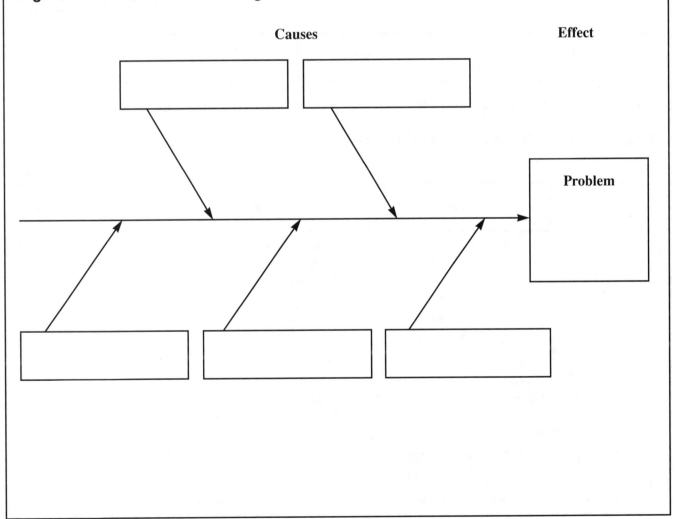

Quality Tools and Techniques, continued

Step 2: Identify and note categories of causes in the boxes of each "fishbone."

Figure 3.5: Fishbone Diagram

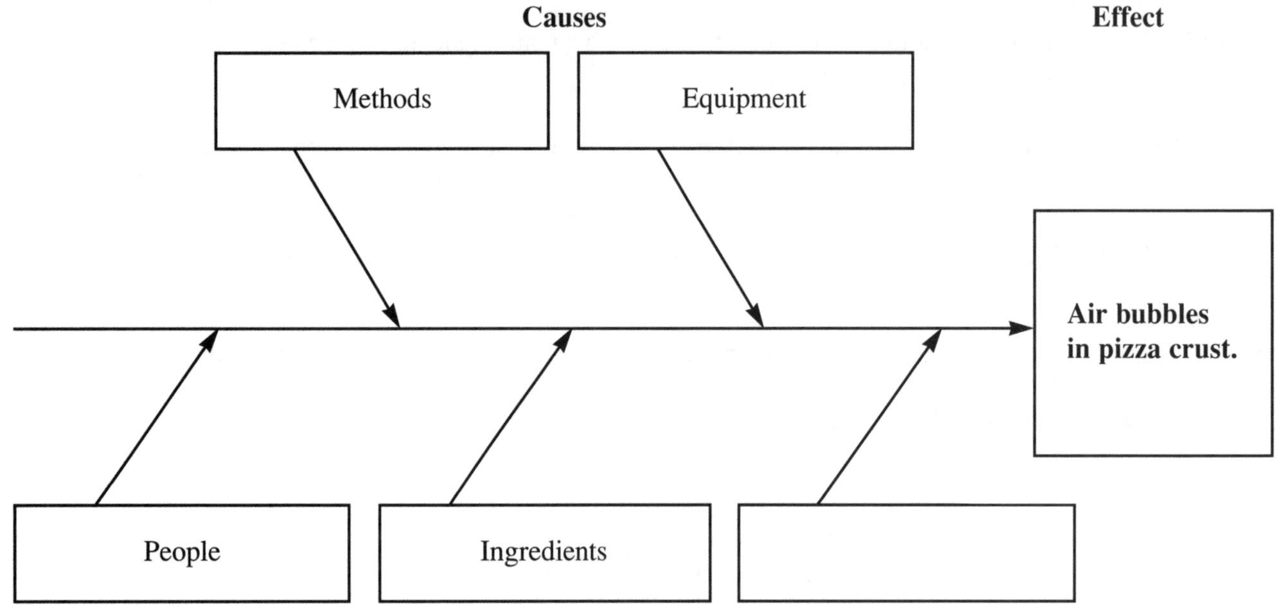

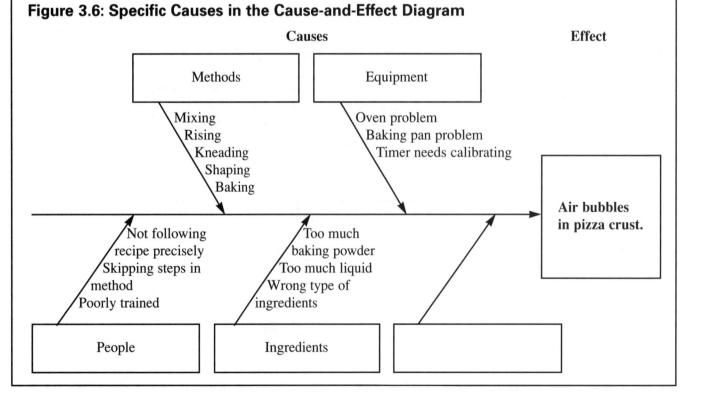

Step 3: Under each category of causes, list all specific possible causes for the problem.

Figure 3.6: Specific Causes in the Cause-and-Effect Diagram

Quality Tools and Techniques, continued

Step 4: Analyze the possible causes by answering the following questions:

• Which of these possible causes is within our control?

• Of those within our control, which items are most likely to have the greatest impact on the problem? List them in rank order.

• What additional information do you need?

Personal Workshop Preparation #15: Cause-and-Effect Diagram

This workshop will teach you how to build a cause-and-effect diagram. Start by thinking of a problem you currently have in your small business. If this is your first attempt at building a cause-and-effect diagram, be sure to pick a problem that is relatively straightforward, such as "paint will not adhere to widgets," as opposed to something abstract and complex, such as "employees are not motivated." Keep in mind that this problem-solving technique will be much more successful if a diverse group of people is involved. After all, you will need to have a variety of perspectives and experiences represented if you want to truly understand the causes of the problem.

 BestBuilt Construction Inc./Pete Jones: I brought our Process Improvement Team together to build a cause-and-effect diagram for one of our most costly problems: not finishing jobs on time. We gained a lot of good information from working through this exercise. The main thing we discovered was that we can't always blame the weather for late jobs—many of the causes for this problem are within our control. Secondly, we were able to identify those reasons which are most likely to occur— the 20 percent of causes that create us 80 percent of the problems. Now we know where to focus our energies for better project planning.

Personal Workshop #15
Cause-and-Effect Diagram

Step 1: Using the template below, identify your problem in the space at center right.

Step 2: Identify and note categories of causes in the boxes of each "fishbone."

Step 3: Under each category of causes, list all specific, possible causes for the problem.

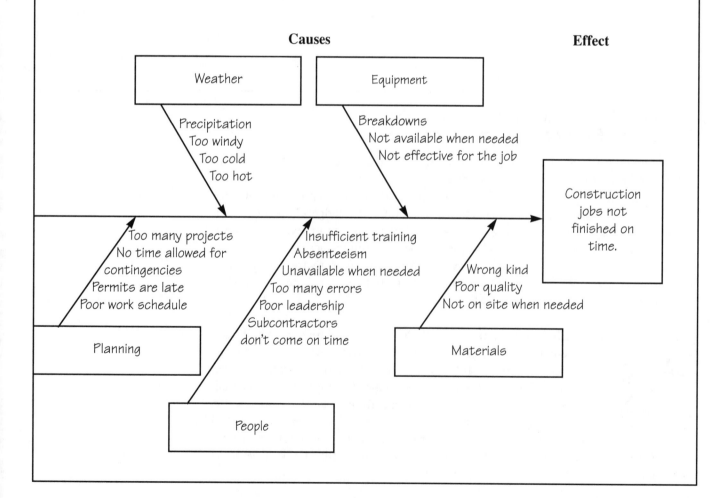

Personal Workshop #15, continued

Step 4: Analyze the possible causes by answering the following questions:

a) Which of these possible causes is within our control?

All, except the weather.

b) Of those factors within our control, which items are most likely to have the greatest impact on the problem? List in rank order.

1. Planning: no time allowed for contingencies.

2. Equipment: breakdowns or not available when needed.

3. People: subcontractors don't come on time.

4. Materials: not on site, wrong kind or poor quality.

5. People: poor leadership and too many errors.

c) What additional information do we need?

We need to look at past jobs and keep better track of future jobs to be sure that these are the most significant causes of our problem. We also need to look at each of our processes—starting with planning—to figure out how we might improve.

THE PURPOSE OF THIS WORKSHOP IS TO IDENTIFY CAUSES FOR A PROBLEM USING A CAUSE-AND-EFFECT DIAGRAM.

Personal Workshop #15
Cause-and-Effect Diagram

Step 1: Using the template below, identify your problem in the space at center right.

Step 2: Identify and note categories of causes in the boxes of each "fishbone."

Step 3: Under each category of causes, list all specific, possible causes for the problem.

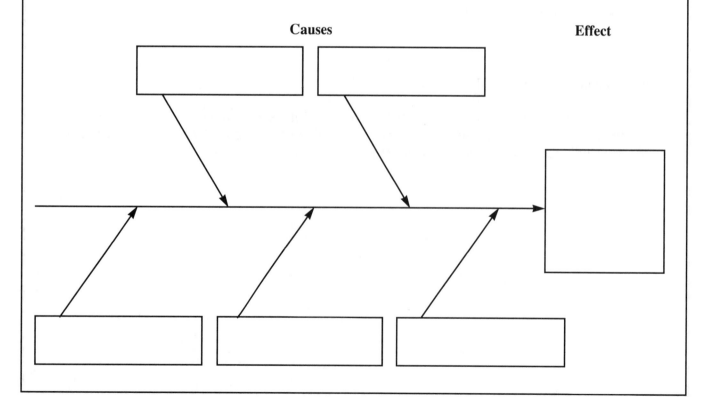

Causes   Effect

Personal Workshop #15, continued

Step 4: Analyze the possible causes by answering the following questions:

a) Which of these possible causes is within our control?

b) Of those factors within our control, which items are most likely to have the greatest impact on the problem? List in rank order.

c) What additional information do we need?

Workshop Follow-Up

✓ Based on what you learned about possible causes for your problem in this workshop, you may now want to gather more information. For example, in the BestBuilt Construction case above, more information is needed before specific action should be taken. By keeping close track of every incident when work is delayed for some reason, Pete Jones will know where his system is weak, and what improvements or changes in the process will have the greatest impact on eliminating the problem. In Challenge 4, you will learn how to use the information you gathered in this workshop to make continuous improvements in your system.

Preparing for Change with Force Field Analysis

Key Word

"In prosperity, prepare for a change; in adversity, hope for one."

—Anonymous

Force field analysis is a team technique for understanding and promoting change. Developed during World War II by a University of Iowa researcher, Kurt Lewin, force field analysis can help team members identify and understand the impact of the driving and restraining forces for any desired change. Once these forces are understood, the team can develop strategies to minimize or redirect restraining forces, while maximizing driving forces. See the Quality Tools and Techniques box for detailed information on force field analysis.

Quality Tools and Techniques

Force Field Analysis

What is it? Force field analysis is a technique for understanding and promoting desired change.

When should you use it? Use force field analysis when the team is having difficulty implementing change or understanding the reasons for resistance to the desired change. Force field analysis allows team members to analyze the forces in effect which either aid or resist the change process, so that strategies can be developed to implement the change.

How do you do it?
Step 1: Using the force field analysis template, team members first identify the issue or problem in the upper left-hand box, and the goal or ideal state in the upper right-hand box. For example, assume a pizza bakery is having difficulty implementing changes that would solve the problem of too many air bubbles in its pizza crust.

Quality Tools and Techniques, continued

Figure 3.7: Force Field Analysis

Issue or Problem	Goal or Ideal
Air bubbles in pizza crust	A flat, tender crust of consistent size, shape, and flavor

Change →

(+) Driving Forces ——————→   ←—————— **Restraining Forces (-)**

(+) Driving Forces	Restraining Forces (-)
• Less waste	• Inconsistent quality of ingredients
• Management support	• Mixing crew not measuring accurately
• Fewer line shutdowns	• Baking crew doesn't see final product
• More consistent product quality	• Costly to have bubbles
• Packing made easier	• Additional research is costly

Action Steps
1. Offer incentives to suppliers who consistently meet our standards for quality ingredients.
2. Develop and deliver joint training sessions for mixers, bakers and packers, so that every employee understands the entire process and their importance to the quality of the final product.
3. First-line management will work more closely with line personnel to ensure changed process is understood and consistently applied.

Step 2: In the left column, team members should use brainstorming techniques to list the **driving forces**—those people, events or circumstances that can aid and support the desired change. In the right column, brainstorm and list **restraining forces**—those people, events or circumstances that are working against or inhibiting implementation of the desired change.

Step 3: Discuss and prioritize (by group consensus or vote), each item on each list in terms of its relative impact on the change. For example, of the driving forces (listed in figure above), the group might decide that management support is most important. In other words, management support could have a greater impact on driving the change than the other forces identified.

Step 4: Starting with the highest priority items, make a list of action steps that will either reduce or eliminate the negative restraining forces, or strengthen or support the positive driving forces for the change.

Step 5: Initiate Action

Evaluating Team Effectiveness

Developing and using teams for decision making in the small business can be time consuming and costly. It makes good sense to evaluate the effectiveness of your teams on a regular basis. There are at least three good reasons for evaluating team effectiveness:

- To understand what progress the team has made in achieving its goals

- To understand how well the team works together and how it might be more effective as a decision-making group

- To give individual members feedback on their team skills

Data to measure team performance can be collected in a variety of ways. You can develop surveys, conduct interviews, request written reports, observe the team in action, or study production data for specific processes over time to understand what impact the team's recommended changes have had. Feedback on team effectiveness can come from team members themselves, from the team leader or facilitator, from members of management, from customers (internal or external), from suppliers, or from anyone else who might be impacted by the team in some way.

Teams need to be accountable and responsible for evaluating their own effectiveness. A high performance team is not afraid of feedback. Team members will continuously seek feedback from a variety of sources, and they will periodically take time to assess how well they are functioning as a team.

Personal Workshop Preparation #16: Evaluation of Team Dynamics

This workshop will give any team in your company the opportunity to assess its effectiveness as a dynamic team. After a team has been working together for several months, ask team members to complete the survey presented in this workshop. The items in this survey are taken from the section in this Challenge called *"Characteristics of High-Performance Teams,"* beginning on page 116. Your team may want to read this section again or use it to develop a set of criteria for completing this workshop. All team members should be encouraged to think of specific incidents or accomplishments that demonstrate the team's characteristics.

One approach for doing this workshop is as follows: each team member could complete the survey and the results could be tabulated for all team members. Then, the team could meet to discuss the results and identify ways to improve its effectiveness. Another approach is for the team members to meet and go through the survey together, discussing each issue as they go, and identifying ways to improve their effectiveness. If the team is functioning reasonably well, either approach should work. If there are some real problems in team dynamics or a lack of trust among team members, then the first approach might be best.

THE PURPOSE OF THIS WORKSHOP IS TO EVALUATE HOW WELL THE TEAM IS FUNCTIONING.

Personal Workshop #16
Evaluation of Team Dynamics

Check the box that best describes the behavior or characteristics of your team.

	Never	Sometimes	Always
1. All team members share a vision for the company.	☐	☐	☐
2. The team has a clear mission and team goals.	☐	☐	☐
3. We have effective team leadership.	☐	☐	☐
4. Our team leader is well organized.	☐	☐	☐
5. Each team member has clearly defined roles and responsibilities.	☐	☐	☐
6. Each team member communicates openly and effectively with others.	☐	☐	☐
7. We abide by a set of ground rules.	☐	☐	☐
8. Each team member is supportive of others and the team as a whole.	☐	☐	☐
9. Team members are interdependent.	☐	☐	☐
10. Each team member has the opportunity to use his or her talents.	☐	☐	☐
11. We achieve synergy as a team.	☐	☐	☐
12. We resolve all conflict immediately.	☐	☐	☐
13. No one is allowed to dominate other team members.	☐	☐	☐
14. We have productive team meetings.	☐	☐	☐
15. Every team member listens intently and respectfully to others.	☐	☐	☐
16. We regularly evaluate our effectiveness as a team.	☐	☐	☐

Workshop Follow-Up

✔ Be sure to discuss the results of your team evaluation as a group, and try to identify areas where additional training or effort may be needed. Remember that your goal is to become a high performance team. Pay attention to those items which might make your team less cohesive or productive. For example, if someone is allowed to dominate the group, certain team members could feel intimidated or less important, and therefore withdraw their participation. Like any process in your small business, there will always be room for improvement in teamwork. But, with your commitment to total employee involvement, wonderful things can happen as the result of effective team-building.

You Have Completed Challenge 3

As the owner of a small business, you need to understand that you cannot implement the quality concept without the help of your managers and employees. At the risk of sounding like a broken record, the change to quality requires a philosophical change throughout your organization. Each and every manager needs to develop team leadership skills that support the quality environment, and each and every employee needs to develop the skills and confidence to make quality decisions every day.

Do not get discouraged if the change process seems slow in your company. Whenever behaviors and attitudes need to change, there will undoubtedly be some resistance, both from managers who are afraid of losing their status and power, and from employees who are afraid to think critically or make decisions on their own. Start by converting one manager at a time, by building one team at a time. Celebrate the little successes, and always move forward. The change may be gradual, but it can and will happen if you persist.

You Leave Challenge 3 with the Following

 Information: This Challenge contained a great deal of information about group processes: the forming of teams, handling conflict, solving problems, and developing team leadership skills. Use this information to begin building strong teams in your business, but keep in mind that your own experience working with teams will be your best teacher. Group processes are complex. It is difficult to teach human relations skills, and it would be presumptuous to say that there is enough information in this Challenge to get you through every tough situation. Practice, read, ask advice, and practice some more. You will eventually accumulate a pool of information that can be used to help develop every employee in your business.

 Tools: Some new quality management tools and techniques were introduced in this Challenge. You learned how to give and use supportive, nonthreatening feedback to help individuals and teams continuously improve. You learned how to use open-ended questions to increase understanding. You were introduced to the cause-and-effect diagram, and force field analysis. Each of these tools or techniques will help the teams in your business solve problems and manage change. Finally, you were given tools for evaluating team effectiveness and team leadership skills. Both of these instruments will serve you well as you transform your small business into a quality organization.

 Learning: It is said that when you teach, you learn twice. By working through the Personal Workshops in this Challenge, you have prepared yourself to teach others many skills that will help them be better leaders, better communicators, better problem solvers, and better employees. By turning your business into a learning organization, you will be giving every employee a gift—the opportunity to grow personally and professionally. Your business will also benefit, since you will be pooling the knowledge, skills and insights of many more people when you build effective teams. Finally, you learned how to use different types of teams in your business and how to develop all types of teams into high performance units.

 Networking: Hopefully you realize by now that networking is what this Challenge is all about. You have gained some skills and implemented tools and techniques that will promote networking and excellent communication throughout your small business.

Networking is nothing more than sharing information and developing resources. When you involve your employees and build teams, that is exactly what you are doing. The synergy that occurs when diverse and talented people work effectively together can benefit your company every single day.

Challenge 3 Self-Assessment

After completing this Challenge you should have a good understanding of how you can effectively develop your managers and involve your employees in the transformation to quality. Check your understanding of the concepts learned by asking yourself the following questions. If needed, go back and review the concepts of team building where you feel you need more practice.

Identify the roles of management in the quality organization.

( ) I have enlisted the help of every manager in the transformation process.
( ) I can explain the importance of being a teacher, a role model, a coach and a cheerleader to every employee.

Pages 93 - 98

Recognize your own team leadership strengths and weaknesses.

( ) I have assessed my leadership skills as a teacher and have identified specific ways to improve.
( ) I have assessed my leadership skills as a role model and have identified specific ways to improve.
( ) I have assessed my leadership skills as a coach and have identified specific ways to improve.

Pages 98 - 106

( ) I have assessed my leadership skills as a cheerleader and have identified specific ways to improve.

Begin building a culture that supports team success.

**Pages
106 - 111**

( ) I am helping other managers develop team leadership skills.
( ) My company has a clear vision and goals, which are customer-focused.
( ) I am working hard to build trust and eliminate fear in the workplace.
( ) I am committed to giving employees the information and authority needed to make good decisions.
( ) I provide supportive feedback to employees, and I receive feedback graciously.
( ) This company is a "learning organization."

Identify the types of teams and how to use them in your company.

**Pages
111 - 115**

( ) I understand that there are several stages in the team development process.
( ) I know the difference between project teams, process improvement teams, problem-solving teams and management teams.
( ) I have identified specific ways to use each type of team in my business.

Apply the following tools and techniques for increasing team effectiveness: brainstorming; force field analysis; and the cause-and-effect diagram.

**Pages
123 - 138**

( ) I have used the brainstorming technique with my employees to complete some of these workshops.
( ) I understand force field analysis and know how to apply it to my business.
( ) I understand the cause-and-effect diagram and can use it to analyze causes for problems in my business.

Evaluate team effectiveness.

**Pages
136 - 138**

( ) I can identify at least three good reasons for evaluating team effectiveness.
( ) I understand the relationship of team dynamics to team results, and know how to use the Evaluation of Team Dynamics in my business.

Take Another Look

Review the results of your checklist. If you feel you need more work in some area, go back into the text and challenge yourself again. Keep in mind that involving all employees and building high performance teams is not going to happen overnight. Keep working on your own team leadership skills, help your managers build their skills, and gradually involve more and more of your employees in the decision-making process through their participation on teams. In Challenge 4, you will learn how to guide those teams through the continuous improvement process, step-by-step.

Challenge 4
A Cycle of Continuous Improvement

"Improvement is the organized creation of beneficial change, the attainment of unprecedented levels of performance."

—Joseph M. Juran

Is there a small business owner alive who doesn't dream of attaining "*unprecedented levels of performance*"? Probably not. The reality, though, is that few business people actually know how to plan for and implement **continuous improvement**, the key to improving performance and the quality of both products and processes.

Key Words

Continuous improvement means getting better every day and in every way. It means gradually eliminating all errors and defects in the products or services produced, as well as eliminating inefficiencies or delays in the production process itself. These problems can be eliminated through the active involvement of your employees in a **cycle of continuous improvement**: studying systems; planning for improvements; trying and testing possible ideas for making things better; and then making those things that work part of the standard operating procedure. Because continuous improvement needs to be ongoing, employee teams continue the cycle by studying the system again, planning for more improvements, and so on. By engaging your employees in these activities, your company will be on its way to attaining the performance levels you dream of.

This Challenge will guide you through the cycle of continuous improvement, step-by-step. You will be introduced to several new quality tools and techniques, and you will be given examples of how those tools you already know can be used in the continuous improvement process.

There are two ways to work your way through this Challenge. First, you may want to work through it on your own to familiarize yourself with the process and the tools introduced. Once you are somewhat familiar with the concepts and the process presented, use this Challenge to guide a process improvement team through a real project. The work you do as a team will be your best teacher of the quality management concepts and the use of the tools presented.

Upon completion of Challenge 4, you will be able to:

- Explain how variation is a threat to quality

- Identify appropriate projects for the continuous improvement process

- Study the system, using a variety of quality tools and techniques

- Identify specific ways to improve the system and plan for that improvement

- Implement your plan and measure results

- Reinforce process improvements

- Repeat the Cycle of Continuous Improvement

Reducing Variation: The Key to Consistent Quality

Key Word

Variation occurs when something is slightly different than another of the same type. When there is variation in a process or in the resources within a system, then there is more likely to be variation in the outputs of that system. For example, if two like products are hand-painted by two different people, you would naturally expect some variation in the final product, the output. However, if two like products are painted by the same piece of equipment using an identical process, the chances of significant variation in the final output are much less. Another example: If the quality of raw materials or manufactured components that go into your product varies, then the quality of your final product will also vary. "Garbage in, garbage out," as they say. If you are interested in improving quality, you need to be concerned about variation in the resources you use in your system, as well as variation in the processes used.

All systems exhibit some variation. A certain amount of variation is natural and does not necessarily mean that the system is unstable or that quality is poor. On the other hand, too much variation or erratic variation suggests an unstable system—one in which the quality of output is inconsistent or unpredictable. This is a dangerous situation for any company, since inconsistent quality will affect customer satisfaction.

To keep customers satisfied, you must continuously improve quality, and to improve quality, you must reduce variation in the system. The continuous improvement process will help you understand where and why variation occurs in a system. Once

FYI

This Challenge is designed to introduce you to the continuous improvement process without overwhelming you with statistical analysis and technical terms. While some prior knowledge of statistics is useful in analyzing and understanding systems, it certainly isn't required. You can begin the cycle of continuous improvement by simply following the steps in this Challenge. Once you have completed this Challenge and your company is successfully involved in the continuous improvement process, you may want to expand your technical knowledge by reading some of the books recommended at the end of this Challenge.

you understand the causes behind variation, you can identify ways to reduce it and stabilize your business operations, resulting in improved quality.

The Cycle of Continuous Improvement

It isn't enough to solve a little problem here, or slightly change a process there, and then forget about it until another problem comes up. Continuous improvement, as the name implies, needs to be ongoing. Continuous improvement means that systems are constantly being analyzed, data is regularly collected and studied, changes are regularly tried and tested, and employees view their work to improve quality as one of their ongoing job responsibilities.

The continuous improvement process should be viewed as a cycle, and teams for continuous improvement need to continue to move through the cycle over the long term. In other words, quality management and employee involvement does not end as soon as one problem seems to be solved. There is always another improvement to be made, another system to be analyzed, or another idea to be tested. The cycle of continuous improvement is shown in Figure 4.1.

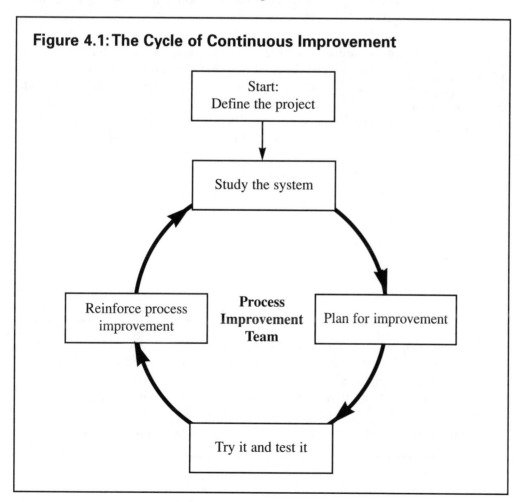

Figure 4.1: The Cycle of Continuous Improvement

Getting Started: Define the Project

When starting the continuous improvement process, pick an initial project that is manageable, and yet significant enough to have a measurable impact on quality. In some cases, a team might be formed to deal with an existing problem. For example, the owner/manager of a small manufacturing company which produces arm rests for automobiles may decide to form a process improvement team when she discovers the company is reworking 40 percent of its output. Or, if a service company owner/manager identifies late payments from customers as a problem, then he might form a team to make changes in the billing and/or collection processes of the company. With a specific project identified, teams can begin their work by clarifying the problem, deciding on the size or scope of the project, and then starting the continuous improvement cycle.

> *"You must identify a problem before you can solve it."*
> —Andrew J. DuBrina

In some cases, a process improvement team may be formed and given a broad or vague mission. For example, the owner/manager might simply form a team to "look at ways to better serve the customer" or to "eliminate errors in production." When this occurs, team members will need to spend their first few meetings more clearly defining the project: clarifying their purpose, setting goals, deciding where to focus their efforts, or identifying one specific issue or problem or point in production to start their investigation.

Denny's Hometown Market/Denny and Mabel Wellman: One of our ongoing challenges is in knowing how many checkers to have on duty so that no customer has to wait in line more than about five minutes. Since the number of customers in the store varies so much from day to day and hour to hour, this is a real challenge. We decided to choose our system for scheduling checkers as our project.

FYI

The concept of a continuous improvement cycle originated with Walter Shewhart who provided the research foundation for Statistical Process Control (SPC) at Bell Labs in the 1930s. Shewhart's cycle of Plan, Do, Check, Act (PDCA) was modified by W. Edwards Deming when he worked in Japan. The Deming Cycle, Plan, Do, Study, Act (PDSA), is widely used to guide businesses through the continuous improvement cycle using statistical process control.

Study the System

Once a project has been identified and the team has been formed, the first step in the continuous improvement process is to study the system. The team's goal is to gather as much information as possible about the system or processes relevant to the project. The purpose of gathering this information is to thoroughly understand the current system, so that the team will be in a position to identify ways to improve the system in the future.

> "A picture is worth a thousand words."
>
> —Anonymous

Several of the quality tools introduced in Challenges 1 to 3 are useful for studying the system, such as flow charts, histograms, and Pareto charts. Several other tools may be helpful, as well, and are introduced in this Challenge. The tool (or tools) you choose to use to help you analyze your system will vary from project to project, depending upon the characteristics of the system and the type of information you need for your project. Before jumping into your study of the system, it might be helpful to list the information you will need to gather for your project.

Personal Workshop Preparation #17: Information We Need

Bring your team members together for a 30-minute meeting to generate ideas about the type of information you will need to gather to do your project. To start the session, post one of the following questions where every team member can see it: What information do we need to gather to _____(describe your project here)_____? What do we need to know about the current system to achieve our project goals? Write all of the ideas down on a board or flip chart—anywhere they can be easily seen by the team. Discuss each item and talk about how you might get the information you need. Record your findings in the Personal Workshop that follows.

Denny's Hometown Market/Denny and Mabel Wellman: Our problem was pretty straight forward: to improve the process of scheduling checkers for better service to our customers. We realized, though, that we needed a lot of information about the check-out system before we could improve the process. The project team held a meeting and we completed the following workshop together. We came up with a list of things that we need to find out about our operations.

Personal Notes

_____

_____

_____

_____

THE PURPOSE OF THIS WORKSHOP IS TO IDENTIFY WHAT INFORMATION IS NEEDED TO COMPLETE YOUR PROJECT FOR THE CONTINUOUS IMPROVEMENT PROCESS.

Personal Workshop #17
Information We Need

Information Needs	How to Get Information
• Average number of customers in store by hour.	• Count customers for one month.
• Average amount of time it takes to check out one customer.	• Have cashiers use a stop watch to measure each check out and record times.
• Average number of customers that can be served by one cashier in an hour.	• Have cashiers keep a tally of customers served per hour on duty, or use the average amount of time per customer to compute customers served per hour.
• Average amount of idle time per hour. Ask cashiers to track and record idle time.	• Ask cashiers to track and record idle time.
• What is an acceptable wait time?	• Survey customers.

THE PURPOSE OF THIS WORKSHOP IS TO IDENTIFY WHAT INFORMATION IS NEEDED TO COMPLETE YOUR PROJECT FOR THE CONTINUOUS IMPROVEMENT PROCESS.

Personal Workshop #17
Information We Need

Information Needs	How to Get Information

Workshop Follow-Up

As your team begins to work through the cycle of continuous improvement, you will undoubtedly become aware of other bits of information needed. Add those items to your list of desired information. Also, as you work through the Personal Workshops that follow in this Challenge, think about how each tool or technique introduced might be useful for collecting and analyzing data, giving you the information needed to successfully move through the cycle.

The Flow Chart

One of the simplest tools for picturing a system or a process within a system is the **flow chart**. Go back to Challenge 2 to review the Quality Tools and Techniques section on flow charts on page 58-59. If the team needs a clear understanding of the relationship between the different steps in the process and the people within the system, then developing a flow chart should be one of its first tasks. By studying a flow chart, the team may discover inefficiencies in the "flow" of the process. For example, perhaps by combining or changing the order of steps or the people involved, improvements in quality can be achieved.

Key Word

 Quali-Temps Inc./Kiki Hermann: We want to improve our process for assigning field associates to our business clients. Occasionally we incorrectly place an associate who doesn't have the specific skills needed. This usually happens because we don't have a clear understanding of what the customer needs ahead of time. Then, when the field associate reports for work, he or she finds out that there is a mismatch, and we have to start over again to find the right person with the right skills. To understand the existing system, our first step was to construct a flow chart which shows who is involved in making the assignments, and what steps are taken to match our field associates to our customers. Figure 4.2 on page 148 shows what we came up with.

By studying this flow chart, we now have a better idea where there might be a breakdown in communication—where we might not be asking the right questions about the specific needs the customer has.

The Run Chart

A **run chart** simply plots data over some period of time. For example, you could use a run chart to show how production levels change from month-to-month, how customer complaints vary from week-to-week, or how sales change from day-to-day. A run chart is an excellent tool for tracking performance over time and for spotting trends or cycles in performance. Information on how to create a run chart is given in the Quality Tools and Techniques box on pages 149-151.

Use common sense in selecting projects. If the project or problem is too complex, the team may find it difficult to get organized or to focus on any single aspect of the problem. Also, if there are multiple causes for a particular problem, any single change made in the system might have a negligible effect. Selecting such a complex problem could be very disheartening for an inexperienced team.

FYI

Figure 4.2: Flow Chart: Process for Assigning Field Associates

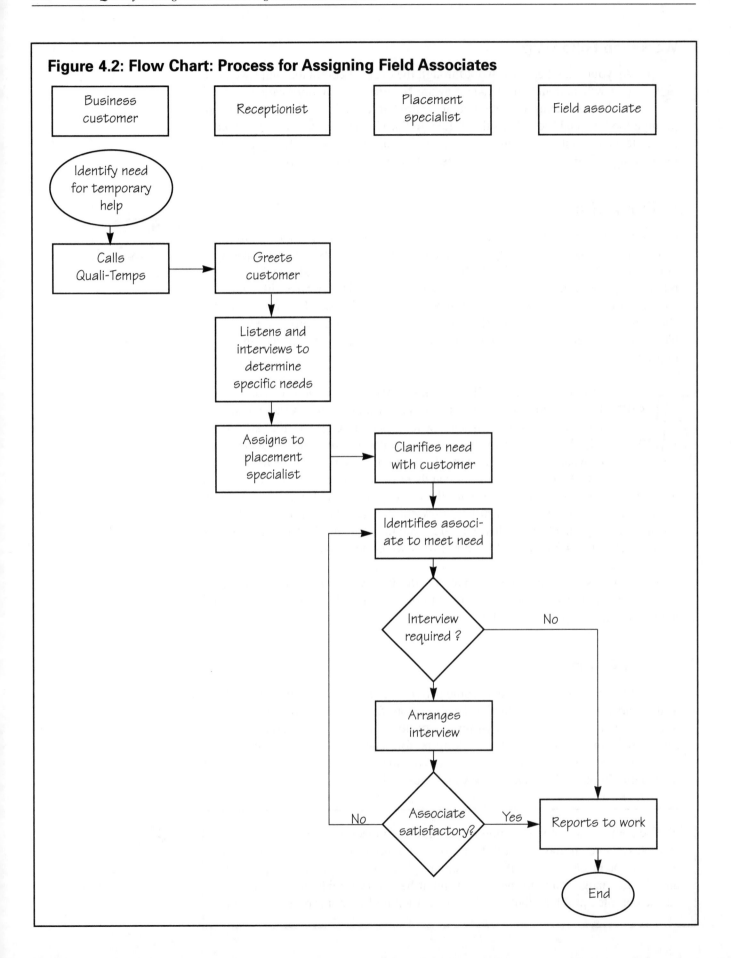

Quality Tools and Techniques

Run Chart

What is it? A run chart is a simple line graph which shows performance data plotted over time. A run chart is one of the seven basic tools for quality management. Run charts are the basis for control charts, which will be introduced later in this Challenge.

When should you use it? Use a run chart when you want a picture of how something performs or changes over time. Use it to spot trends or cycles in performance, or to compare performance before and after you have made a change in a system or process.

How do you make it?

Step 1: Identify what you want to measure and in what increments of time. For example, sales transactions per day, production errors per week, customers served per hour, employee absences per month, and so on.

Step 2: Collect data for a minimum of 20 to 25 points in time. A larger number of data points will help you detect trends or cycles or patterns in performance. Depending on your project, you may be able to use historical data already on record somewhere in your business, or you may want to collect new data. If necessary, develop a simple form to keep track of data on an ongoing basis, such as the one below, which was used to record the number of errors made each work day.

ERRORS PER DAY (JANUARY)

Day and Date

M	T	W	H	F	M	T	W	H	F	M	T	W	H	F	M	T	W	H	F
2	3	4	5	6	9	10	11	12	13	16	17	18	19	20	23	24	25	26	27

Number of Errors

2	1	3	2	5	1	2	2	4	6	2	2	3	1	3	1	1	3	5	4

Step 3: Create a graph with an x-axis (a horizontal line) and a y-axis (a vertical line). Draw the scale for time on the x-axis, and draw the scale for your performance measure on the y-axis. An example is shown in Figure 4.3.

Quality Tools and Techniques, continued

Figure 4.3: X - Y Graph

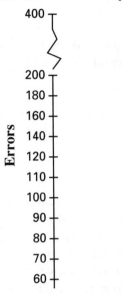

Step 4: Plot the data by making a point that corresponds with the number of errors for each day. Connect the dots as shown in Figure 4.4.

Figure 4.4: Sample Run Chart

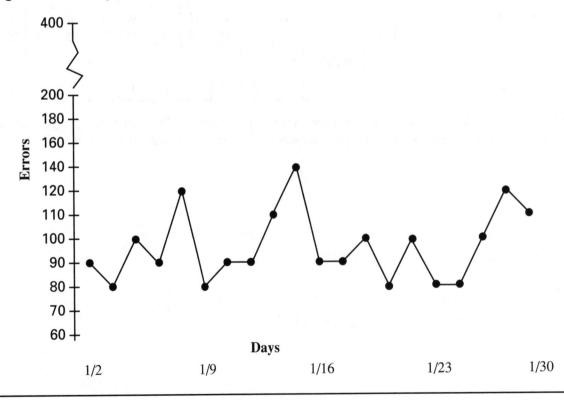

Quality Tools and Techniques, continued

Step 5: Study the run chart. Do the points appear to be random, or does the chart suggest a trend or a cycle or a pattern of some sort? For example, in the sample run chart in Step 4, you might notice a pattern which suggests that, during most weeks, more errors occur at the end of the week. In some cases, you might see a "run," where seven or more points in a row are increasing or decreasing. Patterns or runs aren't necessarily good or bad; but they should always be investigated. They could suggest trends, possible problems, changes in your customers' needs, excessive variation in quality, or any number of other valuable bits of information.

Step 6: Continue to collect data and plot it on the run chart, and watch for any changes that need to be explored.

Figure 4.5: Run Chart with a Natural Variation

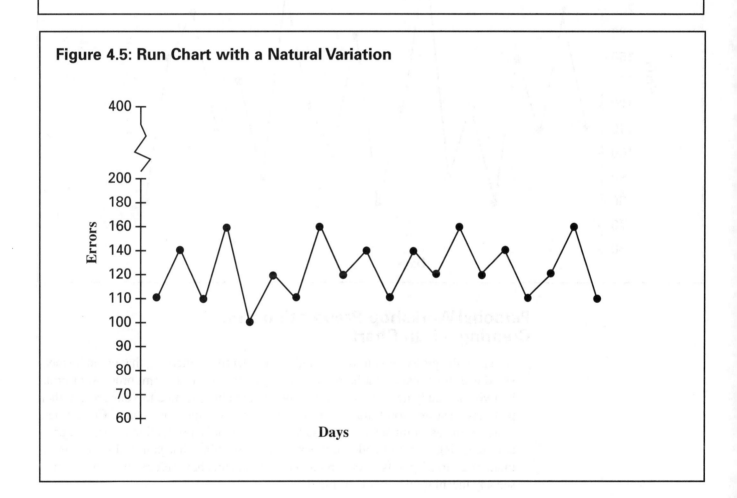

FYI

A run chart can help you see if you have excessive or erratic variation in your system. For example, if all of your points in the run chart are fairly close together, it suggests a stable system with some natural variation. Figure 4.5 shows an example of this.

On the other hand, if the points are far apart at times, close together at times, and inconsistent in general, it suggests that quality control may be a problem because of extreme variation.

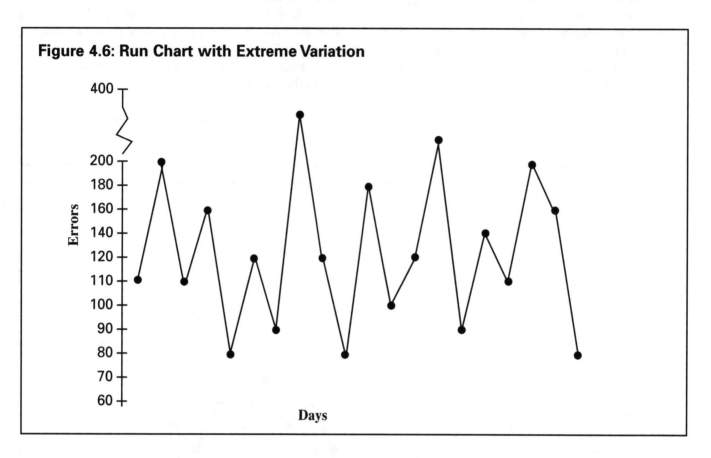

Figure 4.6: Run Chart with Extreme Variation

Personal Workshop Preparation #18: Creating a Run Chart

Based on the project you have selected, try to identify something that could be measured over time that might help you better understand the system, process, or problem you are studying. If you cannot think of something related to your project, then pick any measure you think would be interesting to study over time. Collect data either from past company records (such as sales records, production records, or accident records), or begin collecting new data. Remember that you will need a minimum of 20 to 25 points of data recorded on your run chart before you can expect to see any meaningful patterns or trends.

Denny's Hometown Market/Denny and Mabel Wellman: Our first step for our project (staffing checkers more efficiently) was to develop a run chart to show us exactly when our customers shop with us. We kept track of how many customers we served each hour we were open (7 A.M. until 10 P.M. daily) for a full month, and then we developed a run chart for each day. We learned a lot about our business and the habits of our customers from doing this research. What was really interesting was how the run chart showed us exactly when people were coming in. This was the kind of information we needed to help us schedule our checkers.

Personal Workshop #18
Creating a Run Chart

Step 1: Identify what you want to measure and in what increments of time.
We want to develop a run chart to show us exactly when our customers shop with us.

Step 2: Collect data for a minimum of 20 to 25 points in time. Record data on the template below.

Step 3: Label and scale the x-axis for your time increments. Label and scale the y-axis for the factor you are measuring.

Step 4: Plot the data on the run chart and connect the dots.

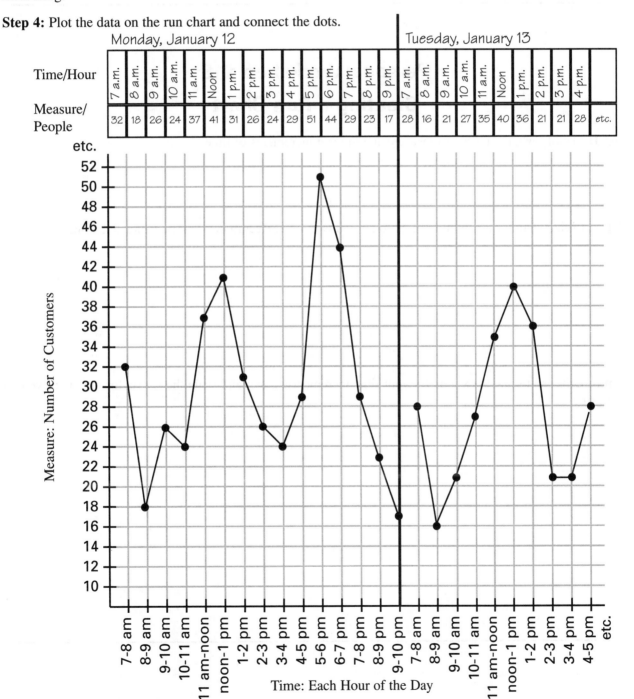

Monday, January 12 — Tuesday, January 13

Time/Hour	7 a.m.	8 a.m.	9 a.m.	10 a.m.	11 a.m.	Noon	1 p.m.	2 p.m.	3 p.m.	4 p.m.	5 p.m.	6 p.m.	7 p.m.	8 p.m.	9 p.m.	7 a.m.	8 a.m.	9 a.m.	10 a.m.	11 a.m.	Noon	1 p.m.	2 p.m.	3 p.m.	4 p.m.	
Measure/People	32	18	26	24	37	41	31	26	24	29	51	44	29	23	17	28	16	21	27	35	40	36	21	21	28	etc.

Measure: Number of Customers

Time: Each Hour of the Day

Personal Workshop #18, continued

Step 5: Study the run chart. What did you learn?

First of all, there is a definite pattern repeated for each week day, with our busiest times being before work in the morning, around the lunch hour, and right after work in the evenings. On the weekends, we found that the heaviest shopping was on mid-Saturday morning and early Saturday and Sunday afternoons. By far, Saturdays and Sundays were our busiest days.

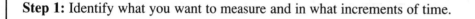

THE PURPOSE OF THIS WORKSHOP IS TO CREATE A RUN CHART.

Personal Workshop #18
Creating a Run Chart

Step 1: Identify what you want to measure and in what increments of time.

Step 2: Collect data for a minimum of 20 to 25 points in time. Record data on the template below.

Step 3: Label and scale the x-axis for your time increments. Label and scale the y-axis for the factor you are measuring.

Personal Workshop #18, continued

Step 4: Plot the data on the run chart and connect the dots.

Time:

Measure:

Measure: _____

Time: _____

Step 5: Study the run chart. What did you learn?

Workshop Follow-Up

 Did your run chart suggest any patterns or cycles in activity, or are there any runs that suggest a possible trend or an unusual circumstance? If so, think about what that pattern, cycle or trend might mean, and what additional information you will need to collect to be sure you understand what is occurring.

If your run chart appears to be totally random, you may want to compute an average (or arithmetic mean) for the data points. Do this by dividing the sum of the measured values by the number of data points. For example, the Wellmans could compute the average number of customers per hour for Monday, January 12, by dividing the total number of customers for that day (452) by the number of data points (in this case, 15 hours) recorded each day. They would learn that they had an average of 30.1 customers per hour on that day. They could also compute the average number of customers for all the Mondays recorded or compute the average number of customers before noon, after noon, or between 4 P.M. and 6 P.M. They can then use this information to determine their usual need for checkers each hour and each day of the week.

You need to decide what information will be useful to you as you work on your project, and then play with the numbers until you feel you have a clear picture of the system. Remember that the purpose of a run chart is to show data over time. If the run chart gives you meaningful information, then consider continuing to collect data and adding to the run chart as long as it is useful.

The Histogram and the Pareto Chart

Key Word

Both histograms and Pareto charts can be helpful for understanding your system or process. Both tools can sort out the significant causes of any problem you might be having in the system. Take a few minutes to step back to Challenge 2 and review the sections on histograms and Pareto charts found on pages 75 and 81, respectively.

 Quali-Temps Inc./Kiki Hermann: Since we want to improve our placement of associates in our client businesses, we needed to know why some placements don't work out. We decided to build a simple histogram to keep track of the reasons why placement mistakes are made. Actually, we just posted this histogram on our "**Quality Wall**" and left it there for six months. Every time we had a problem with placement, we would add a block with the date above the appropriate reason. After six months, it was obvious that our biggest problem was poor communication with the client business in the first place. Now we can use that information to improve our screening process when clients first give us a call.

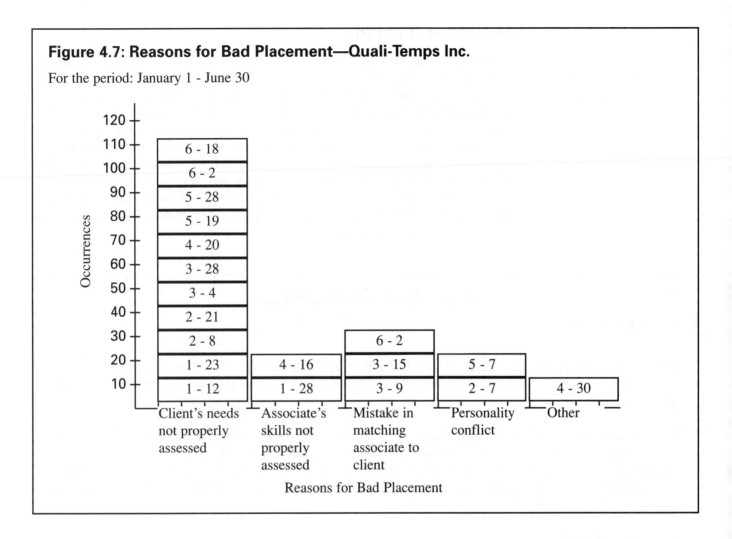

Figure 4.7: Reasons for Bad Placement—Quali-Temps Inc.

For the period: January 1 - June 30

R emember that the more information you can gather, the better your understanding of the system and the problems in the system will be. As you collect data using the different quality tools and techniques, you might want to consider creating a **Quality Wall**: a designated place in your company where flow charts, run charts, Pareto charts, cause-and-effect diagrams, and all of the other tools can be displayed and studied by every employee. Keep the Quality Wall current by updating run charts and histograms on a regular basis.

Key Word

The Scatter Diagram

Key Word

The **scatter diagram** shows a relationship between two factors. Points are plotted on a graph, with each point representing the relationship between two variables. For example, a scatter diagram might show the relationship between the number of sales-people on the floor and the number of sales made, or it could show the relationship between the number of orders that are processed in a day and the number of processing errors made. While a scatter diagram might confirm that a relationship exists between two variables, it *does not* necessarily prove a cause-and-effect relationship between those variables. The points on a scatter diagram often are clustered or in a pattern, though, which can be analyzed by team members to help them understand the relationship. Information on how to create a scatter diagram is given in the Quality Tools and Techniques box.

Quality Tools and Techniques

Scatter Diagram

What is it? A scatter diagram is a graph which shows the relationship between two factors. For example, a scatter diagram might show that the performance of one factor (such as sales) is related to another factor (dollars spent on advertising).

When should you use it? Use a scatter diagram when you suspect there might be a relationship between two variables (or factors) within a system, but you are not sure what that relationship might be. For example, you might suspect that the more dollars spent on advertising each week, the higher the sales will be for that week. A scatter diagram can confirm that a relationship exists between dollars spent on advertising and sales, and it can suggest how strong that relationship is.

How do you make it?
Step 1: Identify the relationship you want to test. For example, assume you want to know if there is a relationship between the amount spent on advertising and gross sales.
Step 2: Collect at least 25 sets of data for the two variables. Too few data sets may prevent you from getting a clear picture of the relationship between the variables. For example, to plot the relationship between dollars spent on advertising and sales, the following data could be used:

Week	Dollars spent on advertising	Gross sales
1	500	15,000
2	375	12,000
3	700	23,000
4	600	19,000
5	450	17,000
6	400	15,000
7	500	16,000
8	550	14,000
9	650	21,000
10	750	22,000
11	575	18,000
12	400	11,000

Quality Tools and Techniques, continued

Week	Dollars spent on advertising	Gross sales
13	525	13,000
14	625	17,000
15	500	19,000
16	475	14,000
17	625	19,000
18	350	13,000
19	425	14,000
20	525	17,000
21	675	18,000
22	650	20,000
23	725	19,000
24	500	18,000
25	375	13,000

Step 3: Draw, label and scale the x- and y-axes for each factor. If you believe one factor is influencing the other, put the influencing factor (called the independent variable) on the horizontal x-axis, and put the factor being influenced (the dependent variable) on the vertical y-axis. For example, since you suspect that the amount spent on advertising influences sales, put advertising dollars on the horizontal axis and sales on the vertical axis, as shown in Figure 4.8.

Figure 4.8: Scatter Diagram

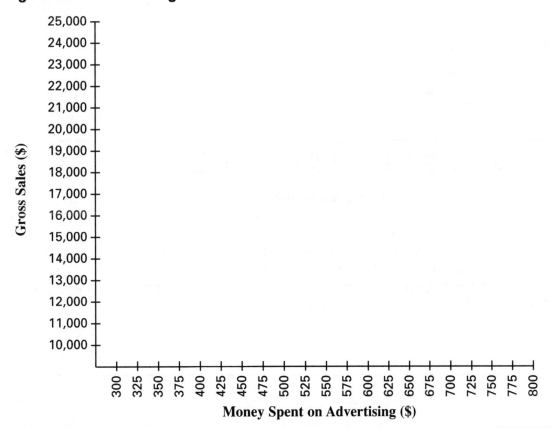

Quality Tools and Techniques, continued

Step 4: Using the set of factors for week one from the data collected in Step 2, plot a point on the graph representing that data set. For example, in week 1, $500 was spent on advertising and gross sales totaled $15,000. Put a point on your graph which corresponds with $500 on the horizontal axis and $15,000 on the vertical axis (see the dotted lines on figure 4.9). Repeat until each set of data is represented by a dot on the diagram. If a set of factors is repeated, you can either clump dots together, or draw a circle around the dot for as many times as necessary.

Figure 4.9: Sample Scatter Diagram

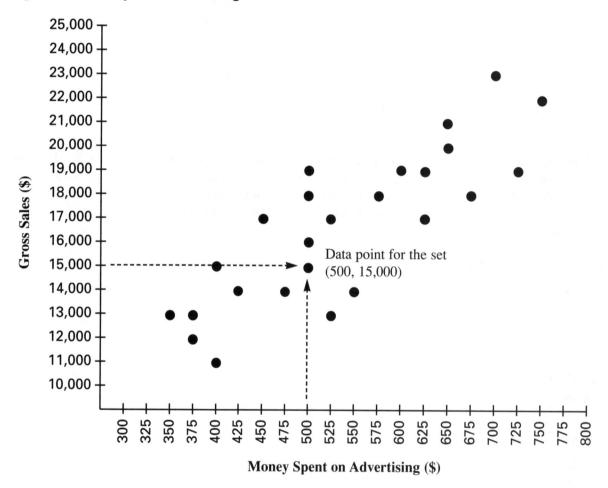

Step 5: Interpret the scatter diagram. If a pattern of dots is apparent, it suggests that there is a possible relationship between the two variables. It *does not* prove, however, that a cause-and-effect relationship exists between those variables. In fact, in the example above, perhaps there is a third unknown variable that is influencing both gross sales and dollars spent on advertising. Be cautious when interpreting a scatter diagram, and remember that it only shows the relationship between two variables in the system.

Quality Tools and Techniques, continued

Some patterns to look for in scatter diagrams include the following:

a) Pattern suggests there is no direct relationship between the two variables.

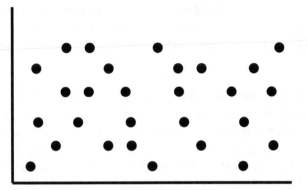

b) A pattern extending from the lower left corner to the upper right corner of the diagram, like that shown below, suggests that a **positive correlation** might exist between the two variables. That is, if one variable increases, the other variable will increase.

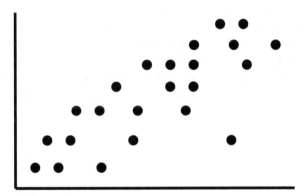

c) A pattern extending from the upper left corner to the lower right corner of the diagram, as shown below, suggests that a **negative correlation** might exist between the two variables. Negative correlation means that, as one variable increases, the other decreases.

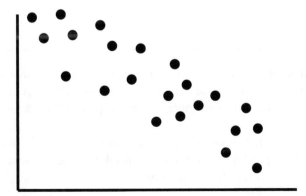

Personal Workshop Preparation #19: Building a Scatter Diagram

Based on the project you have selected, try to identify two variables (factors) that you think might be related in some way. If you believe that an understanding of the relationship between those variables will help you understand the system you are studying, then collect data and build a scatter diagram using those two variables. If you cannot think of something relevant to your project, then pick any two variables in your business that you suspect are related in some way, and do the workshop using those variables.

 Denny's Hometown Market/Denny and Mabel Wellman: We have assumed all along that there is a relationship between how long customers have to wait in the checkout line and their general satisfaction with the store. Specifically, we believe that the longer people have to wait, the less satisfied they are. We decided to use a scatter diagram to see if a relationship actually exists.

We gathered our data by surveying 75 customers (25 each day for three days) as they were leaving the store. We simply stood by the door for a few minutes each hour throughout the day, only surveying a couple of customers each hour. We did this so we would get a good mix of customers, some at busy times, and some at light times. We asked each customer only two questions: "How long would you estimate that you had to stand in the checkout line today before it was your turn to check out?" and "On a scale of one to ten, with ten being the best, how satisfied are you with the service you received at Hometown Market today?" We developed a simple check sheet to record the data. We then worked through the Personal Workshop to build a scatter diagram.

FYI

As with the run chart, a scatter diagram might suggest how much variation is in the system. If the dots on the scatter diagram are close together and form a "clean" pattern, this suggests a stronger relationship with less variation.

If there is a pattern, but it is less well-defined with some "wild" dots outside of the pattern, it might suggest that variation is a problem in the system, or that the relationship between the variables is sporadic.

THE PURPOSE OF THIS WORKSHOP IS TO BUILD A SCATTER DIAGRAM.

Personal Workshop #19
Building a Scatter Diagram

Step 1: What is the relationship in your business that you want to test? Identify the two variables you believe are related.

We feel that there is a relationship between how long customers have to wait in the checkout line and their general satisfaction with the service the store offers.

Step 2: Collect your data.

Wait Time (Minutes)

		No wait	0-1	1-2	2-3	3-4	4-5	5-6	6-7	7-8	8-9	9-10
High	10	IIII	₵HH	III	III	II	I					
	9	I	III	IIII	III	I			I			
	8	III	II	IIII	III	III	II	I				
	7		I	I	I	I	II	I	I			
	6		I		I	II		II		I		
	5		I			I	I	I	I			
	4			I						I		
	3						I		I			
	2				I						I	
Low	1											

Level of Customer Satisfaction

Step 3: Label and scale the x-axis and the y-axis on the template below.

Personal Workshop #19, continued

Step 4: Build the scatter diagram by drawing a dot to represent each set of data.

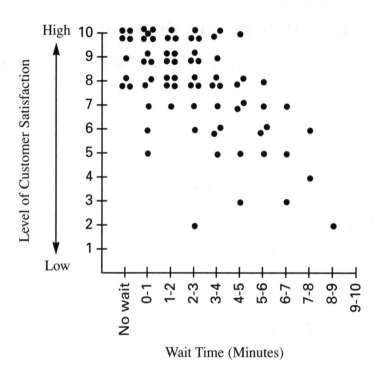

Wait Time (Minutes)

Step 5: Interpret the scatter diagram.

There appears to be a negative correlation between wait time and customer satisfaction. Specifically, the longer the wait time, the lower the satisfaction. Looking more closely, though, the scatter diagram suggests that wait time really didn't appear to have much of an effect on satisfaction until customers had waited for more than three or four minutes. Maybe this means that customers expect to wait a few minutes and aren't bothered by that, but once it gets over three or four minutes, they start to get annoyed.

THE PURPOSE OF THIS WORKSHOP IS TO BUILD A SCATTER DIAGRAM.

Personal Workshop #19
Building a Scatter Diagram

Step 1: What is the relationship in your business that you want to test? Identify the two variables you believe are related.

Step 2: Collect your data.

Step 3: Label and scale the x-axis and the y-axis on the template below.

Step 4: Build the scatter diagram by drawing a dot to represent each set of data.

Step 5: Interpret the scatter diagram.

Workshop Follow-Up

✔ Be cautious when you interpret your scatter diagram, and remember that a relationship does not prove that one variable drives the other. Consider what other factors might influence the relationship you see. For example, at Hometown Market, there were probably numerous other factors that influenced customer satisfaction, such as how friendly the employees were, how easily shoppers were able to find what they wanted, and so on. Also, in that example, the data was based on their customers' perceptions of how long they waited in line, not on actual time in line. It is difficult to know how accurately people estimated their wait time. The scatter diagram can be very helpful for understanding the relationship between two variables in a system, but do not automatically assume that what appears to be true is in fact true.

Control Charts

Key Word

The basic **control chart** is a run chart that includes statistically determined upper and lower limits, which show how much variation is typical in a particular process. Control charts are the most sophisticated of the seven basic quality management tools. There are several different types of control charts that can be developed and interpreted; but the primary purpose of each type is to help you determine whether the system is in or out of control. Information on how to create a control chart is given in the Quality Tools and Techniques box.

Quality Tools and Techniques

Control Chart

What is it? A control chart is a run chart with statistically determined upper and lower control limits which show whether variation in a system is normal and predictable (from a common cause in the system) or abnormal and unpredictable (from a special cause). **Common causes** of variation are shown by points which are randomly dispersed around the average and within the upper and lower control limits. Common causes are inherent in the process itself and can only be eliminated if the system is changed in some way. **Special causes** of variation, which are outside the control limits, are sporadic, unpredictable, and could be caused by human error, changes in the work environment, unusual occurrences, or changes in input, equipment, or measurement accuracy. All special causes of variation should be investigated and eliminated.

When should you use it? Use control charts to assess system stability and to monitor variation in a process over time. Use control charts to understand whether variation in a system is due to a "common cause," or a "special cause," which suggests that the system may be out of control.

How do you make it?
Step 1: Repeat Steps 1 to 4 for making a run chart as shown on page 150-151.

Quality Tools and Techniques, continued

Step 2: Calculate the average, symbolized by $\overline{X}$, (pronounced "X bar"), for the data points on the run chart. Compute $\overline{X}$ by:

a) adding the values of each data point

b) dividing that sum by the number of samples taken

For example, $\overline{X}$ is calculated for this set of data as follows:

ERRORS PER DAY (JANUARY)

Day and Date

M 2	T 3	W 4	H 5	F 6	M 9	T 10	W 11	H 12	F 13	M 16	T 17	W 18	H 19	F 20	M 23	T 24	W 25	H 26	F 27
								Number of Errors											
2	1	3	2	5	1	2	2	4	6	2	2	3	1	3	1	1	3	5	4

$$\overline{X} = \frac{2+1+3+2+5+1+2+2+4+6+2+2+3+1+3+1+1+3+5+4}{20} = \frac{53}{20} = 2.65$$

Step 3: Draw a solid horizontal line on your run chart to denote the average $\overline{X}$. For example, the average of 2.65 errors per day would be shown on the run chart as follows:

Figure 4.10: Some Form of Control Chart

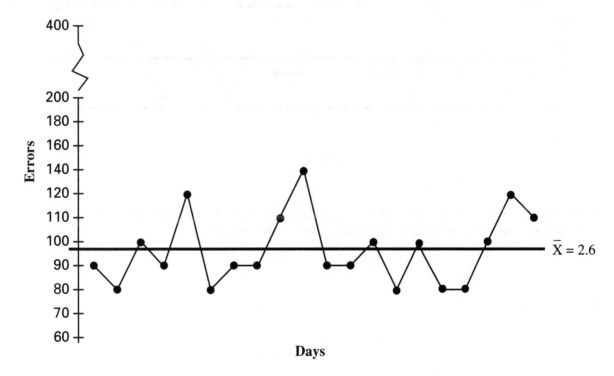

Quality Tools and Techniques, continued

Step 4: Compute the **Upper Control Limit** (UCL) and the **Lower Control Limit** (LCL) for the data. There are several different types of control charts, each with a different statistical formula for computing the UCL and the LCL. Computing control limits, however, is beyond the scope of this book.

For more information on the types of control charts and how to compute upper and lower limits, refer to *The Memory Jogger II* by Michael Brassard and Diane Ritter, or *Total Quality Transformation: Improvement Tools* by Melinda Ball. Both of these books are listed in the Key Resource section at the end of this Challenge.

Step 5: Draw the upper and lower control limits on the chart using a dotted line.

Figure 4.11: Upper and Lower Control Limits on a Control Chart

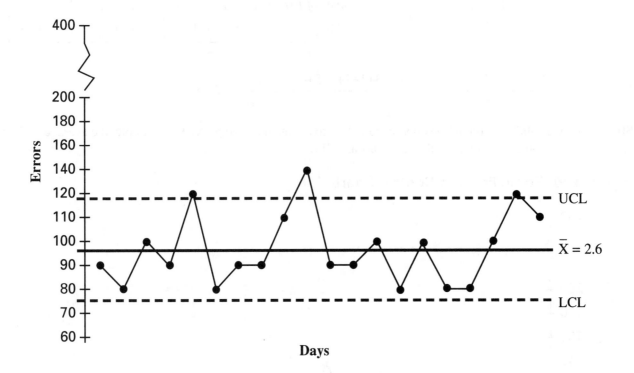

Step 6: Interpret the results. There are several things to look for when interpreting control charts which suggest that the system may be out-of-control, as shown in the following diagrams:

Quality Tools and Techniques, continued

a) Points outside the control limits

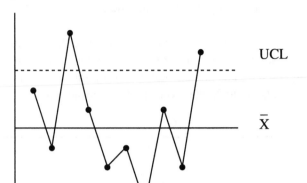

b) Runs of seven or more points above or below.

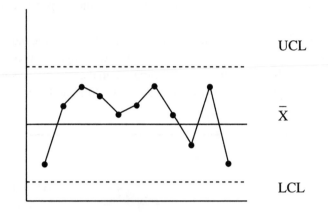

c) Runs of seven or more points moving in the same direction

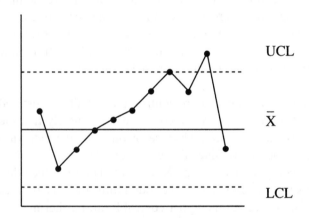

d) A distinct pattern or cycle in the system

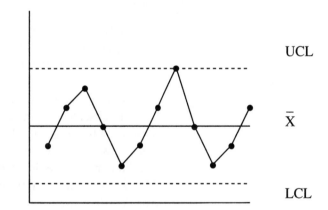

e) Points are either too close or too far from the average

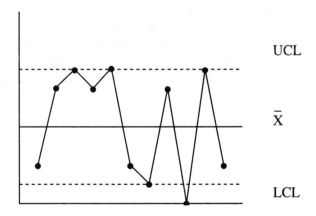

Quality Tools and Techniques, continued

Each of these situations suggests that the system is unstable and that special causes might account for variation in the system. Try to identify what those special causes are and attempt to eliminate them.

Step 7: Reduce variation in the system. Once any special causes for variation have been eliminated and the system is stable, you can consider other ways to change the process or system itself to further reduce variation; that is, to reduce the common causes of variation in the system. Assuming you have an adequate number of samples, the closer the upper and lower control limits are to $\bar{X}$, and the closer the dots are to $\bar{X}$, the more stable the system is.

Recycled Paper Wholesalers/Lindy Hernandez: We constructed a control chart to help track absenteeism in our company, because absenteeism can cause us numerous problems on the production line. Specifically, we were interested in finding out just how many productive hours we were losing to absenteeism each month. We defined absenteeism as being away from work for any reason (sick leave, vacation leave, other authorized leave or unauthorized absence). We dug out our records for the past two years, and we intend to add to the chart on a monthly basis from now on. Our control chart for absenteeism is shown in Figure 4.12, on page 171.

This control chart suggested that our system is out of control. First of all, we lost 400 hours to absenteeism in April, two years ago. We recognized immediately that the reason for this high number was the week-long absence of one of our production workers who underwent surgery that month. Since this was such a "special cause"— a real anomaly—we decided to compute our average $\bar{X}$ based on data from the other 23 months. With $\bar{X}$ at 101 hours lost to absenteeism, we found three months, besides April of 1994, where absenteeism exceeded the upper control limit. Further investigation showed us that in all three cases, the large number of absences was due to people using vacation leave in August and around Christmas. This suggested to us that we need to look more closely at our system for approving leave, since our current system seems to allow too many people to be gone at the same time. The control chart also suggested to us that absences are not random. There seemed to be a cycle, with peaks occurring in August, the heaviest vacation month, and in December. We will continue to study absences over the next year or two. Hopefully, as the result of tracking absences, we will be able to keep all absences within our control limits, which is critically important if we want to keep the line moving and meet demand.

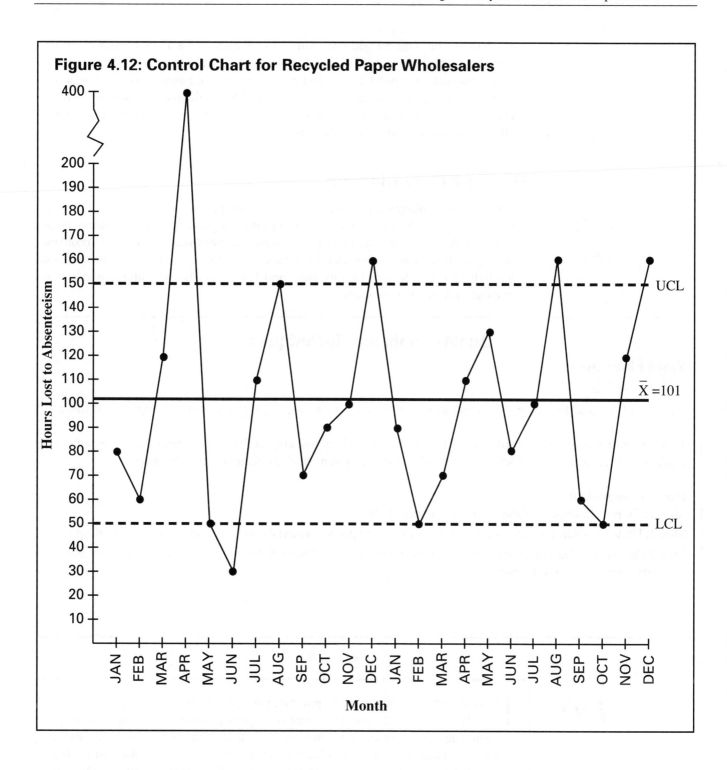

Figure 4.12: Control Chart for Recycled Paper Wholesalers

Incidentally, because we had one point below the LCL, we looked at our records to see what might have caused such low absenteeism that month. We concluded that it was just a heck-of-a-good month, and the low number of absences couldn't be attributed to anything special that we did. Too bad. Our challenge now will be to refine our system so that vacation leave will be more balanced throughout the year, and all other leave will be minimal all the time.

The Work Flow Diagram

Key Word

The **work flow diagram** provides a picture of how people or materials or paperwork move through a physical space, such as an office, a plant floor, or a business establishment. A clear understanding of work flow will help you spot possible problems in a system, such as bottlenecks, backtracking, or the inefficient flow of materials through a process. See the Quality Tools and Techniques box for information on how to create a work flow diagram.

Quality Tools and Techniques

Work Flow Diagram

What is it? A work flow diagram is a picture of how people, materials, or paperwork flow through a workspace.

When should you use it? Construct a work flow diagram when you suspect that the physical flow of people or work is inefficient, or a possible cause of problems in the system, such as accidents or lost materials.

How do you make it?
Step 1: Draw a floor plan of the workspace under study.
Step 2: Draw lines which represent the movement or flow of people, materials or paperwork through the work space.
Step 3: Study the diagram to see if there is a more logical way to arrange the work space in order to minimize movement and increase efficiency.

FYI

In the continuous improvement process, your goal is always to minimize variance in the system. If you have identified special causes for variation, attempt to eliminate those causes first. Once your system is in control (free of special causes), you can begin to make changes in the process or system itself to further reduce the variation caused by common causes. This might involve modifying procedures, materials, equipment, or training for employees.

Quality Tools and Techniques, continued

Figure 4.13: Work Flow Diagram of Workspace

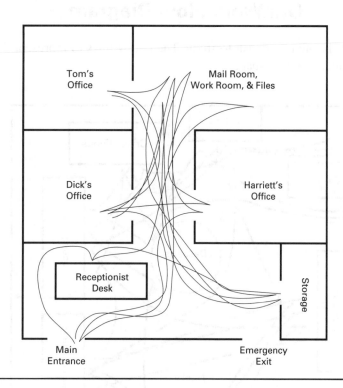

Personal Workshop Preparation #20:
Our Work Flow Diagram

For whatever system you are studying, consider the workspace involved. If it would be helpful to know how people, materials, or paperwork move through the workspace, then sketch out a floor plan and track the flow of work through the area. If work flow is not an issue for the project you have selected, then do this workshop for any work space in your business (it could be a single office, one department or the entire business) and evaluate the efficiency of your current layout.

Denny's Hometown Market/Denny and Mabel Wellman: We decided to study the flow of people through our deli, since it seems like our customers get all bunched up in there at our busiest times. This work flow diagram really helped us spot some problems, and now we are making plans to redesign the deli sometime next year.

Personal Workshop #20
Our Work Flow Diagram

1. Sketch out a floor plan of the area you wish to study. Then draw lines to represent the movement of people, materials, or paperwork through the workspace.

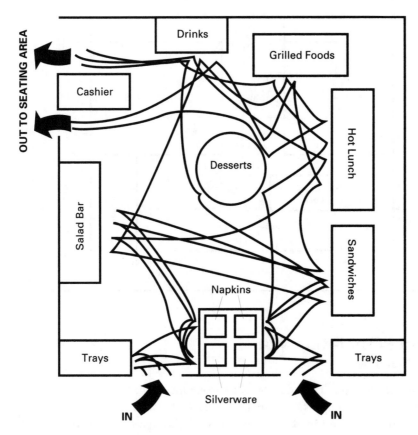

2. Using the work flow diagram note any potential problems or inefficiencies you see in the workplace.

- There's a blockage at the entrances, where people grab trays and then cross in front of the entrance to get silverware and napkins.
- People tend to pick up napkins first, then backtrack to get silverware. They like to place their silverware on top of the napkin so it won't blow off the tray.
- When lines have more than two or three people, they tend to block other counters. For example, the grilled food line blocks the hot lunch counter; the hot lunch line blocks the sandwich counter, etc.
- When busy, the line to check out blocks access to the drinks station.
- There is too much criss-crossing across the room—big potential for accidents.

THE PURPOSE OF THIS WORKSHOP IS TO IDENTIFY PROBLEMS WITH WORK FLOW USING A DIAGRAM.

Personal Workshop #20
Our Work Flow Diagram

1. Sketch out a floor plan of the area you wish to study. Then draw lines to represent the movement of people, materials, or paperwork through the workspace.

2. Using the work flow diagram note any potential problems or inefficiencies you see in the workplace.

Workshop Follow-Up

 Work flow is an important concept in quality management. Based on what you have learned about the flow of people, materials, or paperwork through your system, note ways that you can redesign or rearrange the layout to make it more efficient, more functional, and/or safer.

Check Your Understanding of the System

Before you move on to the next step in the continuous improvement cycle, ask yourself the following questions about the system you have studied:

1. Do you believe you have a clear understanding of the system as a whole and the specific processes in the system?

2. Do you understand which people are involved in the system and how they are involved?

3. Have you identified places where there is variance in the system?

4. Do you have some ideas about the root causes of variance in the system?

5. What additional information or data do you need to gather to help you better understand the system and variance in the system?

Take time now to gather any additional information you might need to thoroughly understand the system. When you are confident that you have enough information to truly understand the dynamics of the system, move to the next step in the cycle, Plan for Improvement.

 Denny's Hometown Market/Denny and Mabel Wellman: It has taken us a good month, but we feel like we have a much better understanding of our system now. Here is a summary of the information we've gathered:

• By tracking our customers for a full month, we now know exactly how many people to expect in our store, on average, hour-by-hour, for each day of the week. We used the data we collected for our run chart to create control charts for each four-hour block of time on weekdays (6:30 A.M.-10:30 A.M.; 10:30 A.M.-2:30 P.M.; 2:30 P.M.-6:30 P.M.; and 6:30 P.M.-10:30 P.M.) since these are our usual shifts. See Figure 4.14 on page 177.

• We did the same for Saturdays and Sundays, which each had its own control chart. We plan to repeat this study once each year, or more often if we sense a change in the market. Hopefully we will be able to spot any changes in consumer habits from these studies.

• For one week, we had checkers keep track of how long it took to check out each customer. They also kept track of their idle time during the week. We decided that the easiest way to do this was to put a small digital clock and a check sheet next to every register. The checkers would jot down the start time and stop time for each customer they served. They also would record idle time, which we

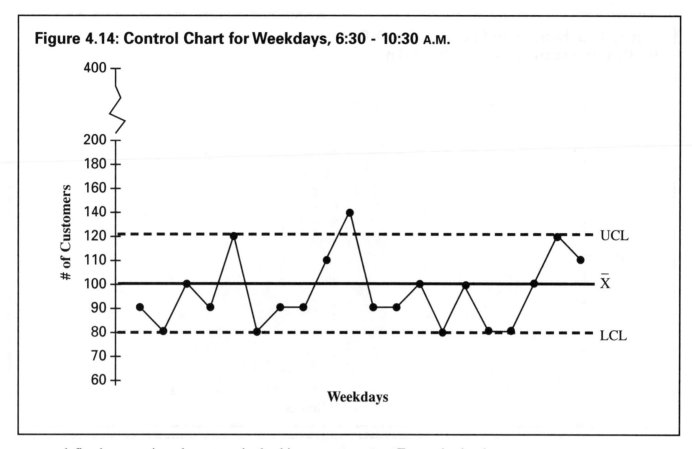

Figure 4.14: Control Chart for Weekdays, 6:30 - 10:30 A.M.

defined as any time they weren't checking out customers. Every checker kept track for a week, and at the end of the week, we had a running list of how time was used at each register. We weren't interested in who was doing the checking, just how long it took. We used this data to build a series of histograms which showed us the frequency of each classification of checkout times (1 min.; 1 to 2 min.; 2 to 3 min.; and so on). See Figure 4.15 on page 178.

• We did a histogram for each hour block of the day (7 - 8 A.M., 8 - 9 A.M.; etc.). These histograms, when put side-by-side, showed us what times of the day our customers are most likely to do their "big shopping" and what times of the day they are most likely to just pick up a few items, like donuts or milk and bread. This information helped us understand how many customers could be served by one checker for any hour of the day.

• Finally, the scatter diagram we developed, which showed a negative relationship between customer wait time and satisfaction, helped us to understand that we need to have enough people checking so that no customer has to wait in line for more than about three minutes. We went one step further and actually used a stopwatch to record wait-time for our customers, and we used that data to develop control charts which showed us the average wait-time per customer for each shift on each day of the week. See Figure 4.16 on page 178.

• With all the data we've gathered, we now feel like we can come up with a reasonable plan for improving our scheduling of checkers at the store.

Figure 4.15: Histogram Showing Check-Out Times for Customers from 2-3 p.m. Weekday

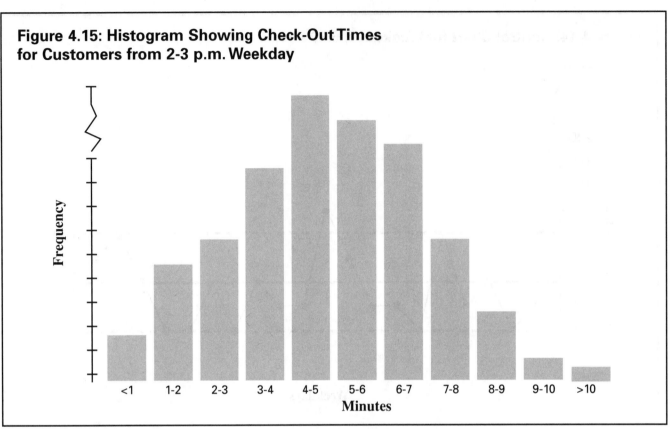

Figure 4.16: Run Chart Showing Average Wait Time for Each Shift (before schedule change)

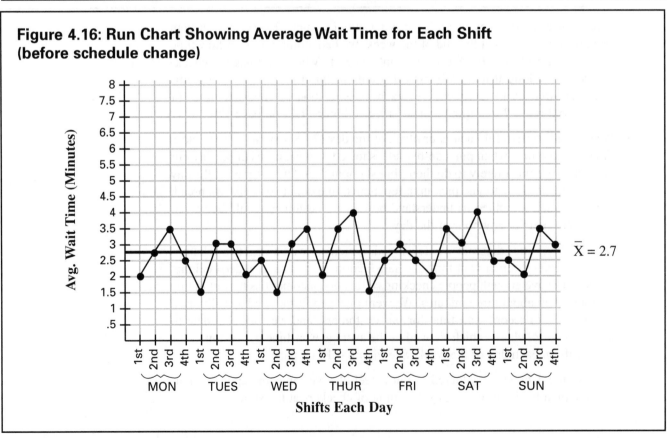

A Plan for Improvement

Once you are confident that you have a clear picture of the system or processes involved, your team will need to analyze the data collected and develop a plan for continuous improvement. There are several tools and techniques available for helping team members sort through data and make decisions about what is important and what is not. Your goal at this point is to identify specific ways to solve your problem and improve the system. To do this, the team will need to make some important decisions about the root causes for the problem and for variance in the system.

> *"Plans are nothing. Planning is everything."*
>
> —Dwight D. Eisenhower

Start by studying and discussing each of the charts and diagrams you have developed so far, including the control charts, histograms, Pareto diagrams, scatter diagrams and/or run charts that are relevant to your problem. What do these tools tell you about possible causes of variation in the system you are studying? Then, use one or more of the following tools or techniques to reach a consensus about what the root causes are: affinity diagrams, or the cause-and-effect diagram.

The Affinity Diagram

The **affinity diagram** is a tool for recording and sorting ideas or issues generated from a brainstorming session. Building an affinity diagram is an effective way to get all team members involved and participating in the decision-making process. See the Quality Tools and Techniques box for information on how to create an affinity diagram on pages 180-181.

Key Word

Personal Notes

_____

_____

_____

_____

Once your team has come to some agreement about the most likely root causes, you may want to take some time to verify what team members believe to be true. This can be done by gathering and analyzing more data using any of the quality tools and techniques, including Pareto diagrams, control charts, scatter diagrams, etc. Your goal at this point is to verify that the problem exists when the root cause is present, but doesn't exist when the root cause is removed. For example, if you believe, as Denny and Mabel Wellman do, that long waits in line are a root cause of dissatisfied customers, then test that theory by measuring satisfaction when that root cause is present and when that root cause is absent.

FYI

Quality Tools and Techniques

Affinity Diagram

What is it? An affinity diagram results from the posting and sorting of output generated in a brainstorming session. Building an affinity diagram is a creative process involving every team member.

When should you use it? An affinity diagram may be used when the issue or problem is complex, or the group is having difficulty organizing its ideas. Also, use an affinity diagram to draw every team member into the brainstorming or decision-making process.

How do you make it?
Step 1: Define the problem or issue and post it in a prominent place for all team members to see. For example, your issue might be, "What are some ways we can improve safety in the workplace?"

Step 2: Ask each team member to spend about five minutes of quiet time "mindstorming"—thinking of ideas to solve the problem. Ask team members to write their ideas down on a piece of paper as they come to mind. As with brainstorming, team members should be encouraged to think of as many different and creative ideas as they can, without taking time to evaluate the ideas.

Step 3: Going around the room, ask each team member to share one idea with the group. Each idea shared should be written down on a 3 x 5 card or on a sticky note.

For example, one card might read:

```
Hold monthly
safety meetings.
```

If a card is used, it should be thrown on a table top, face up. If sticky notes are used, they can be posted on a large sheet of paper or the wall. Continue around the room until all ideas have been shared and posted. As in any brainstorming session, ideas should not be discussed or critiqued at this point. The goal is to generate as many ideas as possible from team members.

Step 4: Team members should now put the cards (or notes) into groups or categories. Team members should move the cards into piles on the table or rearrange the notes so that ideas which seem related in some way are together. Team members should do this without discussion until everyone is reasonably satisfied that the cards are in the right piles. Any single cards not put into a pile should be grouped together in a miscellaneous pile.

Step 5: The team leader or facilitator should read each card in each pile to the group, and the group should decide on a category name or description for each pile, which should be written on a header card.

Step 6: Build the affinity diagram by posting all the cards under the appropriate header card on a large sheet of paper. Draw a box around each category of cards. Give the affinity diagram a heading and date it. See Figure 4.17 on p. 181 for an example.

Quality Tools and Techniques, continued

Figure 4.17: Affinity Diagram

Issue: _____   Date: _____

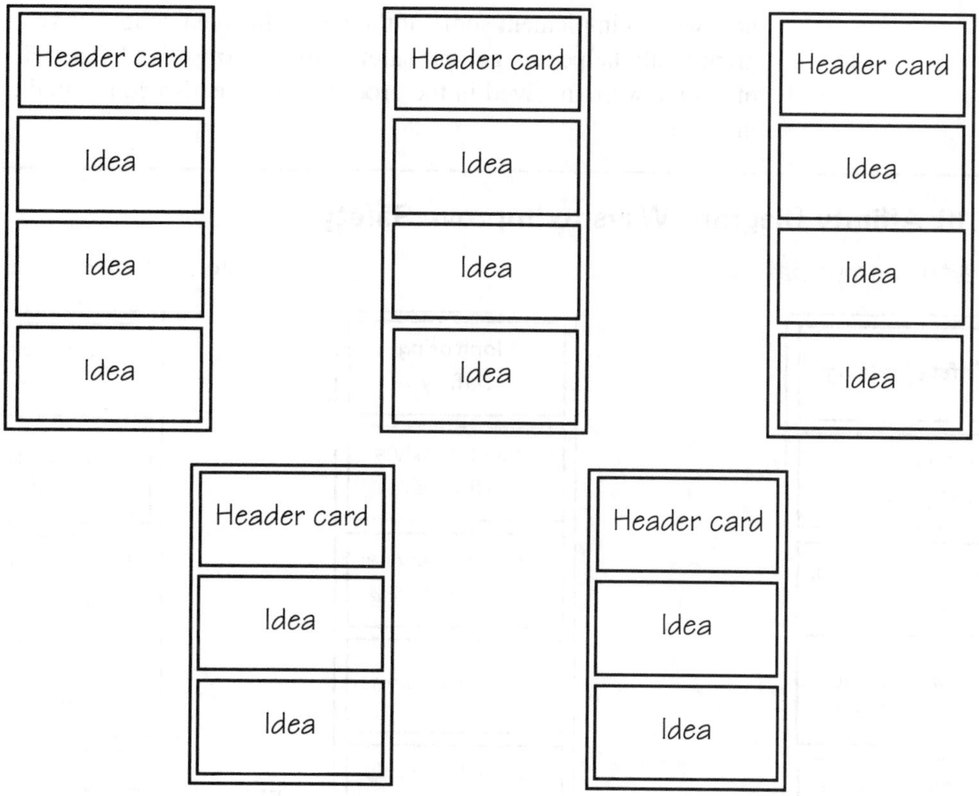

```
┌─────────────────┐     ┌─────────────────┐     ┌─────────────────┐
│  ┌───────────┐  │     │  ┌───────────┐  │     │  ┌───────────┐  │
│  │Header card│  │     │  │Header card│  │     │  │Header card│  │
│  └───────────┘  │     │  └───────────┘  │     │  └───────────┘  │
│  ┌───────────┐  │     │  ┌───────────┐  │     │  ┌───────────┐  │
│  │   Idea    │  │     │  │   Idea    │  │     │  │   Idea    │  │
│  └───────────┘  │     │  └───────────┘  │     │  └───────────┘  │
│  ┌───────────┐  │     │  ┌───────────┐  │     │  ┌───────────┐  │
│  │   Idea    │  │     │  │   Idea    │  │     │  │   Idea    │  │
│  └───────────┘  │     │  └───────────┘  │     │  └───────────┘  │
│  ┌───────────┐  │     │  ┌───────────┐  │     │  ┌───────────┐  │
│  │   Idea    │  │     │  │   Idea    │  │     │  │   Idea    │  │
│  └───────────┘  │     │  └───────────┘  │     │  └───────────┘  │
└─────────────────┘     └─────────────────┘     └─────────────────┘

         ┌─────────────────┐     ┌─────────────────┐
         │  ┌───────────┐  │     │  ┌───────────┐  │
         │  │Header card│  │     │  │Header card│  │
         │  └───────────┘  │     │  └───────────┘  │
         │  ┌───────────┐  │     │  ┌───────────┐  │
         │  │   Idea    │  │     │  │   Idea    │  │
         │  └───────────┘  │     │  └───────────┘  │
         │  ┌───────────┐  │     │  ┌───────────┐  │
         │  │   Idea    │  │     │  │   Idea    │  │
         │  └───────────┘  │     │  └───────────┘  │
         └─────────────────┘     └─────────────────┘
```

Step 7: Discuss the ideas and issues on the affinity diagram. Start by talking about the major categories of ideas (the header cards): Do you need additional categories? Is the team comfortable with the placement of cards in each category?

Do these categories give team members insight into the causes or possible solutions to the problem? Talk about each idea generated. How will each idea help solve the problem? Which ideas, if implemented, will have the greatest impact on the problem? Which ideas can we and should we implement—and when?

Recycled Paper Products/Lindy Hernandez: Safety is always a major issue for us, as it is in most factories. We have a lot of heavy equipment, and we use some hazardous chemicals in our process. And, as far as I'm concerned, one accident is one accident too many. We decided to pull together a good-sized group of people from production to do some brainstorming about safety and we built an affinity diagram to help us get our ideas in some kind of order. See Figure 4.18.

We have now formed a Safety Team to evaluate each of these ideas and to figure out how we can implement some of them over the next couple of years. The affinity diagram really helped us get our safety program organized. And, since a large number of people were involved in the process, they are also committed to what we are trying to do.

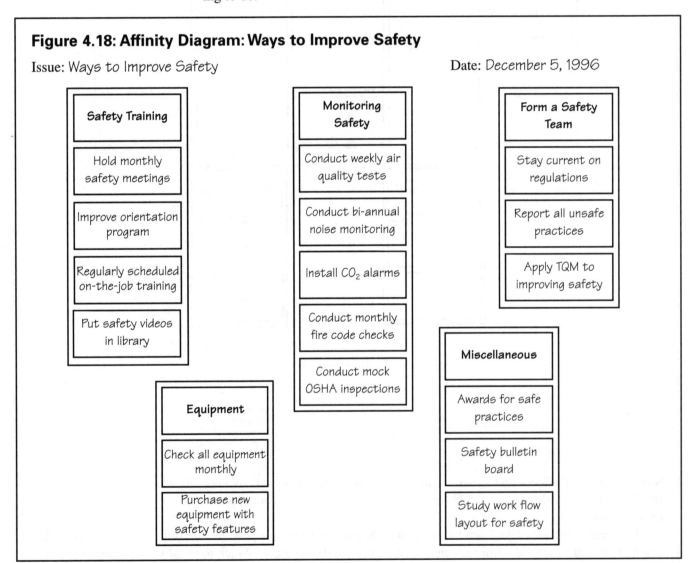

Figure 4.18: Affinity Diagram: Ways to Improve Safety

Issue: Ways to Improve Safety   Date: December 5, 1996

Safety Training	Monitoring Safety	Form a Safety Team
Hold monthly safety meetings	Conduct weekly air quality tests	Stay current on regulations
Improve orientation program	Conduct bi-annual noise monitoring	Report all unsafe practices
Regularly scheduled on-the-job training	Install CO_2 alarms	Apply TQM to improving safety
Put safety videos in library	Conduct monthly fire code checks	
	Conduct mock OSHA inspections	

Equipment

Check all equipment monthly

Purchase new equipment with safety features

Miscellaneous

Awards for safe practices

Safety bulletin board

Study work flow layout for safety

The Cause-and-Effect Diagram

The cause-and-effect diagram is an excellent tool for identifying and sorting out the possible causes of any problem in the system being studied.

Take a few minutes to review the information about cause-and-effect diagrams in Challenge 3 on page 127. Then, think of ways a cause-and-effect diagram might help your team better understand the root causes for the project you have selected. If appropriate, take time now to develop a cause-and-effect diagram for your project.

 Denny's Hometown Market/Denny and Mabel Wellman: Because we are concerned about delays at checkout, we thought it would be helpful to construct a cause-and-effect diagram to identify the major causes of delays. Figure 4.19 illustrates what we came up with.

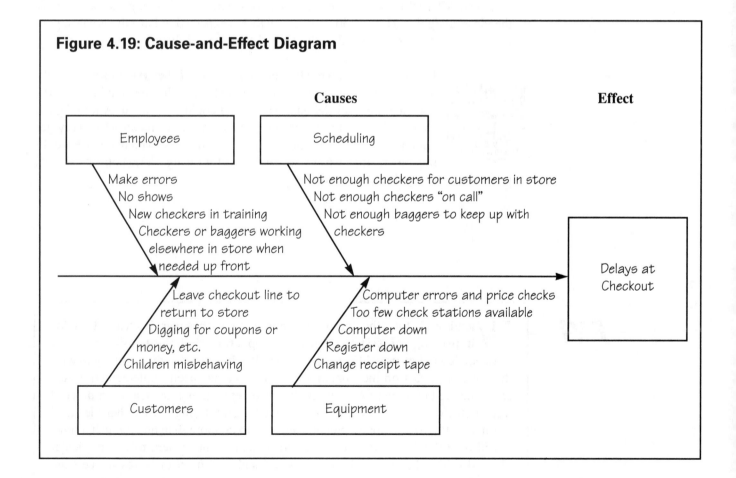

Figure 4.19: Cause-and-Effect Diagram

> *"We do the work; therefore we must find the answers for doing it better."*
>
> —David Carra

The real value of this diagram is that it helped us distinguish between those causes of delay that are within our control and those that are out of our control. As we make plans for improvements in our system for customer checkout, we will be able to address many of the causes we identified here.

Develop Ideas for Eliminating Root Causes

At this point, the process improvement team needs to organize its thoughts about root causes of the problem at hand and ways to eliminate those causes. In other words, it is time to develop a written plan for process improvement.

Personal Workshop Preparation #21: Our Process Improvement Plan

By now, your team should be bursting with ideas and theories about how to improve the process or solve the problem you have selected. Use the Process Improvement Plan form provided in this Personal Workshop to get those ideas and theories down on paper. After all ideas and theories for improvement are listed, go back and rank the ideas, assigning #1 to the idea or theory that is expected to have the greatest positive impact on the process, #2 to the second-best idea or theory, etc.

 Denny's Hometown Market/Denny and Mabel Wellman: Probably the toughest thing for us in this whole process has been holding everyone back until all the data was in and could be studied. A lot of great ideas had been thrown around, and we were all ready to actually get our plan on paper. Coming to some agreement on which idea we would implement first wasn't so easy. The following workshop reveals our plan—with the top three ideas numbered.

FYI

Warning: While the team may come up with several great ideas for improving the system, it will be important that the team implement **only one idea at a time.** Ideally, the team will select the idea that is likely to have the greatest impact on the system. After that idea has been implemented, tested and integrated into the process through reinforcement, then the team can proceed through the cycle of continuous improvement again, trying out another idea, and so on. If your process improvement team tries to do more than one thing at a time, it will be difficult to attribute any improvement in the system to one particular idea. Also, the change will be more radical and may meet more resistance from employees. Start slowly, but persevere and implement ideas one at a time.

THE PURPOSE OF THIS WORKSHOP IS TO DEVELOP A PROCESS IMPROVEMENT PLAN TO HELP YOU GET
YOUR PROBLEM-SOLVING IDEAS ON PAPER.

Personal Workshop #21
Our Process Improvement Plan

Project Title: _Fewer delays in checkout process_

Rank Root Causes Within Your Control	Ideas/Theories
1. Scheduling: not enough checkers or baggers to keep up with high-volume times	a) If scheduling would be based on average volume (# of customers) in the store per hour, then there would be enough checkers and/or baggers available when needed.
2. Scheduling: not enough checkers scheduled to work other positions in store during slower hour(s) of shift, so that they'll be available to check during busier hour(s) of shift	b) Are "on-call" checkers "on call" when needed? c) Train all employees to be "on-call" checkers.
3. Equipment: computer errors and price checks	a) If computers are updated daily, then there would be fewer errors. b) If all errors were reported by checkers when discovered, then they could be corrected immediately.
Too few check stations available	If we remodel our space, then we can accommodate more check stations.
Computer down	a) If we contract with Computer Repair Inc. for 1-hour repair service, then delays will be minimized. b) If we could arrange access to a backup system, then delays should be less than 5 minutes.
Register down	a) If we develop a plan for weekly maintenance checks, then breakdowns should be minimal. b) If we have a service technician on call, delays in repair should be minimal.
Change receipt tapes	If all checkers are trained properly, then there should be minimal delay.

Personal Workshop #21, continued

Rank Root Causes Within Your Control	Ideas/Theories
Employee makes errors	a) If all checkers are trained properly, then errors should be minimal, and checkers will be able to correct them on the spot. b) A manager should be on duty near registers at all times to help solve problems if needed.
Employees don't show up for work	If we develop a reliable list of back-up checkers, then delays due to no-shows will be minimized.
New checkers in training	a) If all new checkers are trained during slowest times, then delays will be minimal. b) If we post a sign, "checker in training," then customers in a hurry can choose another checkout lane.
4. Checkers or baggers working elsewhere in store when needed up front	If manager on duty regularly scans Aisle 8, then she/he can page on-call checkers and baggers before the customers reach the checkout station.

THE PURPOSE OF THIS WORKSHOP IS TO DEVELOP A PROCESS IMPROVEMENT PLAN TO HELP YOU GET YOUR PROBLEM-SOLVING IDEAS ON PAPER.

Personal Workshop #21
Our Process Improvement Plan

Project Title: _____

Rank Root Causes Within Your Control	Ideas/Theories

Personal Workshop #21, continued

Rank Root Causes Within Your Control	Ideas/Theories

Workshop Follow-Up

✔ Once you have decided which idea to implement, then develop a plan for implementing it, for testing it, and for regular meetings to check your progress. Your plan for implementation may be simple, or it may be complex. For example, Denny and Mabel realized that it would take some time and experimentation to come up with a new scheduling plan for their checkers that would accomplish the goal of shortening checkout time for their customers, yet wouldn't significantly increase their labor costs or leave checkers standing around idle for part of the shift. On the other hand, implementing the idea of candy-free check-out lanes, would be rather straightforward and simple.

Check Your Plan for Improvement

Plan carefully for the changes you want to make. Before carrying out your plan for improvement, ask yourself the following questions:

1. Does your plan describe what will happen, when, where and how, and who is responsible for making it happen?

2. If special employee training will be necessary to make the change, have you included that training in your plan?

3. Does your plan include information on how and when you will measure results? In other words, how will you test the system after you have implemented the change? What quality tools or techniques you will use to see if the change has had an impact and has accomplished your goals for process improvement?

When you feel confident that you have a solid plan in place, you are ready to move to the next step in the cycle of continuous improvement—try and test your idea.

FYI

In developing your process improvement plans, the team may find force field analysis a helpful technique for identifying both the driving and restraining forces in the system that might impact test results.

Step back to Challenge 3 and review the section on force field analysis on pages 134-135. If you anticipate the proposed change might meet with some resistance, then take time to do a force field analysis. Use the results of that exercise to help you plan for a smoother transition.

Try It and Test It

With your plan in place, it is time to try out your idea and test to see what impact the change might have on the system and, consequently, on the quality of the product or process involved. Follow your plan for training, implementation, and testing your idea for improvement. Training, if needed, should begin well in advance, so that employees know what changes will take place, how they will be personally involved or affected, why the change is necessary and important, and why it will be important to follow the plan or procedure established.

> *"Come, give us a taste of your quality."*
>
> —William Shakespeare

Test the results of the changes as planned. This involves gathering data and looking for evidence of decreased variation in the system, or any other data that might support an improvement in the process or product being produced. For example, in a manufacturing environment, you may want to collect data and use the quality tools and techniques you have learned to see if by slightly changing a process, there is less variation in the finished product, which suggests better quality control, less waste, and fewer reworks.

In a service business, you again want to collect data and use the quality tools or techniques to see if the change made in your system has resulted in better customer service, which might be indicated by faster service time, fewer mistakes made, or more service for the dollar.

Personal Workshop Preparation #22: Try It and Test It

In this workshop, you need to carry out your plans to try your idea and test it. Understand that it may take you several months or even longer to complete this workshop for your business. How you test the effect your idea or change has had on the system depends upon how you tested the system in the first place. If you developed run charts or control charts to study your system and plan for improvement, then you will undoubtedly want to continue to plot data on those charts throughout the test period. This will give you "before" and "after" data, but it will also give you information on how factors or relationships in the system might have changed as your plan was implemented. If you used histograms or Pareto diagrams in the early stages of the continuous improvement cycle, then new histograms and Pareto diagrams will help you determine if any root causes of variation have changed or been removed. Comparing scatter diagrams before and after the implementation of your plan will, likewise, give you data to support or refute your theory about the relationship between certain factors in your system.

To do this workshop, you will need to decide which data to collect and which quality tools and techniques to use to help you get a clearer picture of how the change you made might have impacted the system. Display your chart in this workshop and write out any conclusions you can draw from the data collected. The goal of this workshop is to see if your theory was correct, and whether the change you made in the system achieved your goals for improvement.

Denny's Hometown Market/Denny and Mabel Wellman: Our number one idea was to base our scheduling system on the average number of customers in our store each hour, so that there would always be enough checkers and baggers available when needed. Our goal was to make no customer wait for more than three or four minutes for checkout. We wanted to make checkout itself as efficient as possible without significantly increasing our labor costs or the idle time of our checkers. Once we came up with a schedule that seemed to meet all of our criteria, we tested it for one month. Each day one of us would use a stop watch to measure the actual wait time of our customers. We would do 40 customers a day, 10 in each shift and rotating checkout stations. The customers, of course, had no idea that we were timing anything. We kept track of the data on a simple check sheet, and we kept an ongoing run chart for the month. We used this data to make several different control charts for the test period. We created control charts for each day of the month (all Mondays, all Tuesdays, and so on), and for each work shift in the month. We also had our checkers continue to track their idle time throughout the month, and we plotted that information and compared it to our earlier data. Some of our new charts are shown in the following workshop.

Personal Notes

_____

_____

_____

_____

_____

_____

_____

_____

_____

_____

_____

_____

_____

Personal Workshop #22
Try It and Test It

Instructions: Try out your idea and collect appropriate data. Use that data to develop charts and graphs, and then note what you have learned from the data.

Description of Chart: Run chart showing average customer wait time for each shift after schedule change.

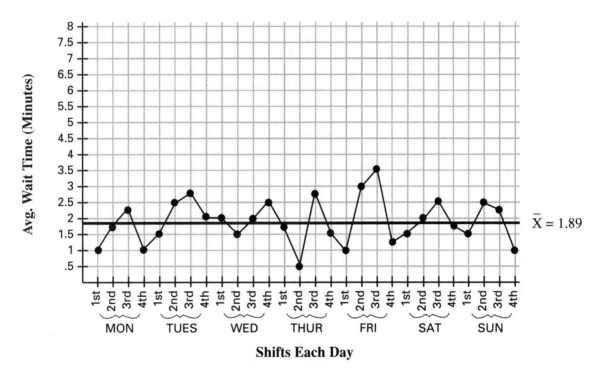

What conclusions can you draw from studying this data?

We learned from this run chart that the average wait time for our sample (10 customers each shift, each day), was less than two minutes. This was a real improvement when compared to the average wait time recorded before we tried the new schedule. Furthermore, by comparing the data from day-to-day and shift-to-shift, it appeared that the schedule worked best for Saturdays through Wednesdays, and that there was more variation in the system on Thursdays and Fridays. It also appeared that wait time under the new schedule was higher on the 3rd shift (our busiest shift on weekdays). We decided to do control charts for each shift and for each day of the week to study this data further.

Personal Workshop #22, continued

Description of Chart: Control chart showing average wait time for 3rd shift

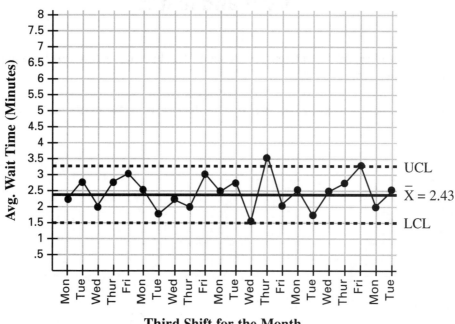

Third Shift for the Month

What conclusions can you draw from studying this data?

By collecting and studying and comparing the data and charts for each day and each shift, we were able to see that our new scheduling system reduced the average wait time for all but the third shift, which remained about the same. We realized, though, that we wouldn't be able to reduce wait time in this shift until we added another checkout station, and that can't happen for a while yet. We also discovered that our new schedule was less dependable on Fridays. We believe that is because Friday is the busiest weekday shopping day. We will have to look at ways to adjust the schedule to get better coverage on Fridays.

Personal Workshop #22, continued

Description of Chart: *Control chart showing idle time in each shift*

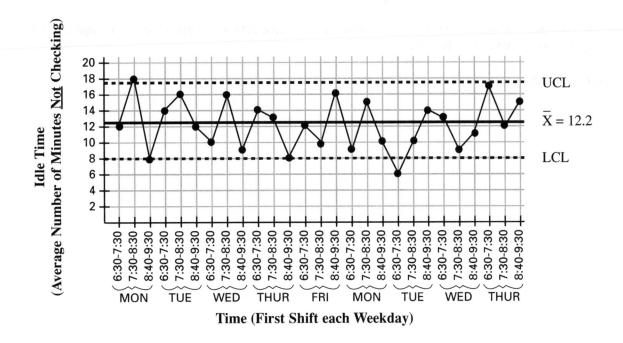

What conclusions can you draw from studying this data?

We learned that with our new schedule, idle time was up slightly in the first and fourth shifts. We plan to stick with the new schedule, though, and we believe this problem will be solved when we have more on-call checkers in the store to pull from in busy times. That will be the next challenge for our team, as well as having other things for checkers to do when they aren't checking.

* Continue to show graphs and write your conclusions on separate paper, as needed.

Personal Workshop #22
Try It and Test It

Instructions: Try out your idea and collect appropriate data. Use that data to develop charts and graphs, and then note what you have learned from the data.

Description of Chart:

What conclusions can you draw from studying this data?

Personal Workshop #22, continued

Description of Chart:

What conclusions can you draw from studying this data?

Description of Chart:

What conclusions can you draw from studying this data?

* Continue to show graphs and write your conclusions on separate paper, as needed.

Workshop Follow-Up

✔ Based on the data collected and studied, you should now have evidence which either supports or does not support your theory for improvement. Go back to your Process Improvement Plan and reread your theory. Does the data you collected support your original idea for solving the problem? For example, the Wellmans's theory statement was, " If scheduling is based on the average volume (number of customers) in the store per hour, then there would be enough checkers and/or baggers available when needed." After testing the new schedule for a month, they found evidence that the average wait time was lower using the new schedule. Although they still have some bugs to work out, Denny and Mabel believe they have solid evidence that their theory was correct. They are ready to make the new scheduling process a regular part of their system.

Carefully Study Your Results

If you have evidence that your idea resulted in an improvement in the system, then you will want to reinforce the changes you have made—in other words, make it a permanent part of the system. Go on to the next step in the Cycle of Continuous Improvement: Reinforce Process Improvement.

> *"Maintaining the momentum can be the hardest task of all if no one is with you; or it can become the easiest when people understand and believe in you and your mission."*
>
> —Joseph M. Juran

If, on the other hand, you find little or no evidence that the system is better as the result of your change, then take some time to analyze why the idea didn't have the expected effect. Review each step you have taken in the continuous improvement cycle, and try to understand why the system didn't respond to the change the way you thought it would. Your team might want to use the force field analysis to help it analyze what happened. Then, go back to the second step in the Cycle of Continuous Improvement: Plan for Improvement. Review and revise your Process Improvement Plan based on the new information you have about your system. Revise your theory, or select a new theory to try and test again.

Reinforce Process Improvement

Your next challenge is to make the change a standard part of your system. The team should start by developing a concise report which describes the new procedure and the impact the change had on the system during the test period. Include in the report copies of appropriate charts and graphs, as well as data that show how the change

FYI

A ny of the quality tools and techniques you have learned could be helpful in reinforcing process improvement. For example, check sheets, control charts, flow charts, histograms, and so on can be used to test the system during and after the implementation of the new process to measure impact. Force field analysis or affinity diagrams can be used to establish recommendations and the plan for implementation.

has affected the system. The team should list its recommendations for making the change, and the report should include a plan for implementation and maintenance of the new system. Maintenance should include periodic testing to be sure the new process is, in fact, achieving the new level of performance.

If the team's recommendations are accepted and implemented by management, then the team will need to follow its plan to monitor the system. It is often difficult to make even slight changes in an established system. By using the quality tools and techniques to monitor the system, you will be able to spot problems or cases where workers have slipped back into the old way of doing things. Your goal in this step is to turn the new process into the standard operating procedure. Remember that careful training and support may be needed to implement the change.

Continue the Cycle of Continuous Improvement

When you are sure the new process has been reinforced and is a natural part of the process, you are ready to continue around the cycle of continuous improvement. You will want to begin by studying the system again, since the changes you made in the first cycle may have changed how the system looks. Then plan for further improvements, and so on.

Denny's Hometown Market/Denny and Mabel Wellman: Once we worked the bugs out of the new scheduling system, we implemented it on a permanent basis. We continue to check wait times and idle time on a fairly regular basis, because we want to be sure that our average wait time stays under two minutes. We plan to count customers per hour once each year, or more often if we suspect that things might be changing for some reason. We started through the cycle again after using our new system for about three months. We studied the system again, and then went on to work on our second idea from our plan for improvement. We are now developing a plan to have more on-call checkers working in the store during our busiest times. We are really confident that when we get this problem solved, it will help us give even better service to our customers—and that, after all, is why we started this in the first place.

You Have Completed Challenge 4

As a small business owner, you know that the survival of your business depends upon your ability to serve your customers better than the "big guys." You can accomplish that by being more responsive to your customers' needs and/or by providing better quality products and services. Continuous process improvement can help you do both. Once you involve your employees and enter the cycle of continuous improvement, you can have better information, fresher ideas, and much better control over processes and quality. You can attain the "unprecedented levels of performance" you dream of.

> *"The journey of a thousand miles begins with one step."*
>
> —Lao-Tse

Process improvement will not happen overnight. Read and learn as much as you can about quality management. Start slowly through the process with manageable and measurable projects. Be persistent. Remember that you can learn as much from your failures as you can from your successes. Once you have started the cycle of continuous improvement, your business will be on its way to getting better every day and in every way. It will take time, but every little improvement adds up—and the end result will be a total quality organization.

You Leave Challenge 4 with the Following

Information: You may be feeling like you are in "information overload" at this point. There is so much information to absorb and try to apply. Remember to start slowly in the continuous improvement cycle with a simple project. Review the information about quality tools and techniques as needed. Read other resources on quality management. As time goes by and you move into the third or fourth cycle in the continuous improvement process, your understanding of the principles of quality management and continuous process improvement will certainly grow.

Tools: You were introduced to five new quality tools and techniques in this Challenge: the run chart; the scatter diagram; control charts; work flow diagrams, and the affinity diagram. In addition, you were shown how to apply many of the quality tools and techniques introduced in previous Challenges to the cycle of continuous improvement. You also developed a process improvement plan, which will be a valuable tool for guiding continuous improvement in the future.

Learning: The cycle of continuous improvement could actually be viewed as a model for learning about your business. At each stage in the cycle, you gathered and analyzed data. From that data, you learned about the system as it existed at that stage. You developed theories for improving processes, and then you tried and tested some of those theories. Each test helped you learn something new about the system, about your business, about your employees, or about your customers. You leave Challenge 4 knowing a great deal more about your business than when you started, and you can continue to learn about your business by following the cycle of continuous improvement.

Networking: This Challenge was set up to guide a process improvement team through the cycle of continuous improvement. While some of the work in this Challenge could be done by individuals, team interaction, brainstorming, and group decisionmaking are key elements in a successful process improvement effort. If you are committed to continuous improvement, you must also be committed to employee involvement and feedback throughout the system. Without effective networking and communication, your efforts to change the current system may be thwarted by confused, frightened, or even angry employees. Use the quality tools and techniques in this book to enhance your networking efforts.

Challenge 4 Self-Assessment

After completing this Challenge you should have a good understanding of how you can begin the cycle of continuous improvement in your company. Check your understanding of the concepts learned by asking yourself the following questions. If needed, go back and review the concepts of continuous process improvement where you feel you need more practice.

Explain how variation is a threat to quality.

( ) I can explain how variation in a system can result in inconsistent or unpredictable output.
( ) I can give an example of how variation is a problem in my company.

**Pages
142 - 143**

Identify appropriate projects for the continuous improvement process.

( ) I can identify specific and meaningful projects.
( ) I can set specific goals for the continuous improvement project.
( ) I can identify the information needed for my project and describe how to get it.

**Pages
143 - 147**

Study the system using a variety of quality tools and techniques.

( ) I can apply the following quality tools to study the system: flow charts; histograms; and Pareto charts.
( ) I can build and use a run chart to study the system.
( ) I can build and use a scatter diagram to study the system.
( ) I can build and use a work flow diagram to study the system.
( ) I know where to get more information on control charts if needed.

**Pages
147 - 176**

Identify specific ways to improve the system and plan for that improvement.

( ) I can use quality tools and techniques to identify root causes of a problem.
( ) I can develop theories for eliminating root causes resulting in process improvement.
( ) I can develop a process improvement plan.

**Pages
176 - 188**

Implement your plan and measure results.

( ) I understand the importance of implementing only one idea at a time.
( ) I can use the quality tools and techniques to test whether a change made has reduced variation or eliminated root causes of a problem.
( ) I understand that trying and testing an idea may take several months.
( ) I can write a report describing the impact of the change on the process.

**Pages
188 - 197**

**Pages
196 - 197**

Reinforce process improvements.

( ) I understand the importance of employee involvement for the successful implementation of any change in the process.

( ) I can apply quality tools and techniques to the system to assure that the change becomes standard operating procedure.

**Page
197**

Repeat the cycle of continuous improvement.

( ) I understand that continuous improvement needs to be ongoing through the cycle of continuous improvement.

Take Another Look

Review the results of your checklist above. If you feel you need more work in some area, go back into the text and challenge yourself again. If you persistently work on continuous improvement, then your organization can only get better and better as time goes on. Work with the quality tools and techniques until you become comfortable with them. Numbers, diagrams, and statistics can give you wonderful insight into your business. Take advantage of the information and tools available to you, and you will be a smarter business owner.

You Have Mastered Total Quality Management Concepts

Congratulations! By actively participating in Challenges 1 through 4 in this book, you have gained knowledge, learned how to use various tools and mastered many of the skills needed to effectively implement the quality concept in your business.

You have learned that quality management is about having a shared vision which gives employees direction and their work meaning. It is about building systems—using the tools and techniques of quality management—to achieve that vision. And it is about solving problems—employees working together to eliminate the errors and variance in the system which threaten quality and your organization's existence.

You have learned that quality is defined by the customer, and unless you consistently meet and exceed your customers' expectations, you will not survive in the long run. Quality is the responsibility of every employee in your business. As owner/manager, you must involve all managers and employees in the quality improvement process. You must be the number-one preacher and teacher of the concepts of quality management. You must guide your company into the cycle for continuous improvement.

Your company's transformation to quality has just begun. Continue to learn as much as you can about quality from a variety of sources. Engage your employees in discussions and decisions about quality. Begin building effective work teams. Initiate the cycle of continuous improvement. Above all, be persistent in your quest for quality. If you do these things, if you transform your business into a quality organization, then it will continue to get better every day and in every way.

Key Resources

The following is a suggested resources and reading list for additional research.

Challenge 1

Aguayo, Rafael. *Dr. Deming: The American Who Taught the Japanese About Quality* (New York: Simon & Schuster, 1991).

Capezio, Peter and Morehouse, Debra. *Total Quality Management* (Shawnee Mission, KA: National Press Publications, 1992).

Deming, W. Edwards. *Out of the Crisis* (Cambridge, MA: MIT Center for Advanced Engineering Study, 1986).

Ernst & Young. *Total Quality: An Executive's Guide for the 1990's* (Homewood, IL: Business One Irwin, 1990).

Feigenbaum, Armand V. *Total Quality Control, Third Edition.* (Cincinnati, OH: Association for Quality and Participation, 1961).

Gabor, Andrea. *The Man Who Discovered Quality* (New York: Times Books, 1990).

Juran, Joseph. *Juran on Leadership for Quality* (New York: The Free Press, 1989).

———. *Juran on Planning for Quality* (Cambridge, MA: The Free Press, MacMillan, 1987).

———. *Juran Quality by Design* (Cambridge, MA: The Free Press, 1992).

———. *Quality Control Handbook* (Cambridge, MA: McGraw Hill, 1951).

Roberts, Harry and Sergesketter, Bernard. *Quality is Personal* (New York: The Free Press/Macmillan, 1993).

Scholtes, Peter and Hacquebord, Heero. "A Practical Approach to Quality" (an article published in Madison, WI: Joiner Associates, 1987).

Senge, Peter M. *The Fifth Discipline.* (New York: Doubleday, 1990).

Walton, Mary. *The Deming Management Method* (New York: Putnam Publishing Co., 1986).

Challenge 2

Albrecht, Karl. *At America's Service: How Corporations Can Revolutionize the Way They Treat Their Customers* (Cambridge, MA: Productivity Press or San Diego, CA: Shamrock Press, 1988).

Albrecht, Karl and Ron Zemke. *SERVICE AMERICA! Doing Business in the New Economy.* (Homewood, IL: Dow Jones-Irwin, 1985).

Connellan, Thomas K. and Ron Zemke. *Sustaining Knock Your Socks Off Service* (New York: AMACOM, 1993).

Howe, Roger, Dee Gaeddert, and Maynard Howe. *Quality on Trial* (St. Paul, MN: West Publishing Co., 1993).

Rosander, A.C. *The Quest for Quality in Services* (White Plains, NY: Quality Resources, 1989).

Willingham, Ron. *Hey, I'm the Customer* (Englewood Cliffs, NJ: Prentice Hall, 1992).

Zemke, Ron and Dick Schaaf. *The Service Edge.* (New York: Plume, The Penguin Group, 1989).

Challenge 3

Bader, Gloria E., Audrey E. Bloom, and Richard Y. Chang. *Measuring Team Performance* (Irvine, CA: Richard Chang Associates, Inc., 1994).

Chang, Richard Y. *Building a Dynamic Team* (Irvine, CA: Richard Chang Associates, Inc., 1994).

Covey, Stephen R. *The Seven Habits of Highly Effective People.* (New York: Simon and Schuster, 1990).

Dyer, William G. *Team Building: Issues and Alternatives Second Edition* (Reading, MA: Addison-Wesley, 1987).

Foundations for Teams (Miamisburg, OH: Productivity-Quality Systems, Inc., 1993).

How to Build a Successful Team, INFO-LINE, American Society for Training and Development, December 1992.

Oestreich, Daniel K. and Kathleen Ryan. *Driving Fear Out of the Workplace* (San Francisco, CA: Jossey-Bass, 1991).

Senge, Peter M. *The Fifth Discipline: The Art & Practice of the Learning Organization* (New York: Currency/Doubleday, 1990).

Scholtes, Peter R. *The Team Handbook: How to Use Teams to Improve Quality.* (Madison, WI: Jointer Associates Inc., 1988).

Wheatley, Margaret J. *Leadership and the New Science* (San Francisco, CA: Berrett-Koehler Publishers, 1992).

Challenge 4

Ball, Melinda J. et.al. *Total Quality Transformation: Improvement Guide* (Dayton, OH: Productivity-Quality Systems, Inc., 1992).

Ball, Melinda J. et al. *Total Quality Transformation: Improvement Tools* (Dayton, OH: Productivity-Quality Systems, Inc., 1993).

Brache, Alan P. and Geary A. Rummler. *Improving Performance* (San Francisco, CA: Jossey-Bass, 1990).

Brassard, Michael and Diane Ritter. *The Memory Jogger II: A Pocket Guide of Tools for Continuous Improvement and Effective Planning* (Methuen, MA: GOAL/QPC, 1994).

Harrington, James H. *The Improvement Process* (New York: McGraw-Hill, Inc., 1987).

Juran Institute of Quality Improvement Tools (Wilton, CT: Juran Institute, Inc., 1989).

Kanter, Rosabeth Moss. *The Change Masters* (New York,: Simon and Schuster., 1984).

King, Bob. *Hoshin Planning: The Developmental Approach* (Methuen, MA: GOAL/QPC, 1989).

Additional Resources

Books

Upstart Publishing Company, a division of Dearborn Publishing Group, Inc., Chicago, IL. Call 800-235-8866 for a free catalog. List of titles include:

Launching New Ventures: An Entrepreneurial Approach, Kathleen Allen, 1995. Innovative entrepreneurship text that enables the students to plan and start a world-class venture. Guide takes the reader from the first basic steps of developing an idea to creating a detailed business and marketing plan. Instructor's manual available. 496 pp., $35.00

Strategic Planning for the New and Small Business, Fred L. Fry and Charles R. Stoner, 1995. This highly practical text guides students through the strategic planning process using case histories and examples of actual businesses. Unique in that it is a strategy book aimed specifically at small businesses. Instructor's manual available. 256 pp., $24.95

Financial Essentials for Small Business Success, Joseph Tabet and Jeffrey Slater, 1994. This text stresses the importance of common sense in overcoming the problems of poor recordkeeping and planning. Step-by-step guidance results in students learning to interpret financial reports and building the necessary financial tools for a profitable small business. Instructor's manual available. 272 pp., $22.95

Business Planning Guide, Seventh Edition, David H. Bangs, Jr., 1995. Designed for both beginning students and more experienced practitioners, this is a vital tool for putting together a complete and effective business plan and financing proposal. Contains three complete sample business plans. Available on CD-ROM. Instructor's manual available. 224 pp., $22.95

Anatomy of a Business Plan, Third Edition, Linda Pinson and Jerry Jinnett, 1996. The step-by-step approach assumes no prior knowledge of a business plan. This basic presentation enables the student or entrepreneur to prepare a start-up plan for a new small business or plan new strategies for an existing business. Instructor's manual available. 256 pp., $22.95

Market Planning Guide, Fourth Edition, David H. Bangs, Jr., 1995. Practical text that shows students how to create an effective marketing plan suited to the business' goals and resources. Features complete marketing plans for two actual businesses. Instructor's manual available. 257 pp., $22.95

Marketing: Mastering Your Small Business, Gloria Green and Jeffrey Williams, 1996. Improve your marketing skills with this "marketing mastery" course. Develop and implement a personalized marketing plan for selling your product or service. Instructor's manual and software available. 288 pp., $22.95

Target Marketing, Third Edition, Linda Pinson and Jerry Jinnett, 1996. Text is a comprehensive guide to developing a marketing plan for your business. Broken into a simple three-stage marketing process of research, reach, and retain. Instructor's manual available. 176 pp., $22.95

Smart Steps to Smart Choices: Testing Your Business Idea, David H. Bangs, Jr., 1996. Helps readers determine if entrepreneurship is right for them. Contains self-assessment workshops. Learning Kit containing book, video, audiotape and software is also available. 192 pp., $22.95

The Start Up Guide, David H. Bangs, Jr., 1994. Walks students through every phase of small business start-up. Text is based on a hypothetical one-year process. 176 pp., $22.95

Steps to Small Business Start-Up, Third Edition, Linda Pinson and Jerry Jinnett, 1996. One step at a time, the student learns the mechanics of business start-ups and gets started on everything from recordkeeping to marketing and business planning. Contains forms, examples, and worksheets. Instructor's manual available. 256 pp., $22.95

Cash Flow Control Guide, David H. Bangs, Jr., 1990. Step by step guide to learning a cash flow control process for the small business. It uses a real-life example of a company that demonstrates how cash flow planning can smooth out some of the small business's roughest spots. 88 pp., $19.95

Finance: Mastering Your Small Business, David H. Bangs, Jr., 1996. Learn the secrets of building a financially healthy business from A to Z. Instructor's manual and software available. 240 pp., $22.95

Keeping the Books, Third Edition, Linda Pinson and Jerry Jinnett, 1996. Hands-on introduction to small business bookkeeping, which may be used with students who have no financial or accounting background. It covers all the essentials and provides numerous sample forms and worksheets. Instructor's manual available. 208 pp., $22.95

Human Resources: Mastering Your Small Business, Jill A. Rossiter, 1996. Learn to recruit, train, manage, and motivate productive employees. Template for employee handbook also enclosed. Instructor's manual and software available. 352 pp., $22.95

Business and the Legal System: Mastering Your Small Business, Scott Minter and Sheri Moore Humphrey, 1996. Learn how to cope with legal challenges that affect small business owners/managers. Instructor's manual and software available. 192 pp., $22.95

Cases in Small Business Management, John de Young, 1994. More than 50 intriguing and useful case studies focusing on typical problems faced by small business managers every day. Problem solving is encouraged through end-of-chapter questions that lead students through an analysis of possible solutions. Instructor's manual available. 288 pp., $24.95

Problems and Solutions in Small Business Management, Editors of *Forum*, 1995. A collection of case studies selected by the editors of the small business journal *Forum*. A problem drawn from an actual business is presented and then followed by three possible solutions written by experts from a variety of areas within the field of small business management. 192 pp., $22.95

Key Word Glossary

Affinity Diagram: A tool for posting and sorting output generated in a brainstorming session.

Affirming Feedback: Information which reinforces performance and builds confidence.

Agenda: A tool for managing meetings which lists topics to be discussed and time allotted per topic.

BFR (Behavior-Feeling-Results) Statements: A technique for giving corrective feedback, which 1) states the behavior 2) states the feeling 3) states the results of the behavior.

Brainstorming: A technique for generating a multitude of ideas, opinions, and/or solutions to any type of problem in a team or group setting.

Cause-and-Effect Diagram: A tool used to aid a team in identifying and classifying the root causes of any problem or existing condition.

Check Sheet: A form developed for gathering and organizing data.

Closed Questions: Questions that can be answered with a simple and direct response, such as "yes," "no," or a simple statement of fact.

Continuous Improvement: The process of continuously getting better by reducing variation and eliminating errors.

Control Charts: A type of run chart with statistically determined upper and lower control limits that is used to analyze the performance of a system.

Corrective Feedback: Information that helps employees focus or redirect their efforts, search for better solutions, and/or improve their skills.

Cost of Poor Quality: The sum of all costs that would disappear if there were no quality problems.

Customer: Any individual or group served by a business.

Customer Loyalty: A long-term, mutually supportive relationship between a customer and a business.

Customer Satisfaction: A short-term state achieved by meeting the customer's immediate needs.

Customer Service Blueprint: A written description or plan for a company's customer service system.

Cycle of Continuous Improvement: An ongoing process involving studying systems, planning for improvements, trying and testing possible ideas for making things better, reinforcing process improvements, and then studying the systems again.

Empowered Employees: People who feel confident enough to make sound decisions when and where decisions need to be made.

External Customers: Individuals or groups outside the company who directly or indirectly receive your services or products.

Feedback, 360-Degree: Information from a circle of people that gives multiple viewpoints about one's performance.

Flow Chart: A picture of a process that uses standard symbols to show the flow of events or steps in the process.

Force Field Analysis: A technique for understanding and promoting desired change.

Frequency Table: A table which organizes data by frequency of occurrence.

Groupthink: A dysfunctional group condition when consensus among team members becomes more important than critical analysis.

Histogram: A bar graph that shows how often something occurs for different reasons over a certain period of time.

Indirect Customers: Individuals or groups who have some stake in your company.

Internal Customers: Individuals or groups inside the company who use the services or receive the product next.

ISO 9000: A set of international quality standards that were established by the International Organization for Standardization (ISO) and have been adopted by the European Community.

Learning Organization: A company that recognizes that continuous learning is the key to continuous improvement and staying ahead of the competition.

Management Teams: Teams made up of members of management and formed for various purposes.

Market Segment: A mass of customers with similar needs and expectations; also called a **customer group.**

Meeting: A gathering of two or more people for a specific purpose.

"Moment of Truth": Any point of contact with a customer.

Negative Correlation: A relationship between two variables that exists when, as one increases, the other decreases.

Open-Ended Questions: Questions that cannot be answered with a "yes" or "no," but typically require more thought and detail by the respondent.

Pareto Chart: A simple bar chart which ranks causes in decreasing order of occurrence.

Pareto Principle: Developed by Vilfredo Pareto, an Italian economist, the Pareto Principle states that 80 percent of the problems come from 20 percent of the causes.

Philosophy for Customer Service: A general statement that will help guide all employees and decision making in the future.

Point of Contact: Any occasion when the customer comes into contact with someone or something that represents your company.

Positive Correlation: A relationship between two variables that exists when, as one variable increases, the other also increases.

Problem-Solving Team: Team developed for the purpose of solving one particular problem.

Process: A series of activities undertaken to obtain results.

Process Improvement Team: Team developed for the purpose of examining and improving a specific process in the system.

Project Team: Team developed for the purpose of planning and implementing specific projects or events.

Quality: The value of your product or service as perceived by your customers.

Quality Concept: An attitude about how to conduct business that centers on meeting or exceeding the customers' wants, needs, and expectations in an efficient way.

Quality Culture: An organizational environment that is customer-focused with a clear vision and goals to guide employees.

Quality Wall: A designated place in a company where quality tools and data are posted and can be studied by all employees.

Run Chart: A simple line graph that records data over some period of time; also called a **trend chart.**

Scatter Diagram: A diagram that shows if a relationship exists between two factors.

Self-Directed Work Teams: Self-managed teams that do their own planning and coordination and evaluation of work.

Statistical Process Control (SPC): A management method involving the use of statistical analyses to control quality in a work system.

Strategic Planning: A company's effort to develop long and short-term goals and action plans for achieving those goals, with the mission and vision of the company as the basis and guide for that action.

Supplier Certification: A system used by some buyers to assure that their suppliers provide goods and services at a certain quality level.

System: A set of interrelated and interdependent entities with a defined purpose or mission.

Systems Thinking: An appreciation for the fact that all parts of a system, small or large, are interrelated and interdependent.

Total Quality Management (TQM): A management philosophy and method for achieving or exceeding the level of quality demanded by a company's customers; variations in name include **Total Quality Control (TQC), Total Quality Improvement (TQI), Continuous Quality Improvement (CQI).**

Ultimate Customers: The individuals or groups to whom a business directly sells its products.

Utility: The condition or quality of being useful.

Variation: A slight difference between items of the same type.

Work Flow Diagram: A picture of how people, materials, or paperwork flow through a workplace.

Zero Defects Management: A concept based on the premise that it is possible to have systems that are totally error free.

Personal Workshops

Your participation in Personal Workshops is a key factor in the success of your mastery learning experience. These workshops provide you with the opportunity to react and respond to the information given in each lesson. As you complete each workshop, you are encouraged to apply your knowledge to your own business experience.

The Personal Workshops presented in this guide are reprinted on the following pages. While the directions needed to complete each exercise are included on each workshop page, the information necessary to prepare you for the activity is not. To fully understand each Personal Workshop, you will need to read the text and the Personal Workshop preparations that precede each exercise.

THE PURPOSE OF THIS WORKSHOP IS TO BECOME AWARE OF YOUR OWN PERCEPTIONS OF QUALITY.

Personal Workshop #1
What Is Quality?

1. What is the best automobile manufactured today?

   What makes it the best?

2. What company do you think of when you think of high quality computer software?

   Why?

3. What company would you hire if you wanted to be absolutely, positively sure something would be delivered the next day?

   Why?

4. What is the best restaurant in your town?

Personal Workshop #1, continued

What makes it the best?

Bonus question:

5. What brand of watch do you consider the best?

What country was famous for making quality watches prior to 1970?

What country has taken over that role in the past 25 years?

Why?

Toughest question (Be honest!):

6. Who do you consider the major competitor for your business?

How do you think your customers view the quality of your product or service compared to that competitor (better or worse)?

Why?

THE PURPOSE OF THIS WORKSHOP IS TO DIAGRAM THE WORK FLOW IN A PROCESS.

Personal Workshop #2
Our Flow of Production

The work flow diagram for:_____

Process Flow Diagram

Process: _____

THE PURPOSE OF THIS WORKSHOP IS TO DETERMINE HOW YOUR COMPANY IS DOING ON DEMING'S FOURTEEN POINTS.

Personal Workshop #3
How Do We Measure Up?

	Things We're Doing Right	Things We Need To Improve	Obstacles We Face
1. Constancy of purpose			
2. Adopt the new philosophy			
3. Cease dependence on mass inspection			
4. End practice of awarding business on lowest price			
5. Continuously improve the system			
6. Institute training			
7. Institute leadership			

Personal Workshop #3, continued

	Things We're Doing Right	Things We Need To Improve	Obstacles We Face
8. Drive out fear			
9. Break down barriers between departments			
10. Eliminate slogans and fluff			
11. Eliminate quotas			
12. Remove barriers to pride of workmanship			
13. Provide quality education programs			
14. Take action in the transformation			

Personal Workshop #4
Quality Leadership Assessment

1. Do you believe that every employee is an asset to your company?

    If not, why not?

    If so, what have you done lately to help develop these assets?

2. Do you have a clear vision and clear values for your company?

    If so, how do you communicate that vision and those values to your employees?

3. Do you involve your employees in decision making?

    If so, how?

4. Are you comfortable letting other people solve problems without your supervision?
    If yes, give an example.

5. Do you promote teamwork in your company?

    If so, how?

Personal Workshop #4, continued

6. Do you effectively communicate with your employees about the plans and activities of the company?

   If so, how?

7. Do you provide your employees with opportunities for education and training?

   If so, what has been done in the last six months?

8. Do the managers/supervisors in your company consistently treat employees with respect and nurture their growth?

   If so, how do you assure this?

9. Do you promote an unwavering commitment to meeting customer needs in your company?

   If so, how do you know what those needs are?

10. Do you promote an unwavering commitment to quality in your company?

   If so, how?

THE PURPOSE OF THIS WORKSHOP IS TO IDENTIFY ACTION STEPS FOR QUALITY TRANSFORMATION.

Personal Workshop #5
Action Steps for Quality Transformation

1. Recognize the informal organization.
   a. List below any informal groups that exist in your company, as well as their leader(s).

   Group(s)   *Leader(s)*

   b. What action steps can you take to win the support of these groups?

2. Seek the active support of a critical mass.
   a. To the best of your knowledge, who do you expect to be the most enthusiastic supporters of quality? Who will be neutral? Who will be the dissenters? List those people below.

   Supporters   Neutral   Dissenters

   b. What action steps can you take to win over the "Neutrals?"

   c. What action steps can you take to negotiate with the dissenters?

3. People don't resist change, they resist *being* changed.
   a. What action steps can you take to understand people's fear of this change?

Personal Workshop #5, continued

4. When possible, change should be planned.
   a. What action steps can you take to ease people into this change?

   b. What is your timetable for implementing this change?

5. Efforts to implement change should be "anchored."
   a. What action steps can you take to assure that people have the support and resources needed to make the change?

6. The more profound the change, the more absolute is the need for the deep understanding and active leadership of top managers.
   a. What action steps can you take to assure that managers have a "deep understanding" of the principles and practices of quality management?

   b. What can you do to assure that managers develop the leadership skills needed to assure the success of your quality transformation?

THE PURPOSE OF THIS WORKSHOP IS TO CALCULATE THE LIFETIME VALUE OF A CUSTOMER.

Personal Workshop #6
Lifetime Value of a Customer

How much does an average customer spend each time he or she makes a purchase? _____

How often does an average customer make a purchase from your business (times per year)? **X** _____

Subtotal **=** _____

How many years will that customer return? **X** _____

Total: The Lifetime Value of a Customer **=** _____

THE PURPOSE OF THIS WORKSHOP IS TO IDENTIFY YOUR INTERNAL AND EXTERNAL CUSTOMERS.

Personal Workshop #7
Who's the Customer?

On the customer diagram below, list the suppliers and the internal and external customers for your company as a whole.

COMPANY _____

Input ———————————————▶ *Processes* ————————————▶ *Output*

External/
Ultimate
Customers

Suppliers

Internal Customers

1.
2.
3.
4.
5.
6.

External/Indirect Customers

1.
2.
3.
4.

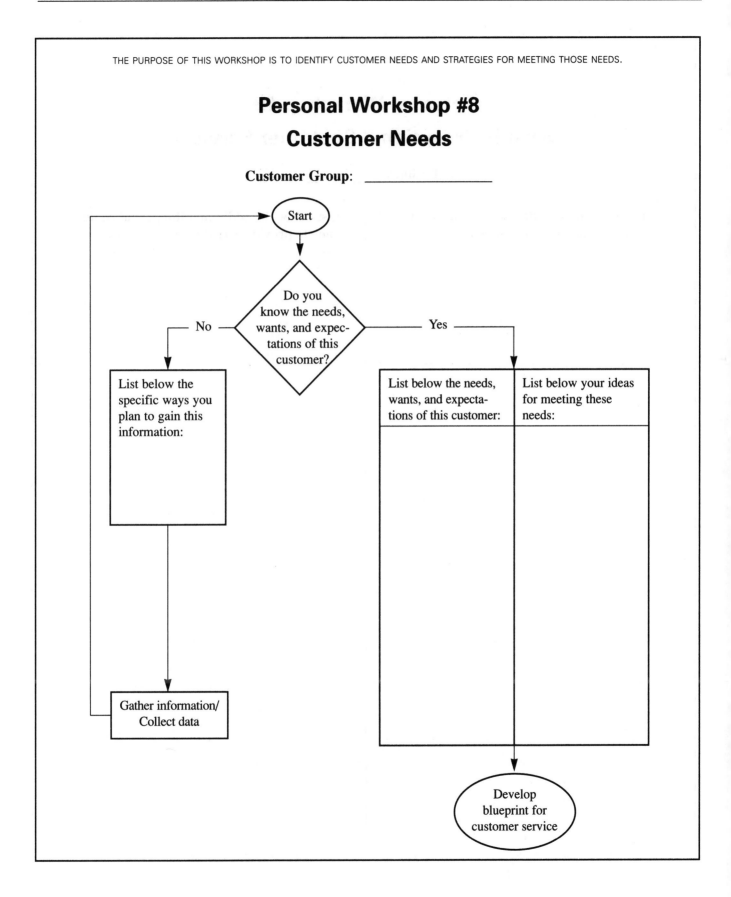

THE PURPOSE OF THIS WORKSHOP IS TO IDENTIFY CUSTOMER NEEDS AND STRATEGIES FOR MEETING THOSE NEEDS.

Personal Workshop #8
Customer Needs

Customer Group: _____

Start

Do you know the needs, wants, and expectations of this customer?

No

Yes

List below the specific ways you plan to gain this information:

List below the needs, wants, and expectations of this customer:

List below your ideas for meeting these needs:

Gather information/ Collect data

Develop blueprint for customer service

THE PURPOSE OF THIS WORKSHOP IS TO DEFINE EXCEPTIONAL CUSTOMER SERVICE FOR YOUR BUSINESS.

Personal Workshop #9
What Is Exceptional Customer Service?

Type of Business: _____

List below what constitutes good customer service for your type of business.	List below the additional things that could be done to provide *exceptional* customer service.

THE PURPOSE OF THIS WORKSHOP IS TO DESIGN A CUSTOMER SERVICE BLUEPRINT TO GUIDE YOUR COMPANY.

Personal Workshop #10
A Blueprint for Exceptional Customer Service

Part I: Develop a statement which describes your company's guiding philosophy on customer service.

Part II: For each ultimate customer group or market segment you serve, describe what you can do to deliver exceptional customer service at each point of contact. Finally, list who is responsible for carrying out each strategy or activity (individuals, departments, or work groups).

Point of Contact	Activities and Strategies	Who's Responsible?

Personal Workshop #10, continued

Point of Contact	Activities and Strategies	Who's Responsible?

THE PURPOSE OF THIS WORKSHOP IS TO BUILD A HISTOGRAM FOR ANALYZING DATA.

Personal Workshop #11
Building a Histogram

Step 1: State your problem.

Step 2: Determine what categories or classes of data you will collect, then collect the data.

Step 3: Format and label the axes below.

Personal Workshop #11, continued

Step 4: Using your data, build the histogram.

Time Period: _____

Frequency

Categories or Classes

Step 5: Analyze the histogram.

1. What does the histogram tell you about your data?

2. What conclusions can you draw (if any) from this information that might help you solve your problem or answer your question?

THE PURPOSE OF THIS WORKSHOP IS TO MAKE A PARETO CHART THAT WILL SHOW SIGNIFICANT CAUSES FOR A SPECIFIC PROBLEM.

Personal Workshop #12
Creating a Pareto Chart

Step 1: Describe your problem or question.

Step 2: Determine the categories or classes of data you will collect and for what time period. Then, collect the data.

(a) List below the categories or classes of data you will collect.

(b) What time period will be studied for this chart?

(c) Collect the data. Use historical data already in your records or collect new data. Record data on a check sheet or in some other organized fashion.

Step 3: Build a Frequency Table. This table will help you organize the data you will need to build a Pareto chart. Use the template below and follow these steps:

(a) In column 1, list categories in descending order, from the category with the most frequent occurrences to the category with the least frequent occurrences.

(b) In column 2, list the number of occurrences for each category. Record the total number of occurrences at the bottom of column 2.

(c) Compute the cumulative frequency of occurrences in column 3. In other words the first category in column 3, the cumulative frequency of occurrences will be equal to the number of occurrences in column 2. For the next category, the cumulative frequency will be the total number of occurrences for both the first and second categories, and so on.

(d) Compute percentages for each category by dividing the number of occurrences for that category by the total number of occurrences for all categories. List these percentages in column 4.

Frequency Table for _____

Problem: _____

Time Span: _____

Categories	Number of Occurrences	Cumulative Occurrences	Percent of Total
Total			

Personal Workshop #12, continued

Step 4: Format the axes of the Pareto chart on the template below. Categories of data should be scaled and labeled on the horizontal axis. Frequency of occurrence should be scaled and labeled on the left vertical axis. Percentages should be scaled and labeled on the right vertical axis.

Step 5: Build the Pareto chart. Transfer the data from the frequency table as follows:

(**a**) Draw a bar that corresponds with the frequency of occurrences for each category for the established period of time.

(**b**) Note the percentages for each category inside its bar.

(**c**) Draw in the cumulative percentage line.

Frequency

Percentages

Problem

Step 6: Analyze the Pareto chart you have created and answer the following questions:

(**a**) Which categories appear to be significant and which appear to be trivial for the problem or question you are studying?

(**b**) What action or strategies can you adopt to eliminate or minimize the impact in those categories which are most significant?

Personal Workshop #13
Team Leadership Skills

Teacher Skills

Part 1: Self-Assessment of Your Ability as a Teacher. For each statement below, put a mark in the space that indicates your behavior.

	Rarely	Sometimes	Usually
1. I keep all employees informed about overall company goals and activities.			
2. I thoroughly explain and demonstrate tasks and proper procedures to employees.			
3. I teach my employees effective team skills.			
4. I teach my employees how to gather and analyze data, how to solve problems, how to think critically, and how to make good decisions.			
5. I evaluate each person's learning to assure the employee has mastered the concepts.			

Part 2: Understanding and Action Plan

1. What strengths do you bring to the role of teacher?

2. What are your weaknesses?

3. List below at least three specific things that you can do to improve your team leadership skills in this role:

Personal Workshop #13, continued

Role Model

Part 1: Self-Assessment of Your Ability as a Role Model. For each statement below, put a mark in the space that indicates your behavior.

	Rarely	Sometimes	Usually

1. I talk about quality, our commitment to the customer, and the importance of teamwork with other employees.

2. I actively look for ways to continuously improve myself and my work, and I seek input from others on how I might get even better.

3. I encourage employees to express themselves openly, even when their views differ from my own.

4. I demonstrate to my employees that I trust their judgment and value their knowledge and opinions.

5. I do not tolerate negative talk, excuses, blaming others, or disrespect in this company.

Part 2: Understanding and Action Plan

1. In what ways do you positively influence others as a role model?

2. What behaviors or attitudes do you need to change because they might have a negative impact on others?

3. List below at least three specific things that you can do to become a better role model for other employees:

Coach

Part 1: Self-Assessment of Your Ability as a Coach.

	Rarely	Sometimes	Usually

1. I work with individuals and teams to set goals and define parameters, but I allow and expect them to solve problems and make decisions with a minimum of interference.

2. I am accessible to employees and easy to talk to.

Personal Workshop #13, continued

	Rarely	Sometimes	Usually

3. I give every employee the opportunity to actively participate on teams and be involved in decision-making.

4. I discuss with employees their performance, their aspirations, and ways they can improve their effectiveness on the job.

5. I provide frequent feedback to employees and teams to guide them and reinforce their accomplishments.

Part 2: Understanding and Action Plan

1. What skills have you developed that make you an effective coach?

2. What weakness do you have as a coach?

3. List below at least three specific things that you will do to become a better coach:

Cheerleader

Part 1: Self-Assessment of Your Ability as Cheerleader.

	Rarely	Sometimes	Usually

1. I praise employees and teams whenever they achieve significant results.

2. I continually talk about our vision with enthusiasm and conviction.

3. I encourage employees and teams to set goals, and I support their efforts to achieve those goals.

Part 2: Understanding and Action Plan

1. When have you exhibited good cheerleading skills in the past?

2. What are some instances when you could have provided more enthusiasm and support?

3. List below at least three specific things that you will do to become a better cheerleader:

Personal Workshop #14
Using Teams in Our Business

Select the type of team you will use. Complete this exercise for each team you selected.

- ❏ Project Team
- ❏ Process Improvement Team
- ❏ Problem-Solving Team
- ❏ Management Team

- Name a specific project or event that could be planned and/or implemented by a project team in your company:

- Describe the purpose for this team:

- Write objectives for this team:

- What people would you put on this team, or which units would you want represented?

THE PURPOSE OF THIS WORKSHOP IS TO IDENTIFY CAUSES FOR A PROBLEM USING A CAUSE-AND-EFFECT DIAGRAM.

Personal Workshop #15
Cause-and-Effect Diagram

Step 1: Using the template below, identify your problem in the space at center right.

Step 2: Identify and note categories of causes in the boxes of each "fishbone."

Step 3: Under each category of causes, list all specific, possible causes for the problem.

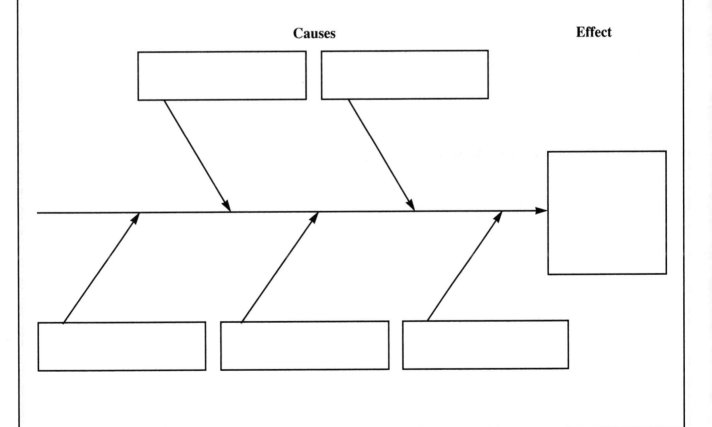

Personal Workshop #15, continued

Step 4: Analyze the possible causes by answering the following questions:
a)   Which of these possible causes is within our control?

b) Of those factors within our control, which items are most likely to have the greatest impact on the problem? List in rank order.

c)   What additional information do we need?

Personal Workshop #16
Evaluation of Team Dynamics

Check the box that best describes the behavior or characteristics of your team.

	Never	Sometimes	Always
1. All team members share a vision for the company.	☐	☐	☐
2. The team has a clear mission and team goals.	☐	☐	☐
3. We have effective team leadership.	☐	☐	☐
4. Our team leader is well organized.	☐	☐	☐
5. Each team member has clearly defined roles and responsibilities.	☐	☐	☐
6. Each team member communicates openly and effectively with others.	☐	☐	☐
7. We abide by a set of ground rules.	☐	☐	☐
8. Each team member is supportive of others and the team as a whole.	☐	☐	☐
9. Team members are interdependent.	☐	☐	☐
10. Each team member has the opportunity to use his or her talents.	☐	☐	☐
11. We achieve synergy as a team.	☐	☐	☐
12. We resolve all conflict immediately.	☐	☐	☐
13. No one is allowed to dominate other team members.	☐	☐	☐
14. We have productive team meetings.	☐	☐	☐
15. Every team member listens intently and respectfully to others.	☐	☐	☐
16. We regularly evaluate our effectiveness as a team.	☐	☐	☐

THE PURPOSE OF THIS WORKSHOP IS TO IDENTIFY WHAT INFORMATION IS NEEDED TO COMPLETE YOUR PROJECT
FOR THE CONTINUOUS IMPROVEMENT PROCESS.

Personal Workshop #17
Information We Need

Information Needs	How to Get Information

THE PURPOSE OF THIS WORKSHOP IS TO CREATE A RUN CHART.

Personal Workshop #18
Creating a Run Chart

Step 1: Identify what you want to measure and in what increments of time.

Step 2: Collect data for a minimum of 20 to 25 points in time. Record data on the template below.

Step 3: Label and scale the x-axis for your time increments. Label and scale the y-axis for the factor you are measuring.

Personal Workshop #18, continued

Step 4: Plot the data on the run chart and connect the dots.

Time:

Measure:

Measure: _____

Time: _____

Step 5: Study the run chart. What did you learn?

THE PURPOSE OF THIS WORKSHOP IS TO BUILD A SCATTER DIAGRAM.

Personal Workshop #19
Building a Scatter Diagram

Step 1: What is the relationship in your business that you want to test? Identify the two variables you believe are related.

Step 2: Collect your data.

Step 3: Label and scale the x-axis and the y-axis on the template below.

Step 4: Build the scatter diagram by drawing a dot to represent each set of data.

Step 5: Interpret the scatter diagram.

THE PURPOSE OF THIS WORKSHOP IS TO IDENTIFY PROBLEMS WITH WORK FLOW USING A DIAGRAM.

Personal Workshop #20
Our Work Flow Diagram

1. Sketch out a floor plan of the area you wish to study. Then draw lines to represent the movement of people, materials or paperwork through the workspace.

2. Using the work flow diagram note any potential problems or inefficiencies you see in the workplace.

THE PURPOSE OF THIS WORKSHOP IS TO DEVELOP A PROCESS IMPROVEMENT PLAN TO HELP YOU GET YOUR PROBLEM-SOLVING IDEAS ON PAPER.

Personal Workshop #21
Our Process Improvement Plan

Project Title: _____

Rank Root Causes Within Your Control	Ideas/Theories

THE PURPOSE OF THIS WORKSHOP IS TO COLLECT AND CHART DATA TO STUDY THE IMPACT OF YOUR CHANGE ON THE SYSTEM.

Personal Workshop #22
Try It and Test It

Instructions: Try out your idea and collect appropriate data. Use that data to develop charts and graphs, and then note what you have learned from the data.

Description of Chart:

What conclusions can you draw from studying this data?

Personal Workshop #22, continued

Description of Chart:

What conclusions can you draw from studying this data?

Description of Chart:

What conclusions can you draw from studying this data?

* Continue to show graphs and write your conclusions on separate paper, as needed.

Index